THE LOST ART
OF FEEDING KIDS

THE LOST ART
of FEEDING KIDS

What Italy Taught Me
about Why Children
Need Real Food

Jeannie Marshall

BEACON PRESS
BOSTON

Beacon Press
Boston, Massachusetts
www.beacon.org

Beacon Press books
are published under the auspices of
the Unitarian Universalist Association of Congregations.

16 15 14 13   8 7 6 5 4 3 2 1

This book is printed on acid-free paper that meets the uncoated paper ANSI/
NISO specifications for permanence as revised in 1992.

Text design by Ruth Maassen

Library of Congress Cataloging-in-Publication Data
Marshall, Jeannie.
   The lost art of feeding kids : what Italy taught me about why children need real
food / Jeannie Marshall.
      pages cm
   ISBN 978-0-8070-3299-2 (hardcover) — ISBN 978-0-8070-3300-5 (ebook) 1.
Children—Nutrition—United States. 2. Children—Nutrition—Italy. 3. Food
habits—United States. 4. Food habits—Italy. 5. Food industry and trade—Health
aspects. I. Title.
   RJ206.M279 2013
   613.2083—dc23
                                        2013001973

For James and Nico.
My fellow adventurers.

Contents

Introduction

ON A TYPICAL Saturday morning in Rome, my small son, Nico, and I wander through our local, outdoor food market. He's eating a few sections of a blood orange that a fruit vendor gave him. It's early winter, so we're looking over the red and green cabbages, tangled heaps of chicory, spinach, and broccoli rabe, and dark-green bunches of Tuscan kale. I'm imagining the kale for lunch, prepared the way Carlo, the farmer who grows many of the vegetables we eat, told me to do it one of the first times I bought some—cooked in water until tender, then sautéed for a few minutes in a pan with some olive oil, sliced garlic, and a little salt, and finished off with a squeeze of lemon. Then Nico spots someone snapping the ends off green beans. He likes them steamed and dressed with olive oil and lemon. "*Dai mi mezzo chilo,*" he tells her. She laughs at this bean-loving child and hands him a few fat, red Sicilian grapes, likely the last of the season, to eat while she weighs the beans. He thanks her and asks how much longer he has to wait until cherry season. We carry on like this, buying what we need for the next few days and indulging in a few whims here and there—some arugula for a pesto, and some wild mushrooms for a risotto.

I like coming here in the mornings. It reminds me that food doesn't need to be complicated. Nico loves being here because it gives him some say in the food we buy, and because someone always hands him something good to eat, like the orange, the grapes, and those memorable cherries in summer. The choice of treats is between a sweet mandarin orange and maybe a lumpy rennet apple. Nothing is packaged; there is only food here in this market, most of it requiring washing and chopping and cooking.

We might stop at the butcher shop on our way home. I'll ask for a piece of pork to roast, and the butcher will point to a few different parts of the portion of a pig lying in the refrigerator case, then cut the chosen piece from the animal's body and tie it with string and sprigs of fresh rosemary. There is no attempt to hide the fact that what I'm buying is a piece of flesh, and this uncomfortable knowledge—not to mention the high price—keeps me from buying and eating this flesh more than once or twice a month, which is good for our health. I'll cook it for dinner on Sunday as he suggests, browned in a pot with onions, celery, and carrots, and then simmered in red wine and vegetable broth with garlic cloves and rosemary.

This is exactly what I thought food shopping would be like in Rome when I moved here from Canada in 2002: market stalls overflowing with fresh, local produce; people shouting *buongiorno* to each other; blood-streaked butchers who know everything about the meat they sell, including what the animal ate and where it died. The market has given me an education in Roman cooking.

When our son, Nico, was born nearly three years into our stay, I began to see how Italian parents introduced their children to real foods instead of the packaged-food products for babies and children that I was used to seeing in North American supermarkets. I watched mothers feeding their babies and toddlers healthy, flavorful foods such as savory beans cooked in herbs, and the all-important pasta with numerous variations on vegetable sauces. I loved that you could take a baby or toddler into a really nice restaurant and that you would be treated like a royal family, complete with special tours of the kitchen and dining room for the little prince or princess. But as Nico began school, I realized that he and his Italian peers were being waved off the traditional path of healthy food and directed toward a new food culture, one far too similar to the one I thought I had left behind in North America.

It is heartbreaking to see Italian children eating hamburgers, hot dogs, french fries, potato chips, chocolate bars, and candy instead of seafood risotto, *spaghetti al ragù*, and green beans cooked in tomatoes. Rather than having a ceremonial drop of wine in a glass of water at Sunday lunch, children are drinking Coke and Pepsi. As my old culture threatens to overtake my new culture, I wonder if these children will be able to carry on the traditions of Italian cooking and the Italian way of eating.

Of course, this change in children's eating habits is happening all over the world, and childhood obesity statistics are growing even in the poorest countries. Long-standing food cultures, traditions that have provided pleasure and good health to people all over the globe, are disappearing because of this rapid change in children's eating habits. Children are key to changing a culture for better or worse. But children need help from the adults in their homes and communities. If children are to carry on traditional food cultures or reinvent them in places where they've been lost, they need to learn the simple pleasures of the table and to appreciate the taste of real food.

ONE

Discovering a Food Culture

The Adventure Begins

PEOPLE COME TO Italy for the food. They also come to see the Colosseum and the Sistine Chapel in Rome, the Uffizi Gallery and the statue of David in Florence, and Saint Mark's Basilica and those handsome gondoliers in Venice. But I think far fewer of them would come to Italy if there were not such good food to eat between the churches and galleries. All this can lead some people to dream of living in Italy. It's usually a dream with roots in a long-ago visit on a hot afternoon, a spring day spent lost and wandering narrow cobblestoned streets lined with ancient crumbling buildings covered in a purple haze of thick wisteria vines. The late afternoon light falls softly on the ocher and pale yellow *palazzi*; the cloudless sky seems blue with a touch of lavender. Inevitably, in this dream or hazy memory, there is a waiter in a crisp white apron. "*Prego*," he says, sweeping his open palm invitingly toward a table for two set against a vine-covered wall in the shade with a view of pedestrians strolling past. It's late afternoon but too early for dinner. You stand there, wondering whether to stop or keep walking, when he offers you a glass of Franciacorta. You give in and sit down. You taste one of the fat, briny olives the waiter puts on the table, and then you sip the cool, bubbly, Champagne-like wine from the mineral-rich soil of Lombardy, and you cannot believe how gentle, how fruity, how sophisticated and utterly unique it tastes. You put away your guidebook and your map, and you stop trying to remember which emperor did what. You chat with your

1

companion—the one you were arguing with barely a half hour earlier—about what you have seen, how different it is from your daily life, and how you would like to take some of this tranquil feeling, this mingling of heart-stopping beauty and fizzy wine, home with you.

Later that night, you find a lovely little restaurant hidden away down a maze of twisting streets from which you are certain you will never emerge, where you spend hours eating small plates of food. There are some marinated vegetables and a few parchment-thin pieces of prosciutto that melt like butter on your tongue, then some homemade ravioli stuffed with ricotta and spinach, served in a pool of melted butter with crisply fried sage leaves. You sip on the excellent, cool, and refreshing Pecorino, a wine from the Abruzzo, a place you can't even imagine. And then the waiter brings you a plate of thin, flat pieces of chicken breast that have been seared quickly and seasoned with salt. The chicken has a slight hint of garlic and lemon, and it goes nicely with the herb-stuffed Roman artichokes the waiter talked you into ordering. After dinner, you skip dessert and have cheese instead, likely a sheep's cheese of some kind, a Pecorino, lightly drizzled with honey from bees that have been feasting on fields of wild thyme. You think this has all been absolutely perfect, but then the waiter insists that you try the amaro, which at first you think sounds like "love"—*amore*—but a few minutes later, thankfully before you have embarrassed yourself, you realize is the word for "bitter." It's delicious, even if you will need a second espresso to clear your head in the morning. When you and your companion leave the restaurant and walk slowly, arm-in-arm, back through the narrow streets, you secretly wish that you will never find the way out of these serpentine paths. You do all of this again once or twice over the next few days. Then you go home, turn on your computer, and Google "Jobs in Italy."

Or something like that. Almost every non-Italian person I meet who lives in Rome has a variation on this story. People from Ireland and England, Norway and Germany, Cameroon and Zambia, Canada and the United States have all talked to me about our common attraction to Italy, where the drudgery of ordinary life is transformed into a series of beautiful, artful, life-sustaining rituals. My husband, James, will tell you that it was work—his work—that brought us to Rome nearly a decade ago and not any sort of romantic ideal, and that is true, but certainly the romance played its part. James, who is a journalist and documentary filmmaker, was offered a series of contracts to make some films for the BBC with the United Nations Food and Agriculture Organization based in Rome. Then he won a job to head the broadcast unit at the International Fund for Agricultural Development, another UN agency. This is the unromantic, practical reason for how we came to live in Italy. But in making the decision to come here, there is no doubt that our memories of warm afternoons, cloudless blue skies, and amazing spaghetti had an influence.

The idyllic image of the life people lead in Rome, their evening strolls among ancient ruins, and their shared pleasure in something as simple as a plate of spring asparagus was attractive to two Canadians who grew up in modern cities without a clearly defined cultural food heritage. The food lured us here, it seduced us with its sensuous pleasures, and its artistry continues to hold us. But the food in Italy is more than just something to eat. It is embedded in life here. It's a simple pleasure on the surface, but one that is in reality a complex web of history, place, religion, family, health, and community. It is a cohesive *food culture*, which is something much greater than the individual cooks and eaters who live within it. And we wanted to be a part of it.

Learning by Eating

Our early days of living in Rome were filled with work—my husband's at the UN and mine as a freelance journalist—and our nights were filled with exploration, with an *aperitivo* after work, a walk, and eventually dinner. This was before we were parents, when we had our evenings to ourselves, to spend exactly as we pleased. We favored old, neighborhood restaurants, off-the-tourist-track *trattorie* that featured the standards of Roman cuisine. We ate the classic pasta dishes: *cacio e pepe*, which is sheep's cheese,

3

pepper, and olive oil tossed with hot pasta to make a creamy sauce; *carbonara*, that rich mixture of raw egg, cheese, and pancetta tossed with hot spaghetti; and *amatriciana*, a slightly spicy sauce of tomatoes, pancetta, and chilies. We ate *broccoletti e salsicce*, where the *broccoletti*, essentially turnip greens, are cooked in salted water, then drained and squeezed and cooked again in a pan of warm olive oil with garlic and chilies. The greens become the perfect, flavorful bed for a link or two of slightly peppery, not too greasy, pork sausages. And we ate *pollo alla romana*, which is a simple stew of chicken with sweet peppers. We felt we really ought to try *trippa alla romana*—a honeycomb-textured cow stomach cooked in tomatoes, onions, carrots, celery, and mint—because Roman cuisine is known for it and so many people love it. Well . . . the sauce was lovely and even though the actual parts of the stomach were mild-tasting, neither of us could stop thinking of them as parts of a stomach. We ordered extra dishes of wonderful Roman artichokes, when in season, stuffed with herbs or fried *alla giudia* (in the Jewish manner); winter greens like *cicoria* (dandelion greens), *spinaci* (spinach), or *bieta* (Swiss chard); and salads in summer with green tomatoes and salt. We laughed at how every menu had the same six pasta dishes and the same few second-course meat options. But we soon learned that the differences came in the skill of the cook and the quality of the ingredients. There were certain restaurants we went to for the *cacio e pepe,* where the olive oil was green, fresh, and pure, and the sheep's cheese freshly grated; and others for the simplicity of a perfect tomato sauce made with chopped fresh San Marzano tomatoes, a big splash of olive oil, and a generous pinch of salt.

With such culinary inspiration all around, I started to experiment in the kitchen. While I liked the flexibility that freelancing gave me, I wasn't earning as much money as I had in Toronto, so I wanted to make up for it by filling the house with enticing aromas. Since James had to go out and work hard every day, since he had taken this job partly because *I* wanted to live in Rome (he speaks Spanish and was more interested in

South America), since I had more time than he did, and because I wanted to make our life in Rome as rich as possible, I started to cook.

I had cooked when we lived in Toronto, and so had he, but this was cooking of another sort. In Toronto, we experimented during the week, making trial runs of complicated dishes we wanted to serve at weekend dinner parties; or we tried to make simple, after-work meals like barbecued fish (even in winter) with salads or vegetables both steamed and roasted, or chicken breasts with herbs, garlic, and lemon slices baked in parchment paper. James likes spicy foods and sometimes cooked Indonesian dishes like *nasi goreng*, with rice, chilies, and a fried egg on top, or he made fresh spring rolls with shrimp, crunchy vegetables, and coriander all rolled up in thin rice wrappers. Given that we lived in Toronto, one of the most multicultural cities in the world, our cooking was all over the map.

Here in Rome, I tried to focus on Roman cooking. I was trying to understand a system, a specific language of food spoken by the Romans, their culture of food. I sought out the best ingredients I could find, brought them home, and tried to figure out what to do with them. In the beginning, I used Marcella Hazan's cookbooks as my guide and interpreter. Marcella, as everyone seems to refer to her, grew up in a small village in Emilia-Romagna. She married an Italian American and spent her life traveling back and forth between the two countries, giving cooking lessons and writing cookbooks for an American audience. She is considered one of the greatest authorities on Italian cooking and has had an enormous influence on the way many of us North Americans think about Italian food. I had given James a copy of her *Essentials of Classic Italian Cooking* years ago in Toronto, never imagining that one day we would use it in a Roman kitchen, spattering its pages with Sabina olive oil and Lazio tomatoes.

The apartment we were renting was near the Colosseum and was owned by a woman named Stefania. It had high ceilings, big windows, and great light, as well as a big dining and living area, two bedrooms, and a decent-sized kitchen with the tiniest fridge I had ever seen. Stefania pointed out the small fresh-food market a few blocks away, where there was also a butcher, a fish shop around the corner, and a fresh-pasta maker at the end of the block. If I needed more, she said, there was a big outdoor market, which also had places for farmers, in the nearby neighborhood of San Giovanni. Stefania and her husband had raised their daughter in this apartment, and she told me that I would find everything I needed within a few blocks. She suggested I start my day at the bar across the street for a cappuccino around eight o'clock, then go to the fresh produce market, then buy meat or fish, and pasta or bread if I needed it, and I could be back home and ready to work before nine.

That's how Stefania had done it with her family, and I assumed, rather naively, that's how parents all over Rome were still shopping and cooking.

Learning by Shopping

The tiny fridge in Stefania's apartment meant that I had to go to the market at least every other day. As I started to learn more Italian, I began asking for help from the people who sold, and in some cases the people who grew, the fresh produce. I soon found that I couldn't always go out with a recipe in mind and expect to find everything I needed. I didn't have a good sense of seasonal cooking in Italy, since where I came from I could buy rock-hard strawberries all year round. I had to go to the market and buy what most appealed to me, then come home and find a recipe or some guidance to help me cook it. Stefania had several years' worth of the glossy food magazine *La Cucina Italiana*, but the recipes were too complicated and my Italian not yet good enough to carry them out. It was the ordinary cooking that interested me anyway—*la cucina casalinga*—the meals people prepared in their own homes for their families.

My goal was to figure out and try to copy what the old ladies in the market were planning to cook. Though, once, I thought I would make the classic French dish *coq au vin* for a change, and I went to the market

6

and asked the butcher to cut up a chicken. He held the bird up for my inspection, chopped off its head and feet (and offered them to me for making soup), then asked me how he should cut it up—what was I going to make with this bird? He was not pleased when I answered *coq au vin*. He told me I should make something else with this Italian chicken and not that fussy old French dish. He told me to brown some pancetta in olive oil in a deep pot and then remove the pancetta. Then I should brown the chicken pieces, adding some salt as they cooked, and remove those as well. Then I should cook some carrots, onions, and celery in the pot until they were soft. After this, I should add a little flour to thicken the sauce and two cups of the broth that I would be making with the chicken bits that I was secretly intending to throw out as soon as I got home, a whole bottle of white wine, some herbs, a fresh laurel leaf, and one or two chopped, fresh tomatoes. Then I should throw the chicken, pancetta, and their juices back in the pot and let it simmer for forty-five minutes to an hour. I could, if I wished, add some small potatoes to the stew to cook toward the end. The butcher then yelled to the vegetable vendor at the stall across from him to bring me an onion, a carrot, some celery, and whatever fresh herbs he had. The butcher cut a fatty chunk of pancetta from a piece that was hanging on a hook behind him. He wrapped the whole works up and only charged me for the chicken. He said I would have to buy the wine myself at the *enoteca* on the corner, but if I told them what I was making, they would recommend both the perfect bottle for cooking and another for drinking. This, he told me, was a *cacciatora* (a hunter's dish), something I might find in a country restaurant, though I hadn't at that point ever tasted it. It was a useful recipe that could be made with pheasant or any other game bird I might shoot during a walk in the woods.

A few days later when I passed through the market, the butcher called me: "*Owww! Ragazza canadese! Vieni qua.*" He wanted to know how the chicken had turned out, if my husband liked it, and whether I understood now my error in thinking I could make a French recipe with an Italian chicken. Of course, I thought he was funny and charming and slightly bats in the way that Italians can be when they talk about food. But since then, I've come to see his point. The ingredients all came from the same area: the chicken, the pancetta, the vegetables, the olive oil, even the wine was from the Castelli Romani and tasted better than expected—at least it worked with the dish. If I were going to make *coq au vin*, I would have been using Italian ingredients, and I would have had to search for French wine or I would have made it with Italian wine, which would have changed the flavor and turned it into something Italian. Whenever we take a recipe created in one country and make it in another, it tastes different; at least it ought to taste different if the food is grown locally. A *cacciatora* can also be made with red wine instead of white, bringing it even closer to the French recipe. But the origins of the two recipes are different: the Italian version was made with a wild bird; the French was made with the old rooster who was past his prime. Both were created to make a tough bird tender in a flavorful sauce. Either way, I was buying a free-range chicken from a butcher. But his point was really true: food will taste of the place where it was grown and raised. I could have followed the French recipe (in this case, I had Julia Child's), and it probably would have tasted fine. But to any self-respecting Frenchman, it would not have been *coq au vin*. Besides, this was a girl chicken, the butcher told me, and not *un gallo*.

Learning by Cooking

James, though appreciative of my culinary investigations, used to laugh at me during this period and say, "Would you ask the butcher in Toronto how to cook the chicken?" or, "Would you ask the supermarket cashier how to make a tomato sauce?" And of course, I would not. But here it seemed as if I could ask anyone how to make anything. I could ask the postman or the bus driver about food and come home with a pretty good recipe for lasagne (way less meat than I thought) or correct instructions for eating fava beans (bite the raw bean, then a chunk of Pecorino Romano, and wash it down with Prosecco). Every Italian is attuned to subtleties in a way that I was not. Italians can tell—just by tasting—whether a squeeze of lemon juice or a few scrapings of lemon rind were added to the soup. They are not foodies, as we have in North America—or maybe they are; maybe everyone here is a foodie. It's more of a common passion than a competitive sport. They have grown up with a set of flavors that come from the region where they live. Italian cooking is very regional. Not only can Italians tell good olive oil from bad at a sniff, but they can recognize all kinds of subtleties of taste among the good ones. It is a rich, flavorful world they live in. It took me, with my galumphing Canadian palate, a long time to appreciate this fact.

There is something so elemental in the way people eat here. We all connect to it; we weave fictions and fantasies about it. The Italians capture something universal and essential in their food traditions. I don't know of anyone who comes to Italy who doesn't feel it. In another age, it was the art that pulled you up, forced you into a confrontation with yourself and your life, and made you fall to the ground in a dead faint. But few people suffer from Stendhal syndrome anymore. We've seen Botticelli's *Primavera* on placemats and Leonardo da Vinci's *Annunciation* on postcards and fridge magnets. Now it's the food, the daily ritual of preparing and eating it, that stops us short, because it's missing in our own lives.

What Is a Food Culture?

The longer we live in Rome, the more complex the role of food appears. Early on in our life here, when I casually remarked on the way Italians become excited by a pasta dish they have been eating forever, James suggested that it means something to them that we will never completely understand since we didn't grow up with it. So along with all the shopping, cooking, and eating, I've taken to analyzing. I'm always trying to figure out how it works. I've tried to get closer to knowing what the daily plate of pasta as well as the other foods they eat mean to people who have lived with them all their lives. They know something that the rest of the world might like to know about enjoying food. But how could I define something that is almost invisible, even to the people who live within it? At one time, I would have thought a collection of recipes, a few signature dishes such as *spaghetti al ragù* in Italy or *cassoulet* in France, would have been the whole definition. I thought a food culture was the food. But now that I live in one, I can see that is not the case. For instance, I asked two women how to make a *ragù*. One started to tell me that I had to begin by browning a little sausage, but then the two of them started arguing over what kind of sausage, then they argued about how many tomatoes to chop up. One said you add a little wine to the sauce and the other said no wine if it's for children, and the first one said of course you add the wine for the children. Their voices became loud and shrill over the question of how long to simmer the sauce. I never did get my recipe. The structure is not as rigid as I might at first have thought. It bends and sways, allowing individual cooks to experiment and improvise; it is flexible. Recipes are more art than prescription and are interpreted differently by each person who takes them on.

But in another way, a food culture *is* the food because it is the ingredients. The food is local and seasonal, mainly because for hundreds of years it had to be. Sure, we have had international trade in spices for centuries, and we all know the tomato is not indigenous to Italy; but the way that meat, fish, fruits, and vegetables have become such a big part of global trade, the way we ship crops around the globe and breed things like strawberries and tomatoes for their durability rather than their flavor is a recent phenomenon. Since living in Rome, I've learned to taste the difference between the pale-green, ridged, sturdy, milder-tasting variety of zucchini grown near Rome and the dark-green, smooth-skinned, slightly stronger-tasting ones that come from farther north.

A food culture has something to do with recipes and something to do with the ingredients, but there are also rules. A food culture organizes your eating instead of allowing you to graze, nibble, and snack all day long. Yes, *spaghetti al ragù* might be part of the culture, but you don't eat it at any time, and you don't get an order of it to take away in a plastic container and then eat it on the bus on the way home from work. By the traditional rules of this food culture, you eat at a table at the appropriate time of day with other people. (Italians feel sad when they see someone eating alone.) The food culture sets rules for consumption that put limits on our tendency to overindulge. When I first came to Italy, snack foods were still fairly limited. We didn't see the racks of packaged snack foods that have since appeared in the coffee bars and *tabacchi*. If you went into a shop that sold slices of pizza at around four or five o'clock in the afternoon, the person behind the counter would offer to cut you a very small piece, about six to eight bites in size, and you'd have to coax and persuade him with stories about the meagerness of your earlier lunch before he'd give you anything bigger.

Generally, a food culture sets prescribed mealtimes. Yet you don't feel deprived because you're not really thinking about food all the time, which might seem counterintuitive since you're surrounded by all this great food. But if you don't constantly see advertisements reminding you to eat, and if you don't see people eating all the time, if it's not acceptable in the culture to walk around eating and drinking, you don't do it. For instance, a good friend of mine, Brenda, came to visit us from New York shortly after we moved to Rome, and she really wanted to try a creamy pastry that she saw in a *pasticceria*. The man who sold it to her wrapped it beautifully in paper and ribbon. Brenda took it outside, unwrapped it on the street, and started to eat it as we strolled around Trastevere. Within two bites, she became extremely self-conscious, aware of the disapproving glances directed toward her, and she realized that eating a wonderful creamy pastry on the street wasn't really done. It's not culturally acceptable. It's not that Italians disapprove of pastry, but there is a time and a place for it, and that is after dinner. This might be why American adults associate chocolate cake with guilt, while the French associate it with celebration.

A food culture is also about community. In Italy, there are special food festivals—*le sagre*—that run from fall through spring to celebrate single

11

foods. In the late fall, there are olive festivals to celebrate the olive harvest and the new season of olive oil; in spring, you can find celebrations of the artichoke. We have stumbled across them by accident in piazzas in central Rome and have made a point of visiting some of them in small villages to taste the food—which is usually prepared by the people who live there, not by professional chefs—and to see how people, from the oldest to the youngest, come out to mingle, eat together, and talk. We visited an ancient hill town toward the Lazio-Umbria border where the whole population comes to the central piazza on summer Saturday evenings to bake pizzas together and dance.

Those are the elements of a food culture, as far as I've observed. But there's more below the surface. Just as the slow-cooked mingling of freshly chopped tomatoes, fruity fresh olive oil, and sea salt produces a flavorful sauce that defies those simple ingredients, so too do the health benefits of a food culture go far beyond the nutrients in the food. "History" and "tradition" are other words for the accumulation of hundreds, sometimes thousands, of years of food and health knowledge contained in a food culture. But this knowledge is not always (or even often) consciously understood, and it's not the main point; rather, it's the flavor, the aroma, the pleasure, the sense of hunger satisfied in the company of people close to us that keep a system like this going. Italians don't eat the way they do because it's healthy, but because it tastes good and because it tastes familiar. Health is a side benefit.

I didn't become so fascinated by the food culture of Rome because of its health benefits (there are certainly many cultures that are even healthier). I was attracted to it because of the tastes and the sociable aspects of the culture. While I was out smelling the fruit and admiring the vegetables, the fact that this food is linked to the health of the people who eat it never really entered my mind.

TWO

The Packaged-Food Revolution

The Taste of Soup

OF ALL THE things I ate during my first year in Italy—like the grilled whole fish with the crackling skin and a green salad by the seaside, the handmade fettuccine with earthy-smelling black Umbrian truffles shaved on top, and the slice of crisp pizza topped with buffalo mozzarella, ripe tomatoes, and basil—it was a bowl of soup that really linked my present food-filled Italian life with my small-town Ontario childhood.

In the winter of our first year here, we went to Tuscany for the weekend with some friends. We all stayed together in an old stone house in the Val d'Orcia. It was early December and it was cold. The wind whipped through the valley below the old house and sent gusts of chilled air through the cracks around the windows. We decided to seek warmth and dinner in the nearby village of San Quirico.

The six of us bustled into a restaurant and asked for a table near the open fire. We soon thawed out, thanks to the fire, a bottle of red wine from nearby Montepulciano, and a basket of bread. At the urging of Giuseppe, one of our friends at the table, we ordered a farro dish to start. Farro is a grain that tastes rather like barley but is denser. It had been cooked slowly in a broth the way you make risotto and was served with mushrooms and Parmesan cheese. We ate it while someone cooked our meat—small pieces of pork and lamb—over the fire beside our table. When the meat was done, it was served to us with rosemary-scented roasted potatoes and big plates of leafy green vegetables that had been

13

cooked in salted water, then drained and squeezed, and cooked again in a pan with olive oil, garlic, a few chilies, and a sprinkling of salt. It was simple, well-prepared, comforting food.

It was the next afternoon at lunch that I ordered the soup. I had to be convinced to order it because I thought I didn't like soup. It was a *ribollita*, which simply means "reboiled," with white beans and barley cooked with a little bit of *guanciale* (pork cheeks), tomato, and dark-green *cavolo nero*. There was so little liquid that it was more of a stew than a soup, but it reminded me quite forcefully of food from my childhood.

Maybe it took nearly a year to make this connection because my palate needed that time to recover from the barrage of flavors that I frequently ate in Canada (and missed, I must admit): the spicy Asian foods, the hot wasabi with sushi, and likely the ramped-up artificial flavors in the processed foods I wasn't even entirely aware I was eating, things like crackers with rosemary flavoring, bottled spicy Szechuan peanut sauce, flavored yogurt, industrial bread, and adulterated bagels.

The soup was savory, earthy, and rich, full of subtle flavors that blended smoothly and created this satisfying, comforting, homey dish on a wintry day. I've tasted this before, long ago, I kept thinking, as I spooned up every last drop of the soup, while knowing that I could not possibly have tasted this exact soup before. But I had tasted something like it. Soups like this are classic country dishes the world over. They are made with leftover bones or the last remains of a scrawny, too-tough chicken. Leftovers go into the soup pot; small bits of fatty meat add flavor to an otherwise grain, legume, and vegetable soup. The Tuscan *ribollita* is the natural extension of winter soups from the Middle Ages, made in the region from cabbages, turnips, greens, onions, garlic, and fat (olive oil or animal). Hearty soups like this were originally made by people who couldn't afford to waste food. They are peasant dishes, loved by everyone. With the skill and knowledge that come from eating them and watching how they are made, each generation keeps the pot simmering. Soups like this are found in kitchens everywhere—in Arab countries, where they might use couscous and mutton; in the southern United States, where bacon and cayenne pepper are added to bean soup; in Quebec, where pea soup is made with a ham bone. Such basic soups vary with the region and the season. Marcella Hazan, my helpful guide in the Italian kitchen, wrote that the ingredients in a vegetable soup "can tell you where you are in Italy almost as precisely as a map."

Well, here I was, sitting in a restaurant in the heart of Tuscany, eating soup that reminded me of the soup my mother made in Jackson's Point, Ontario, in the late 1960s. Hers was influenced by the soup her French-Canadian mother made for her family in Toronto in the 1930s, and the soup her French-Canadian grandmother had made for her fur-trapping family in Northern Ontario at the end of the nineteenth century. Of course, the soup I was enjoying in Tuscany tasted of hearty *cavolo nero*, which is that long, rippling Tuscan kale, olive oil, and Parmesan, while my mother's tasted of her own chopped, preserved tomatoes, barley, beans, cabbage, and, most likely, bacon or lard. Both soups were thick, with a slightly meaty-tasting stock and with beans and grains that absorbed the liquid and most of the flavor. My mother's soup sat on the back of the stove simmering away (an accidental *ribollita?*). We would eat some and let the rest keep simmering. There was always a pot on the go; in fact, it seemed that everyone had such a pot in those small towns, because I can remember eating chicken soup at a friend's house. Her mother was famous, not least among children, for her rich, savory soup, which was thick with some kind of grain and carrots.

In the intervening thirty-odd years, I had forgotten all about soup. We moved to Toronto in the early 1970s, and we started to eat different-ly. Canned soup came into the house more often. It was such a time saver for my busy mother, who was raising a family on her own (my father died when I was a baby). Why would you spend hours simmering soup when you could simply open a can, heat, and eat something that, well, maybe it didn't taste as good, but didn't really taste bad? Why would you go to the trouble? With the exception of turkey soup, which my mother made with the remains of the Thanksgiving and Christmas birds, she rarely made soup anymore. And I guess that's why I stopped eating it and somewhat unconsciously avoided it on menus.

The Change in North American Food

But really, how could the foods of Italy evoke my childhood meals in a small Ontario town? It's the authenticity of very simple, well-prepared food, I suppose, that links these two disparate culinary worlds. Canadians and Americans have rarely thought of our countries' culinary past in the way you might think of the food history of Italy. The food in Canada and the United States was heavily influenced by the foods of their diverse populations and then by big industrial producers of fast and processed foods.

Before the processed foods though, before industrial farming and the food industry dominated food and eating, North American and European foods were more alike than different in a few fundamental ways. There was no chemical fertilizer or pesticides on North American farmlands when those areas were first being settled. There were no biotech foods, no chemical additives and preservatives. The food was grown and raised locally, and most of it was prepared and consumed at home. Culinary techniques and recipes brought from diverse parts of the world were handed down through families. The best of American and Canadian cuisine, which really is a fusion of various cooking styles with local foods, springs from this tradition. Some of it still exists, though it is no longer the norm.

By the 1950s, the food industry was working hard to figure out how to convince American women to use packaged foods, to change their view of themselves as cooks, even to convince them that they didn't have time to cook. The food historian Laura Shapiro says the industry manufactured a sense of panic about cooking, creating the idea that women neither enjoyed cooking nor had time for it. The fast-food industry pushed that even further by making fun, tasty food cheap and easily available in family-friendly environments.

I remember as a child in the 1960s going to a restaurant on occasion for a hamburger and French fries. But I also remember that this was a treat. French fries were hard to make at home, so we ate them out. In the 1960s, many people were still cooking without food products. New immigrants to Canada and the United States were cooking, reinventing, and adapting dishes they were used to making in their home countries to the ingredients they found around them. Sondra Gotlieb, the irreverent writer and somewhat undiplomatic wife of a former Canadian ambassador to the United States, even titled one of her cookbooks from the period *The Gourmet's Canada* and dedicated it to "the gastronomic resources of [Canada] and the wealth of its culinary traditions."

Canada had culinary traditions? I might have sneered at Gotlieb and thought her book an exercise in stretching a point, had it not been for my Proustian moment with the bean soup. But the soup brought back memories of the table set for dinner every night, of my older brothers coming home for Sunday dinner, and of the frosted, double-layer cakes that my mother made for those dinners every week. It wasn't what we later came to call gourmet food, but it was built around hearty soups and stews, roasted meats and root vegetables, vegetables fresh or frozen in winter, and summer salads from the garden.

In the 1960s, my busy mother used to bake bread two or three times a week. After we moved to the city in the 1970s, she rarely, if ever, made it. By 1970, only 15 percent of all flour sold in the United States was for home baking, while in 1900, it had been 95 percent. I assume a similar pattern existed in Canada, where the cult of convenience was so firmly taking hold. Why would a mother make her own bread when she could find it sliced, wrapped, and waiting in the supermarket? This was the beginning of the period when time spent in the kitchen was considered time wasted.

Women wanting to liberate themselves from their domestic obligations, particularly in the kitchen, certainly played a role in this shift. My mother never called herself a feminist, but feminist ideas would have resonated with her. Betty Friedan's *The Feminine Mystique*, published in 1963, describes the malaise of women who had to give up entirely on the idea of a family if they wanted a career, or who had to give up on a career or any sort of expression of their own individuality to serve their families. My mother actually liked to cook and she was a good cook, but like so many women of her generation with children, women who were working outside the home, or women like my mother who were trying to go to school while raising a family, she welcomed anything that could make her life easier. I remember that she made very simple meals for us, and that she involved her children in the cooking as we got older, but she also felt the pressure to take shortcuts. It was in the era of the working mother that packaged food really found its niche. What busy mother has time to coax her children to eat a dinner that she has carefully prepared from scratch? All she has to do is open a package and, considering the amount of salt and flavor enhancers that went into that package, children were sure to eat up. Packaged foods fit into the discourse of the day. They were convenient and they seemed nutritious, and that was almost all that mattered.

Cookbooks from the 1960s and 1970s reflect both the excitement and the anxiety about these packaged foods. My mother's very popular *Better Homes and Gardens Casserole Cook Book* (published in 1968) is all about opening cans and packages to make dinner for the family. *Betty Crocker's Picture Cook Book* was produced by General Mills in 1950 and became a standard in American kitchens throughout that period. Recipes in magazines urged women to serve wedges of canned meat glazed with marmalade, and to broil sausages and serve them with canned peaches.

In Canada, Madame Benoit, famous across the country in her day with her own TV show, published *Madame Benoit Cooks at Home* in 1978. At first glance, she seems to endorse authentic home cooking—she praises the superiority of beans baked in a clay pot overnight in a brick oven—but she also seems quite excited about the time-saving possibilities inherent in instant mashed potatoes, and includes canned beans and ketchup in a recipe for Bean Pot Pork Chops. For a while, Madame Benoit seemed poised somewhere between a Canadian version of Julia

Child (she even trained at the Cordon Bleu in Paris) and Betty Crocker, but she eventually gave in entirely to the faster-is-better trend and wrote a book on microwave cooking. My mother had some of her books in our kitchen.

Of course, not everyone was giving into convenience foods. In 1966, the popular Canadian historian Pierre Berton and his wife, Janet, published *The Centennial Food Guide*. They were clearly in the anxiety camp: "In a country that produces the world's finest fresh meat, we submit to a dozen equivalents of Spam, all of them appalling," they wrote with obvious disapproval. "We squirt fake whipped cream on our frozen strawberries and douse our instant pancakes with ersatz maple syrup." The Bertons, who were clearly in the minority, feared that the way things were going, the art of cooking would soon become the art of stirring, and that babies would eventually be born without taste buds because they would no longer need them.

The Bertons had seven children to feed, and the soup pot was always bubbling on the stove. What to eat was a constant question in their family, a constant source of pleasure. At least that's how they presented it in print. In fact, the stories throughout the book are about cooking with their children, coming up with big feasts for the family, and sitting down to a good, cooked breakfast on the weekends. There are also stories about serving more elegant meals, though still composed of local ingredients, when the occasion called for it. There's nothing about feeding children differently from adults, about hiding their vegetables in chocolate cake or cutting their sandwiches into the shape of a Venetian gondola. It's probably safe to assume that the Berton household was free of specially prepared foods for children.

In Britain, Elizabeth David brought life to stodgy English food after World War II with her Mediterranean recipes and books on French and Italian cooking. In the United States, Craig Claiborne was writing about food in the *New York Times* through the 1960s, bringing recipes and techniques from countries like Mexico and India, as well as Italy and

France, to the page for his readers to try. (He is also known to have said, "I have learned that nothing can equal the universal appeal of the food of one's childhood and early youth." In his case, it was the foods of Mississippi and, in particular, his mother's Chicken Spaghetti, a dish that combined chicken, ground beef, ground pork, tomatoes, cream, and many, many other ingredients, that he yearned for.) Claiborne is often credited, along with Julia Child, whose introduction to the world of French home cooking was published in 1961, with bringing a kind of artfulness to the kitchens and pleasure to the tables of America. Claiborne's and Child's influence, though profound, was nothing compared to the bulldozing influence of the food industries that were then gaining such a foothold.

What these cookbooks of the 1950s and 1960s make clear, though, is that before the 1970s, people cooked real food. They might have been trying to recreate ethnic dishes from faraway places—and by that I mean Italian recipes in New York, French recipes in Quebec, and German recipes in Pennsylvania and southwestern Ontario—but they used the local, fresh ingredients they had at hand, and in the process they were creating something unique.

Children Are the Gatekeepers

I've been deliberately indulging in nostalgia with my memories of soup and homemade bread. Nostalgia has a bad reputation, especially in the ongoing debate about food. But nostalgia is important for reminding us of another time, when things were done differently; otherwise we accept our present state as completely normal. It reminds us that there may be something we're missing. We can try to find the thread of traditions that ties us to our ancestors, that goes far beyond the people we actually remember. We can pick up those dropped threads before they disappear completely. Nostalgia can also remind us that the path we're on now is not inevitable, and it is still possible to change course. Children are essential to this process. Children are the gatekeepers of culture; they hold the key to changing the culture for either good or bad. It's up to the adults to include children in a culture of real food if the tradition is to be revived in North America or continued in Europe. The old ladies in my favorite Roman markets will soon be gone, and I often wonder who will be left to keep the pots simmering.

Just as Proust's madeleine opened his memory and released hundreds of pages of reminiscence (or as Remy's ratatouille brought back happy memories of childhood to Anton Ego), a very happy period of my own childhood seemed to rise up along with the steam from a bowl of Tuscan bean soup. I remembered things I didn't know I had forgotten. An image of the dining room of the house where we lived until I was nine years old came back to me, complete with its fussy, flowered chairs and curtains. I could see the beautiful table laden with food, and I remembered quite clearly what it was like to be the youngest child at the table with all my older siblings, listening to the unimaginably exciting tales of their lives, and realized how all of these experiences had a hand in shaping my adult life and personality.

But what of children who won't have such memories because they won't have regularly enjoyed the pleasures of the communal or the family table? A family that sits around a table sharing the simplest of foods that someone has taken the time to cook will have memories that go beyond the food they actually consumed. Children who learn to read package instructions so they can microwave their own separate dinners might not be so fortunate.

Living in Italy has allowed me to remember a part of my own history, almost to reexperience it. It's also allowed me to see the schism that occurred, changing food for the worse and sending North Americans down an unhealthy path. It makes me fear for the future of Italy, as I see now what we lost and realize how easily we gave it all up, and how difficult it is to get it back.

The Canadian and American slide into becoming fast-food, industrial food cultures was a gradual process. We didn't change overnight. We adapted bit by bit, and we made use of the many time-saving products available to us. The industry capitalized on our apparent needs by of-fering solutions with ready-made meals that were fast (if speed was the issue), that were adapted for special diets (if losing weight was the prob-lem) or were appealing to children (if picky eaters were the concern). The food industry seemed to have all the answers—answers to questions we didn't know we were asking.

THREE

Scientific Mothers

The Baby Is Coming

IT WAS SPRINGTIME in 2004 when I found out that we were going to have a baby. Originally, the plan was to return to Canada around that time, but really it felt as if the adventure was only beginning. Now the adventure was magnified several times by our coming child. There would be doctors to find, baby clothes to buy, and, eventually, play dates to organize and schools to decide on. It changed us, though we didn't wholly realize it at the time, from being two people exploring a foreign country to a family making a life here.

Once my profile started to take on that recognizably pregnant, just-swallowed-a-melon look, my neighbors began to show an interest in my health. At the market in Trastevere, Bruno, one of the fresh-produce vendors, reminded me every day that I needed to eat more greens, and Marco at the coffee bar, who had two small children himself, introduced me to the *latte macchiato* (steamed milk with a drop of espresso) to ease my caffeine withdrawal. My doctor told me to eat organic food and to wash my vegetables well to avoid insects and parasites. If I had to eat nonorganic, he said to wash them doubly well to avoid insects, parasites, pesticides, and other chemicals. He also told me to have a small glass of wine with dinner occasionally to help my digestion, which made some of my North American friends practically jump out of their skins. I welcomed their advice because I had absolutely no idea about pregnancy or babies. Some of it might have seemed like common sense to some people, but not to me. James and I are both youngest children in large families, and both our mothers were old women by then and far away. We were separated by distance from our families and felt a world away from our own culture. Our neighbors seemed happy to fill in with helpful advice. I also found a midwife, Valeria, who could monitor my pregnancy and ease my way through both this strange experience and the Italian medical system. Valeria took care to remind me constantly that what I was going through was completely natural and that it would be no different for me than it had been for women of all previous generations.

While I mostly thought about the food I ate during pregnancy as nourishment for the baby, I learned that a child's taste for foods also starts developing in the womb. Somewhere in the sixth month, the fetus learns to swallow. It swallows some of the amniotic fluid, which tastes of the foods the mother has been eating. I had read about this and assumed I should be careful to eat a lot of fresh fruit and green vegetables for the baby's health, but Valeria encouraged me to think about the way this might shape the future tastes of the child as well. She emphasized that I should be eating the freshest foods possible and taking advantage of what each season had to offer. It's the first step in teaching the baby to like the foods of its culture.

This baby was certainly going to have a taste for cherries, which I ate by the kilo throughout that late spring and early summer, for oven-roasted *rombo* (turbot) and asparagus, for *pappardelle con ragù di cinghiale* (wild boar sauce) and *fettuccine al tartufo nero* (black truffle sauce), both of which I ate on fall weekends in Umbria, and for the roasted meat I ate in the winter with rosemary potatoes and dark leafy greens with fresh green olive oil. This child was really going to love Sicilian blood oranges and fig gelato. James and I took a holiday—our last holiday on our own without a child—to Emilia-Romagna, where we sampled the richer foods of that region. We ate the famous prosciutto of Parma in Parma and tried a slow-cooked Bolognese sauce in Bologna. We learned of the simple pleasures of mortadella on bread and peppers cooked in the sweet and justly famous balsamic vinegar of Modena. James traveled to London and to Burundi for work during that period, but I was very happy to remain in Italy throughout my pregnancy.

Valeria also started preparing me to think about the process of breast-feeding my son and assured me that my diet during that period would also continue to influence his tastes. It is a fact that flavors like garlic and broccoli pass from the mother's diet into breast milk, and there is a lot of evidence to suggest that children tend to gravitate toward those flavors once they are weaned. The health benefits of mother's milk aside, this was the next step in the gentle process of raising a child to appreciate the tastes of his particular family and the region where he's being raised.

Many of my friends in Canada who already had children said they changed their diet while breastfeeding to avoid spicy or really strong flavors that might upset the baby, but the Italian women I met never did this. Maybe it's partly because Italian food, though complex and flavorful, is rarely overpowering in any way, other than the array of bitter flavors in the greens. Garlic is used sparingly and chilies offer just a slight degree of heat, nothing too strong. I met a Sri Lankan woman in Valeria's waiting room during that time who said she intended to continue eating spicy food while nursing her child because it hadn't occurred to her not to do so. Women around the world continue to eat the foods of their regions while pregnant even if those flavors are strong and spicy. This might actually help their children adapt to the local cuisine.

Whether I would nurse the baby or give him a bottle of infant formula was never really a question. When you go to a midwife—especially one as firm as mine—you prepare to nurse. Valeria told me that unless I died in childbirth, there was no reason for my baby to have anything other than his mother's milk.

I was e-mailing daily at that time with my friend Elizabeth in Toronto who'd had a baby almost exactly one year before my due date. She was breastfeeding her son, Aiden, without trouble. Elizabeth was like a long-distance sister during that period. She sent me her maternity clothes, bought me a nursing bra, and shipped boxes of tiny baby clothes to get us through the first few months of rapid baby growth. She also kept me connected to the concerns of North American women when it came to pregnancy, childbirth, and breastfeeding versus formula.

It seemed like everyone I met during that period was talking about breastfeeding (or maybe it was just me). A woman with an extremely demanding job at the World Food Programme in Rome told me how she had nursed her two sons throughout her few months of maternity leave, and then continued after she went to work by expressing milk and having the nanny bring the babies to her office once a day for a feeding. An American journalist friend living in Rome, who had her baby a few months before mine was due, established breastfeeding during her meager six weeks of maternity leave and then kept it up well into the second year with the aid of a breast pump and her husband, who occasionally rushed the baby to her office for the odd emergency feeding. Certainly it was easier for those who didn't have to spend all day at work, but even those who did seemed to take it remarkably in stride.

All of us had clearly gotten the message that "breast is best" for the baby's health, that everything from a strong immune system to higher IQ levels later on are associated with breastfeeding. But we don't often really think about the role breastfeeding plays in shaping our children's food preferences too, the way it influences what they eat later and how that consequently affects their health. In a place like Italy, or even more specifically Rome, there is a range of tastes and a sort of coherence to the way foods and flavors work in the overall diet, so breastfeeding is an obvious way to pass those flavors along at the earliest stage of life, as long as everything else falls into place.

The Birth of a Boy

Over the six months that I spent checking in with Valeria before the baby was born, we talked about the details of actually giving birth. She suggested that I endure most of my labor at home, where I would be more comfortable, and finish up at a clinic about a twenty-minute drive away. She encouraged me to forgo pain-relieving drugs in favor of natural childbirth. She told me it was going to hurt like nothing I'd ever experienced before and that I would beg for mercy and scream for drugs, and that she wouldn't give them to me. I told her I didn't buy into the romantic view of natural childbirth as an experience not to be missed. I would be happy to miss that kind of pain. But when she said, "It's not for you; it's for the baby," she had me. It still shocks me that I agreed to do it.

Valeria worked with a doctor. He would be there at the birth to monitor the baby and be ready to jump in if I needed a Caesarean section, but mostly it was all going to be up to me. The one thing I really wanted was to give birth in water, and Valeria said she could arrange for this at the clinic. I assumed I would labor for a few hours at home, James and I would drive to the clinic where we would meet Valeria, I would hop in the tub with a few howls, yells, and pushes, and the baby would be born.

Instead, my water broke at 3:00 a.m., but I wasn't in labor. I waited an hour before waking James (I was in another room because I was having trouble sleeping). Our moods swung between intense excitement and terror for about half an hour until at 4:30 a.m. we finally phoned Valeria and asked her what to do. She came over, and we sat and waited and waited. Then, around noon, she called an acupuncturist to come over and jump-start my labor. He jabbed me with needles and stimulated my ankles and wrists with a weak electric current, and my first contraction came within ten minutes. The contractions came and went in waves of energy-draining pain all afternoon and into the night.

In the meantime, the doctor was there, Valeria was there, the acupuncturist was there—they were all hanging around the house waiting for me to do something. Valeria encouraged James to go out to the market to get the ingredients for a late lunch. He came back and made a big salad, cut up some bread, and made a plate of fresh fruit and cheese. The doctor left and said he would meet us later at the clinic. James offered wine, but everyone refused since they were working. Later, Valeria told James he ought to think about what to make for dinner. He cooked some pancetta in olive oil with red chilies and then added chopped tomatoes. Valeria told him to wait and add the salt once the tomatoes had completely softened. He cooked some spaghetti in properly salted water (Valeria made sure) and prepared another salad. Valeria told him to cut up some bread because the acupuncturist was "old-fashioned" and would expect to see bread on the table at dinnertime. James offered wine, and I think that this time they might have had a token sip or two. I still think Valeria was trying to keep James busy so that he wouldn't worry about me and the baby. He still believes that she was just hungry and needed someone to cook for her.

Around eleven o'clock that night, everyone found places to sleep and I stayed in the living room hugging my yoga ball, moaning, and cursing. I was awake for the rest of the night. In the morning, James started making *cappuccini* for everyone and then decided he had really had enough cooking and shopping, and suggested we just go to the clinic and birth the baby. We went to the clinic, and I continued to yell and scream for the rest of that day. I blamed Valeria for encouraging this ludicrous idea of natural childbirth. I didn't ask her for drugs because I knew it would be pointless. Instead, I grabbed the doctor by the lapels of his white coat and told him to give me a Caesarean. He sympathized with me but said Valeria would kill him if he did it.

Since my water had broken so early, I was at risk of infection and couldn't go in the birthing tub during labor. I stayed in my room, screaming my way through contractions and frightening the other women who were in the earlier stages of childbirth. Later that evening, when it seemed that I had progressed far enough that it would be safe to go into the water, we went down to the delivery room. Valeria had lowered the lights. She brought a lamp to give a soft, cozy glow to the room and draped scarves over hospital partitions. The birthing tub was actually a giant wine vat that Valeria had bought from a wine producer in the Castelli Romani (brand new, never actually used for wine), and she filled it with hot water using a green garden hose. I climbed into it carefully, and for a few minutes, the hot water soothed my battered and aching body, and I almost relaxed. I closed my eyes and listened to birds chirping and monkeys shrieking and a loud humming of insects. The doctor had put on a CD of jungle sounds to go along with my animal wailings. He was convinced that it would help and, if it didn't help, it would at least amuse us. The whole thing was so strange and charming that I felt encouraged to go on (not that there was really any other direction in which to go) and within an hour finally gave birth to our little Nicolas Matteo, soon to be known as Nico. The doctor pronounced him whole and healthy. Valeria wrapped him in a soft sheet and handed him to me.

Just as nothing else in this birth scenario went according to plan, my squirming, screaming little treasure refused to nurse. After all the talking with Valeria about the naturalness of nursing a child, after several preparatory La Leche League meetings, and discussions with other new mothers, it seemed I couldn't feed my son. He just wouldn't "latch on," as they put it; he didn't seem to know how. So after a few days of trying and being frustrated and watching his little baby rolls disappear, we gave him some infant formula. I hated to do it, but I didn't see an alternative.

It struck both James and I as painfully ironic that after all that long and agonizing labor that I endured so that the baby would start his life without any foreign substances in his system, after all that healthy and fresh Italian food I had been passing on to him in utero, here we were, barely a few days into his new life, going down to the supermarket to buy a box of infant formula off the shelf for him. Formula, after all, is the first industrially produced food for children that begins to interfere with the food culture. Mothers turn to it when the child doesn't latch on, as in my case, or later when they think the child isn't getting enough milk, or if they need a break, or if they have to work and cannot make arrangements to nurse. Infant formula has even been called a sort of "pediatric fast food" because it is now considered an acceptable alternative to breast milk rather than a special and important substance to be used to save infant lives in an emergency. My situation wasn't exactly an emergency, but we needed to give the baby some food for a few days while we worked at teaching him how to nurse.

I didn't want to give him formula, but there are no wet nurses left in Rome these days and certainly no milk banks. Fortunately we only used it for a short time, and with Valeria's persistence in helping us, he did learn to latch on after a week and was able to nurse for his first year. But during that frightening first week, we had no alternative: it was my milk or the ones made by Nestlé or Similac.

As I found out, formula has a sort of plain, chalky, milky, and slightly sweet taste. (Since I was giving it to my infant son, I thought I should try it.) Just like a McDonald's or Burger King hamburger, it tastes the same all over the world. It tastes the same every day, whereas a breastfed baby with a Roman mother tastes different foods at each meal. That baby is tasting garlic, rosemary, basil, sage, olive, lemon, tomato, eggplant, bitter greens, melon, squash, *prosciutto crudo,* cod, turbot, anchovies, octopus, and so on—varied flavors that, though they won't give him a taste for foreign foods, will make him more inclined to eat the foods that are found in plenty in his environment. And since traditional diets from long-established food cultures tend to be healthy, the child is likely to grow up healthy.

Formula and Infant Mortality

During pregnancy, I focused solely on my plans to nurse my baby, so I knew very little about the milk I was buying off the shelf. I was curious about this product that got us through those first few days of our son's life, and I discovered that infant formula was originally developed to lower infant mortality, which was nearly one-third in parts of the United States toward the end of the nineteenth century. Doctors at the time blamed the problem on inadequate or even "poisonous" milk being produced by the mother or by the wet nurse, who would have nursed the baby if the mother could not. The best mother's milk was recognized as being superior to anything else, but doctors at the time believed that few women were capable of producing the best milk.

Mother's milk seems to defy replication by scientists. They can analyze it, break it down into its component parts, and create a mixture that synthetically contains all those parts, and yet mother's milk is still vastly superior. Just as a food culture is more than individual foods and a recipe collection, the benefits of mother's milk for an infant are far greater than a chemical analysis would suggest. Formula is an industrially manufactured product that is made for infants, the most vulnerable among us, and yet few infants genuinely need an alternative to mother's milk. For those few who do need it, formula can be lifesaving if a wet nurse or milk bank cannot be found. As it turned out, the high infant mortality rate, the original rationale for producing formula, had everything to do with poverty and poor hygiene and nothing to do with poisonous breast milk.

Women's magazines in the nineteenth century reflected the growing interest among mothers in the science of feeding babies and children. Articles written by women urged mothers to ignore instinct and tradition and turn to the chemists and doctors (invariably men), who gave them scientifically formulated infant formula, for nutritional advice. Books and pamphlets of the period urged women to look to science, not to older female relatives. It led them to accept the teachings of science as superior to their own experience, their observations, and the cultural knowledge that would have been passed down through generations. This led to an enormous number of babies being raised on food that was often bad for them, killed some of them, and was certainly completely unnecessary in the majority of cases. This is exactly what is happening now with artificially fortified foods for children, which are being advertised around the world. Science again is being used as a marketing tool to convince parents that these children's foods are superior to the traditional foods that previous generations have eaten.

Even though breast milk did not turn out to be poisonous, the formula industry has not only survived but flourished. The one thing that infant formula has over mother's milk is packaging, and with packaging come health claims and exciting added ingredients like probiotics, omega-3, and omega-6. But it tastes the same whether it's being given to a baby in Madrid, Mafraq, or Medicine Hat.

The nineteenth century, when formula was being developed, was an intense period of scientific research on nutrition and disease. It was also the period when women moved away from the romantic ideology of domesticity toward the notion of "scientific motherhood." It seems like the place where we are stuck today. We read the health pages of the newspaper for advice on which nutrients we need or we read the labels on boxes to find out what to eat instead of following the traditional wisdom of our culture. It's why we head off to the often ironically named "health food store" for a dozen different artificial supplements to replace eating a well-balanced diet or to supplement our well-balanced diet. We have come to think that food alone is inadequate. (And in some cases, it *is* less adequate than it used to be. The wild greens that are still eaten in the Mediterranean region, for example, the prickly mixture of weeds, the *misticanza*, that Italians eat with spinach in the late winter, or the Greeks' steamed *horta*, which is eaten with olive oil and lemon, are far more complex than vegetables produced by chemically intensive industrial agriculture. Plants that have to defend themselves against pests produce more phytochemicals with antioxidants and anti-inflammatory effects.) We've become so versed in the pseudoscientific language of nutrition that we no longer know, and we certainly do not trust, a well-balanced diet when we see it.

Nestlé was among the first makers of infant formula in the nineteenth century. It used the milk of Swiss cows fed on Alpine grasses, which would have been great had Nestlé been feeding baby cows. It is now the biggest processed-food company in the world and derives most of its profits in its infant-nutrition division from the sale of infant formula. The nutrition division of this Swiss company had sales of CHF 7.2 billion (or around US$7.5 billion) in 2011. The company boasts of "double digit growth in emerging markets for both infant formula and infant cereals," which are products that very few babies actually need. But we are so used to seeing formula on the shelves. In supermarkets in Rome, it's stacked up with disposable diapers on one side of it and jars of baby food on the other. We're all so used to seeing babies drink formula that it seems quite natural.

Strangely enough, it's actually the sight of a woman breastfeeding that sometimes brings shocked stares. In 2009 in Detroit, security guards kicked a woman out of a Target store for breastfeeding her four-week-old infant. They thought that what she was doing was against the law. While most people felt the security guards' actions were excessive, there are still many who believe that women shouldn't breastfeed in public. And yet anyone who has ever had a four-week-old baby knows that babies need to feed all the time. If you never fed your baby in public, you would be a shut-in. In 2008, a Vancouver woman nursing her fussy infant in an H&M store while her husband tried on clothes was told to stop because she was making people uncomfortable. The clerk told her it was store policy, even though Canadian women have the right to breast-feed in public. In response, a few days later, women with babies in arms packed the store and fed their babies all at once. Though I nursed Nico in Rome throughout 2005 without being publicly humiliated, three years later a hundred mothers in Rome held a nurse-in to protest what they felt was a growing intolerance toward publicly nursing babies.

And what about Nestlé's double-digit growth in sales of infant formula and cereals in emerging markets? And what about the fact that in 2012, Nestlé bought Pfizer Nutrition, stating that it was delighted by the fact that 85 percent of Pfizer's infant nutrition sales are in emerging markets? Nestlé says it adheres to the World Health Organization's (WHO) International Code of Marketing of Breast-milk Substitutes, which is a set of rules developed in 1981 to counteract aggressive marketing by infant formula companies (including Nestlé) in underdeveloped countries. The idea behind the code is that babies are much better off if they are breastfed, not only for nutritional benefits but also because many of these places lack the clean water and hygienic conditions necessary to prepare formula.

Organizations like WHO and UNICEF try to get the "breast is best" message out to women in poorer countries, while refining the message to reflect that breastfeeding isn't so much best as it is normal and that the alternative is substandard. Yet, as Nestlé's growing sales figures testify, the message isn't being heard clearly, perhaps because the message is muffled somewhat by marketing and product labels that suggest infant formula is superior to mother's milk and will give these poor children an advantage in life. Sometimes parents in these countries turn to formula because it seems modern, which is a compelling image in cultures still living with the legacy of colonialism in an era of globalization.

Despite the introduction of the WHO code, these problems have worsened with increasing sales of infant formula. When the Philippines adopted the code in 1986, only a handful of infant formulas were available in the country. Now there are more than sixty different kinds, and only 16 percent of babies are breastfed exclusively for their first four to five months. In Bangladesh in 2007, a doctor complained that 70 percent of admissions to his hospital were formula-fed babies suffering from diarrhea and vomiting, figures far worse than when the International Code of Marketing of Breast-milk Substitutes was originally written. In the United States, fewer than half the babies are breastfed at six months, and only 13.3 percent of them are exclusively breastfed to that point. Canada is hardly any better, with only 14.4 percent of babies exclusively breastfed to six months.

Even when formula is properly prepared with clean water, it is still linked to health problems and obesity. It also cuts off children from the tastes of their culture, which they would otherwise find in breast milk. Rather than embedding the flavor of fish sauce, curry, or rosemary deep in the baby's brain, formula causes the baby's tastes to acclimate to a highly processed product made in a factory.

Though breastfeeding is natural, I learned firsthand that it is not always easy. I only managed to nurse my son because of the efforts of an aggressive Italian midwife. Even though I wanted to nurse, when I realized how much bother it would be to get the baby to latch on, that nursing meant that *I* always had to be the one to get up in the middle of the night to feed the baby or spend my precious few moments alone expressing milk so that James could feed him, I was tempted to give up and turn to formula. It seemed like the simple way to get through that physically demanding first year. Formula seemed so liberating and such an undeniably modern way to get on with our lives. While James was supportive of breastfeeding, he enjoyed being the one to give Nico the formula during those early difficult days when I wasn't yet able to nurse. He was a little sorry to hand that responsibility back to me.

In retrospect, I'm glad we didn't succumb to temptation. The first year passed quickly enough, and Nico's dependence on me lessened substantially after six months, when he started to eat some solid foods. Many women enjoy breastfeeding. It can be a welcome break from a busy working life, and it is a time to bond with your child. I was less romantic and nursed Nico more out of a sense of obligation. Even though it didn't cost me that much, I admit I felt the pull of the easier solution.

FOUR

When Children Learn to Taste

Babies' First Foods

AFTER NICO WAS born, I started going to a mothers' group with women from the United Kingdom and the United States. There were also a few women from Italy. It was one of those things I never imagined myself doing, but it was the very thing that saved my sanity during that first year with a baby. We shared tips on how to get our babies to sleep, and we comforted each other when they didn't sleep. And when our babies were approaching six months, we talked about what to give our children for their first taste of solid food.

The English-speaking mothers all introduced foods one at a time. We started with a little bit of rice cereal for a week, then added cooked apple to the menu, then zucchini, then mashed banana, and so on, adding one new food a week so that any allergic reactions would be easy to identify. Who knows why we all did it this way, maybe because we were all reading the *What to Expect* books. We were all excited about seeing our babies try food for the first time, but the babies' reactions were mixed. I remember that little Sam liked fruit, ate some green vegetables, but hated potatoes, and that Alice liked broccoli and cauliflower but not pears.

When Rocco's mother took the lid off the container of his lunch, the room filled with a heady smell of savory vegetable and herb soup. Rocco's arms waved happily and his mouth opened, ready before his mother had tied his bib on. All the Italian babies ate these aromatic lunches based on a traditional recipe, and all responded with great enthusiasm. One mother told me she thought our method was strange, that it was as though we were teaching our babies not to like food. She thought it was more important that they eat something tasty. For them, it wasn't explicitly about health; it was all about taste and pleasure. Even my midwife, who ascribed to the allergy theory, was dismayed by the blandness of the single-food offerings. She would frequently suggest adding a little olive oil and Parmesan to the mushy broccoli.

Our pediatrician had given me the recipe for the traditional Italian baby meal when Nico was nearly ready to start eating solid foods, but I didn't make it at first because I thought it sounded like too much work for something that he would very likely spit out. But after a few weeks of watching Italian babies eagerly devour their lunch, I decided to try it. The recipe starts with a *brodo*, which is a nutritious broth made by simmering chopped vegetables like carrots, onions, celery, and a little of whatever else you have on hand for an hour or two. The broth is the liquid basis of the baby's meals. Most people make it a couple of times a week and either keep it refrigerated or freeze it.

One night when I was making a squash risotto to go with roasted chicken and steamed broccoli, I took some of the risotto with the squash cooked into it; some of the chicken that I had stuffed with lemon, garlic, and rosemary; and some of the plain, cooked broccoli and combined them in a food processor. I poured some of the broth in a steady stream, adjusting the texture as it processed to make it easy to swallow. I put the whole works into a bowl, drizzled a little olive oil on top, and mixed in a spoonful of freshly grated Parmesan. The meal is known as the *pappa*, a word that makes Italian babies drool with anticipation. Sometimes parents will cook a few vegetables in the broth and then purée them into a thick soup. When babies are around eight or nine months old, parents mix in a little *stelline* (tiny, star-shaped pasta) with olive oil and Parmesan. Italian babies are usually receptive to these flavors since they have been steeped in them since they were but dots on the ultrasound.

James set the table and put Nico into his high chair. He was a little bit older by then—maybe nine months old—and had tried most of the vegetables and seasonal fruits with varying levels of enthusiasm. We set out our plates and put Nico's bowl in front of him. We fed him with a spoon, but he also dipped his fingers into the bowl and fed himself. The food was really good. We enjoyed it and so did he. I won't say it was a peaceful meal, because eating with a baby is rarely ever tranquil, but it was a pleasure to eat with him and to watch him enjoy the same food that we were enjoying.

I had been thinking only about nutrition and getting vegetables into the baby, like a dose of medicine. But the Italian mothers were training their babies' tastes, which would lead them to the foods that were good for them. Since the baby eats what the rest of the family is eating, it can actually be a fairly easy regimen to follow. You don't have to make anything special, but someone does have to cook. You can't do this with frozen dinners or takeout Chinese.

The first time we ran into difficulty with this method was when Nico was about eleven months old and we came to Toronto for Christmas. We were staying at other people's houses and I wasn't cooking. It wasn't always easy to make the *brodo* ahead of time or to slip in and purée part of dinner for the baby. Even when I did, the food didn't taste right to Nico. There was nothing wrong with what we were eating. In fact, I remember salmon with honey-mustard crust, which was very good, but it was all foreign to Nico's tongue. He liked his fish done with rosemary, garlic, and lemon. So I went to the supermarket, where I was amazed and, I admit, quite excited by what I saw.

In Italian supermarkets, you find several shelves of baby food, but mostly single vegetables like zucchini or carrots, or cooked meat like rabbit, beef, horse, lamb, or fish. It's becoming more common to see Italian parents use them like convenient ingredients for the *pappa*. If they haven't cooked meat for the family meal, they will stir a couple of spoonfuls of horse meat or rabbit into the puréed vegetable and broth mixture.

At an earlier time, they wouldn't have felt the need to give the child meat at each meal. Now that it is so conveniently available, many parents make use of these baby foods in this way. I was never very tempted to use them because I didn't really need it. But in a Toronto supermarket, I was more than tempted. I bought jars of food that contained entire meals. They sounded so good: chicken casserole with vegetables, sweet potato, and turkey, even lasagne with meat sauce and pasta primavera. I warmed them up and tried to feed them to Nico, but he would hardly touch them. At nearly a year old, his tastes were already becoming set, and clearly his tastes were influenced by Italy.

Though I had been cooking Nico's food, I was never really opposed to buying a jar of baby food from a health standpoint, because it's a fairly safe product. Commercial baby food is homogenized and pasteurized, meaning it is passed at high pressure through small holes and heated to a high-enough temperature to sterilize it and kill off any micro-organisms. It is mostly made without unhealthy additives. But you still have to read the labels and try to figure out what the ingredients list means. You can buy organic baby food, too. But it is made in a factory, so you don't have control over the quality of the ingredients, the processing method, or the taste.

Homemade Italian baby food tastes really good; it tastes like real food. It's fresh because it's made at the same time as the family meal. Commercially prepared baby food, not surprisingly, tastes like something that's been mass-produced in a factory and then passed through tiny holes at high pressure and squirted into airtight jars. And you never really know what's in baby food unless you've made it yourself. A European study that tested the nutritional value of the fruit in jars of baby food found that the quantity of fruit varied substantially and that there were often additives like sugar and starch. Food in a jar has that bland, processed-food-in-a-jar taste. If we feed babies food like this, even though it might not be bad for their overall health, that's the taste we are teaching them to like.

The Italian mothers' emphasis on taste rather than on an abstract notion of nutrition or fear of allergies is really about passing on culture. Italian parents think about nutrition in a broad sense and try to ensure that their children eat a wide range of foods, but they also assume that the foods of their culture are healthy. Fruits and vegetables are eaten every day in Italy, and many meals include legumes, some dairy, and a little meat here and there. In Rome, there is also a tradition of eating certain foods on certain days: on Wednesday, you eat pasta with lentils; Thursdays are for gnocchi; and, being a Catholic country, there's always fish on Friday. The children learn to love the flavors but also the rhythms; they learn about the range of foods available in a given season and they learn about the times of day when it is appropriate to eat them. They are learning to be members of a group—a vegetable-eating, olive oil–loving, Parmesan-revering group.

The Link between Tradition and Nutrition

Italian parents make a *brodo* not because they are cleverer than the rest of us, but because it's tradition. It's the *tradition*—the accumulated knowledge passed from generation to generation—that is clever. Contemporary mothers use a food processor, whereas their mothers used a potato masher or a mortar and pestle, but the idea is the same.

Today, even Italians—and pretty much everyone else—are becoming mesmerized by *nutrition*. Food manufacturers emphasize the nutritional benefits of their packaged children's foods to persuade parents to buy them. Even those parents who aren't normally swayed by advertising get caught up in the hype over children's nutrition. It causes parents to second-guess their traditional knowledge and do what they are told is in the best interests of their children.

A baffling trend in Italy—one that is much more developed in North America—is that once babies start eating solid food, their parents start buying them processed foods from outside their culture, because the foods promise good health, calcium, iron, and probiotics. Though yogurt is part of Italian food culture, and you can find fresh cow's milk, goat's milk, and buffalo milk yogurt at farmers' markets and in cheese shops, you also find brightly packaged, artificially flavored yogurt with added nutrients for children in the supermarket. Products like Danone's Danito Yogoloso, which has brightly colored candy on top; Nestlé's Mio products, which claim to be *Piu' Ricco in Frutta, Fonte di Vitamina B6*; and Kinder's Fetta al Latte, which is often described as a "milk sandwich," but in which the "bread" is really a spongy chocolate cake. Advertising and packaging that emphasize the nutritional content of packaged foods have eroded the confidence Italian parents have long had in their own food traditions. Packaged foods for children—including baby food, the specialty yogurts, the chocolate snacks—all have labels that radiate health, that proclaim them as tasty carriers of vitamins and nutrients. Of course, fresh food has vitamins too, but they're not listed on a stalk of broccoli. There is no label stating that it naturally contains vitamins A and C as well as other things that are good for us that we don't yet fully understand. It's easy to see where buying into the claims of packaged-food labels can lead. The tastes that have been slowly building over the baby's short life and that should help the child to understand the foods from his region and culture can be sidetracked by the pursuit of proper nutrition. Instead of developing a taste for the sourness of natural, fresh yogurt poured over early summer cherries for breakfast, the child develops a taste for sweet yogurt with artificial cherry flavoring. Because strained peaches are available all year round in a jar, and pasta primavera, which is a dish made with spring vegetables, is on the shelf in December, the child does not learn to connect certain foods with the seasons.

Independent Eaters

Jean Anthelme Brillat-Savarin, the French food philosopher, described our sense of taste in the early nineteenth century in entirely positive terms, without a trace of anxiety or the mistrust that afflicts those of us trying to eat in the twenty-first century. It strikes me now as a kind of innocent wisdom: "[T]aste as nature has endowed us with it is still that one of our senses which gives us the greatest joy. . . . Because, finally, in eating we experience a certain special and indefinable well-being, which arises from our instinctive realization that by the very act we perform we are repairing our bodily losses and prolonging our lives." Brillat-Savarin didn't have to contend with a food industry that perverts our natural senses from earliest childhood for profit. The toddler stage of childhood ought to be an exciting time of food exploration. Children ought to be wobbling around doing exactly as Brillat-Savarin suggests: learning to take pleasure in the food that will prolong their lives. In an ideal world, parents and the larger community would encourage children to love their local foods and to take pleasure in the rare sweetness of some of them. There are all these first tastes and new textures to experience. And the child finally has a chance to feed herself a little bit, to pick up food with her hands, to make her preferences known. It's up to parents to teach children to like the things that are good for them (not just to endure those foods, but to like them), and in most parts of the world, those are the foods that grow around them. It's a big challenge because children so easily like the things that are not good for them. And side-tracked by their obsession with nutrition, parents hide green vegetables in homemade chocolate brownies so children get the nutrition but don't have to deal with the taste. Parents buy biscuits with calcium, iron, thiamine, riboflavin, and niacin. Doing so doesn't teach children to like vegetables; instead it teaches them that brownies and biscuits are healthy.

Food scientists are becoming more interested in understanding the toddler stage of a child's development. I spoke with Gabriella Morini, who is a food scientist teaching at the Slow Food–affiliated University of Gastronomic Sciences in northern Italy, to see why small children so readily eat food that is bad for them and shun the food that is most nourishing. It seems counterintuitive. Wouldn't it make better biological sense if we liked the foods that are good for us and didn't like the ones that clog our arteries? "We like what we become used to eating early in life," she told me. "Vegetables are good for us, they are less caloric, and they have lots of vitamins and nutrients. But they are the hardest things to get young children to eat." No kidding!

Children are the most open to trying new foods when they are first being introduced to them. Once they start to walk, they enter a phase that Morini describes as "neophobia," where they become wary of certain tastes, particularly the bitter taste of many vegetables. Of course, this is an old survival technique. Children who could walk could poke around in the forest by themselves and put whatever they liked in their mouths. Their natural instinct to spit out anything bitter could save them from being poisoned. "It's an old model," said Morini. "It doesn't work so well anymore, but it's not going to change very quickly." The taste of salt was a good sign because it's something we need in small doses, it was harder to find, and our bodies can't store it. Sweetness represents energy, so children naturally like sweet flavors and fats for the same reason. Of course, our bodies are designed more for food scarcity than for abundance, so we like the high-calorie foods that were harder to find, and we are more wary and discriminating about the abundant green stuff that was all around us, some of which could have been dangerous.

According to Morini, children become settled in their preferences around age two. They can learn to like new foods, but it's much harder to get them to like new tastes. So if we don't establish a taste in toddlers for the bitterness of vegetables, they are not likely to change their preferences until past adolescence. Morini fears that many parents give up with vegetables after one or two attempts. Children, she explains, might keep spitting them out on instinct eight to ten times, but eventually they will come around.

She thinks the Italian *pappa* is a good way to teach babies to like the taste of vegetables because it mingles, without diluting or overpowering, the bitter taste with the more desirable fatty taste of the olive oil and the salty taste of the Parmesan, though she fears that even the fresh vegetables we buy at the market here in Italy have now been bred for a milder flavor. Many of the dark greens, like the varieties of *cicoria*, are quite bitter to my taste, but she says they are less bitter than the wild varieties that people used to eat (and still do, to some extent). Since the vegetables are often grown for export, they have to be milder to appeal to people outside the Italian food culture. She fears that future generations will lose the taste for those strong greens such as *cicoria*, *broccoletti*, and, for the wintertime, *puntarelle* (a bitter and pungent mixture of pale green chicory eaten raw with garlic and anchovies and found almost exclusively in and near Rome).

Many parents think that if they don't give their children sweets and fatty foods, they will never develop a taste for them. And they are often quite dismayed when they discover that their whole-grain-and-vegetable-fed toddlers will devour a bag of potato chips with gluttonous pleasure the first time they encounter one. Morini explains that we're programmed to like these foods; it's the other stuff that we have to learn to like. But if children develop a taste for the good, they might be able to deal with the bad when they get a little older.

We were fortunate to be living in Italy during Nico's "neophobic" phase because there are not too many recognizable "toddler foods" yet available in Italy. But I knew they were out there in other parts of the world. I would see tourists giving their children little packages of snacks to eat in their strollers. American friends would return to Italy from visits to New York and Los Angeles with bags of Goldfish crackers, small packages of miniature cookies for babies on the go, and little jellied fruit things.

The Outsiders' Perspective on Roman Habits

When Nico was around eighteen months old, I met a woman from Connecticut who had two children close to the same age, and we became good friends. Lydia and I would spend our days watching Nico, Henry, and Lilly explore the flowers and trees in Rome's botanical garden, and we would talk about the minutiae of our domestic lives. The world is small when you have little kids, and the most interesting conversations tend to be about ways to make that domestic life a little more peaceful. At first we talked wistfully about convenient toddler foods and wondered why we couldn't find any in Italy. We both imagined how much easier it would be to get our children to eat if we could only buy tasty and "healthy" snacks.

Neither of us at that time was really thinking about the benefits of local food or how the food culture affected our children. We just wanted them to eat. We were both drawn to snack foods because of our own general cultural familiarity with them. We bought into the idea of packaged health foods. But at the same time, we were uneasy about the idea of packaged snacks in this environment. We kept thinking that Italians, with their rich food culture, must have devised some tasty toddler foods, too, that we hadn't yet discovered. Her American and my Canadian cultures have been separating people into demographics for a long time now, and so we naturally thought of babies, toddlers, and very young children as requiring their own special foods. In fact, we had trouble imagining a world without them. But if the Italians were making them, we weren't finding them. Other than the sweet yogurts, breakfast cereals, and milk products, there weren't any specific toddler snacks, the sort of things we thought would be convenient for our children to eat in their strollers or in the car. We relied quite a lot on fresh fruit (and occasionally dried fruit) for snacks, on lightly cooked green beans, and on freshly baked, whole-wheat bread with crusts as hard as wood. We had to endure tantrums from small tyrants who did not want to eat carrots or cherry tomatoes. While we were romanticizing Multi-Grain Cheerios (which, as it turns out, have more sugar than regular Cheerios) as a fun toddler food, Lydia noticed that the Italian children didn't eat in their strollers the way our children did. Italian children developed their fine motor control while eating cooked chickpeas and cannellini beans at their designated snack time. At a very early age, they were able to amuse themselves by shelling peas and eating them, and they liked things like pasta with lentils for lunch. Italian parents also fought with their children about food, and they became as exasperated as we did when their children wouldn't eat their beans, vegetables, or fruit, but neither the parents nor the children had an alternative. Eventually the toddlers learned to eat, and to like, what was given to them.

45

Lydia and I adopted some of these practices quickly because we had to, but also because once we were able to push aside our cultural expectations of what constituted good toddler foods, and our sense that snack foods should be plentiful and convenient, we had to acknowledge the obvious: chickpeas and lentils are pretty healthy foods for children. So Henry and Lilly, along with Nico, began to eat like the Italian children, and we forgot about those dreams of easy, packaged snacks.

If you asked Italian parents what nutrients are in these beans, lentils, and peas, few could really tell you, though they might talk about how good they taste and that they like to eat them as part of a meal a few times a week. But if you asked parents who bought a package of Gerber Graduates Fruit Puffs, which are made by Nestlé, they would know all about the nutrients because that's the main reason they bought them. "Made for Babies and Toddlers" it says on the product website. "First step to healthy independent eating, Melts in baby's mouth, Perfect first finger food." The label says that these handy little snacks are made with whole grains and real fruit; they're a good source of vitamin E and zinc and contain iron for healthy brain development. They also carry Gerber's NUTRIPROTECT seal, which indicates that this product contains "Nutrition for Healthy Growth & Natural Immune Support." And yet they look suspiciously like candy. They're sweet like candy, too. Even if these snacks are as nutritious as the label says they are, they are also training children to seek out sweet snack-food products.

Graduates Fruit Puffs are an example of a food that is designed to appeal to a baby, with their bright colors, small size, and sweetness, but the label is designed to appeal to the nutrition-conscious parent. It's the perfect nonfood food. If someone handed a package of candy to a parent and said, "Here, feed this to your baby as a regular snack, she'll love it," I'm pretty sure the parent would refuse. But all the nutritional claims on snack foods for babies blind us to the fact that these products aren't very different from candy.

The Italian parent has grown up with a system developed over a long time that includes healthful foods incorporated into meals. The system also includes teaching babies and toddlers to enjoy these foods, too. There is a lot more pleasure in a system like this one. The system in which I grew up, based so much on science and food products, has divorced nutrition from food. It's intensified to the point where we now talk about the nutritional components of food rather than the food itself. I've even heard North American children talk about consuming protein and calcium rather than nuts and milk. They learn to consume nutrients rather than food, and to see food and food products mainly as nutrient carriers. Then they grow up and talk about bananas, as a friend of mine recently did, as potassium rather than as a tasty fruit that makes a nice snack or part of a good breakfast. My friend wasn't thinking about meals or the pleasure of food when she reached for her potassium from the fruit bowl; it was more like she had a checklist of nutrients to consume each day, and she randomly grabbed foods and packages that met her requirements. It's the kind of thinking that leads us as parents to buy food products like those fruit puffs, because we've read somewhere that small children need zinc or iron. And using those products reinforces the system by teaching children to seek nutrients rather than teaching them to eat food at mealtime.

As an example of the way we let our nutrient knowledge spoil our lunch, I once made white bean and vegetable soup for visiting Canadian friends and served it with Lariano bread made by a local Roman bakery. It's a traditional bread made with roughly ground flour, almost like whole wheat, a little salt, water, and olive oil, and it rises with natural yeast, which is really just fermented bread dough. It's allowed to rise for a very long time, which gives it texture and makes it easier to digest. It's then baked in a wood-fired oven. This bread is so good, it makes you swoon. But no one ate the bread because they all believed, as the latest diet and media reports have told us, that carbohydrates make you fat.

No one thought about how good the bread would taste with the soup. If anyone did think about how soups like the one I'd made are always served with bread, they might have dismissed the tradition as something we did in error before we knew that carbohydrates make you fat. But no one thought about the fact that soups with beans are traditionally served with bread to form a complete protein. The nutrition scientist in us might like to know that certain proteins lack particular amino acids, but if you add another protein lacking different amino acids to the meal, you have the complete protein. This is why the Italians have created dishes like *pasta e fagioli* (pasta with beans), *pasta e ceci* (pasta with chickpeas), and, the one most loved by children, *pasta e lenticchie* (pasta with lentils).

Maybe carbohydrates do make you fat. But Italian adults eat bread, they eat pizza, and they eat pasta nearly every day. Some people eat pasta twice a day. Yet Italian adults are not particularly overweight (though obesity statistics are rising in Italy as well as the rest of the world as diets change). I've tried to figure out why, but I really can't find a definitive answer. An Italian nutritionist suggested that it was because the bread is usually made with natural yeast and is freshly baked every day. An Italian chef told me that it was because their bodies have adapted to this high-carbohydrate diet in the way the Inuit adapted to the high fat content of whale blubber. An Italian friend said Italians believe that overcooked pasta will make you fat, but when it's cooked al dente, it's fine. Maybe they're not overweight because they're not given to snacking between meals, or because they eat carbohydrates as part of a meal and perhaps eat less of other fat-producing foods as a result. What this really says is that culture and tradition are a way of living, and nutritional knowledge is only one tiny little part of the picture. We worship nutrition sometimes to the detriment of our health and that of our children.

I exchanged e-mails with a Brazilian doctor and nutrition professor, Carlos Monteiro, who has been researching the idea that the most significant factor linking food with health and with disease is not so much the food itself or the nutrients in the food but the processing. His hypothesis is that it's the processing the food undergoes before we buy it and feed it to our children that could be damaging, and there is no way we can know this by reading the labels on the package. The processing changes the food. We already know that an apple is quite different from apple juice made from nothing but apples, with absolutely no added ingredients. The process of extracting the juice concentrates the sugars and leaves the beneficial fiber behind.

If we separate nutrition from food, and food from place and culture, we're only getting part of what is good for us, and we suffer from what is missing. Children are soaking up knowledge constantly, and children who eat within a food culture are soaking up knowledge that perpetuates their traditions, connects them to the past, and establishes healthy food habits to keep them going in the future. If we look at the history of nutrition science and see how vitamins were discovered, we can see that this knowledge and more were already known and contained within the accumulated knowledge of mature food cultures. When we take this knowledge and we focus too much on the vitamins and nutrients without thinking about the food and its context, when we bring in food products fortified with extra vitamins and nutrients to replace real food, we risk losing (and in some places, we have irretrievably lost) the knowledge that keeps us alive. When we assume the experts at the giant food companies know better how to feed our children than we do, we might be cutting our children off from vital knowledge they need to thrive. When we consult the media for the latest in nutrition news, we are doing exactly as those women in the nineteenth century did when they embraced infant formula and the science of motherhood.

FIVE

The Art, Science, and Tradition of Eating

Taste and Memories

AFTER WE HAD spent a few years in Rome, after we had gotten to know the rhythms of the yearly cycle, we really started to feel as if we had a past in this country. We also had good friends who we could say we had known for years. Whereas I had been cooking dishes that were new to me, there came a point when I realized I was making dishes with a history that included me.

For instance, I recently made a summer pasta that has become a favorite over the years. I chopped up some fresh San Marzano tomatoes and threw them in a pan with olive oil to cook while the pasta water heated. Once the tomatoes started to break down a little, I added some salt. When the pasta was ready, I took the sauce off the heat and threw in handfuls of torn-up basil leaves. Then I tossed the pasta in the pan with the sauce, put it on the plates, and grated some soft and creamy ricotta salata on top. We first had this pasta one July weekend with our friends Elisabeth and Massimiliano. I watched Liz throw it together so effortlessly, while a bunch of us stood in their tiny kitchen eating oven-cured black olives and drinking a cool glass of white wine. Massi tossed a salad and put a whole fish dressed with herbs and lemon in the oven. They had invited us to come for lunch, and within half an hour we were sitting down to a feast. I loved the creaminess of the cheese and the intense, barely cooked flavors of the tomatoes and basil. When I ate this pasta again with James and Nico, none of us thought about the flavonoid content of the tomatoes or about the protein, calcium, or vitamin A in our meal. Instead, we ended up talking about Liz and Massi. We told Nico about that lunch we had with them in their tiny house near the lake in Bracciano when he was a tiny baby. We talked about how much we like them, and how we'd really like to see them again soon. The pleasurable experience we had the first time we ate the pasta made the food taste even better.

A History of Nutrient Exploration

The science of nutrition has yielded some interesting facts, but it has also changed our relationship with food. While there's nothing wrong with trying to understand the nutrient content of our food, it seems a far less enjoyable task than preparing a particular dish because it reminds you of your friends.

When the German chemist Justus von Liebig broke food down into its chemical compounds in the nineteenth century, he was trying to understand what were the essential elements in food that sustained us. It was an intellectual query. Liebig, who was also one of the first to make infant formula, identified the percentages of protein, fat, carbohydrates, and water that he thought were needed in a healthy diet. He believed that those were the important elements of nutrition, that it didn't matter what foods people actually ate as long as the balance of protein, fat, carbohydrates, and water was achieved. Liebig's work really marks the point at which food left the kitchen and entered the laboratory.

Another food scientist who followed Liebig was Stephen Babcock, an American who suspected that there was more to food than Liebig's four components. He had been working with dairy farmers to devise a method of measuring the amount of butter fat in milk. Babcock noted that the farmers believed their cows were healthiest when they were allowed to graze on a wide variety of plants, which is traditionally the way that cows were fed. The farmers, through experience and observation, knew something the scientists didn't, and Babcock set out to shed some scientific light on the farmers' theory. He divided cows into four groups: one group was fed only corn; another group, only wheat; another, only oats; and the fourth group was fed a mixture of all three grains. All the diets contained the same amount of protein, fat, carbohydrate, salt, and water. (The one thing Babcock didn't do was allow them to graze on grasses and plants, which is what the farmers believed to be best for the cows.) If Liebig was correct, the cows should all have fared about the same. At first they seemed to be fine, to be growing, and to be healthy. Later, when these cows were bred, their calves proved to be extremely different from each other. The calves of the corn-fed group were mostly fine, but the calves of the other three groups were weak and sick. All the calves of the wheat-fed group were blind. This demonstrated that there was more to food than just the simple chemical components Liebig had identified.

The study of vitamins (a word that wasn't applied to these nutrients until the twentieth century) moved in increments throughout the nineteenth century. A big revelation came when scientists realized that certain ailments were caused by something lacking in the diet. Diseases such as rickets, which softens the bones, scurvy, which mainly afflicted naval explorers, and some kinds of childhood blindness and infections were all caused by something missing in the diet. It took a long time for scientists to see that these diseases were caused by a dietary deficiency, because they were used to viewing infections or viruses as the cause of illness. Rickets, as it turned out, was prevented and even cured by sunlight or cod-liver oil, both of which stimulated the body to produce a hormone that is somewhat mistakenly known as a vitamin: vitamin D. Scurvy could be prevented and cured by eating citrus fruits or other foods that were high in vitamin C. Adequate levels of vitamin A in children's diets encouraged proper eye development and greater resistance to infection.

Focusing on single nutrients in this way has been important for the scientific understanding of how such nutrients keep us healthy, but it has led to a very narrow view of nutrients in health. There's nothing wrong with understanding how vitamins function in food and in our bodies; the problems come from what has been done with this knowledge. Rather than recognizing the importance of variety in diets, the scientific approach often leads to a fixation on single nutrients apart from the foods that contain them. For example, the discovery that vitamin A deficiency in children causes vision problems and blindness and makes them more prone to dangerous infections such as pneumonia has led to widespread vitamin A–supplementation programs. Half a billion vitamin A capsules are produced and distributed to 200 million children every year. The idea, of course, is to eradicate vitamin A deficiency. It sounds simple enough, but it hasn't worked. If a child is vitamin A deficient, it's likely because he doesn't have a wide enough variety of foods to eat, which will cause him to be deficient in other nutrients, too. A body that isn't well nourished often cannot absorb the vitamins in supplements as well as it could the vitamins in food. Also, some children are receiving too much vitamin A because of the supplements, and this is creating different health problems. When children get their nutrients from food rather than supplements, overdosing on vitamins doesn't occur.

In some parts of the world, children who are deficient in vitamin A are surrounded by foods high in the vitamin, but the children either don't have access to them or they've lost the traditional knowledge that would have led them to know what to eat. For example, there were children in a region of Brazil who were taking vitamin A capsules while there were bushes and trees all around them bearing fruits rich in vitamin A, such as *buriti* and *pequi*, among others. A nutritionist living in the area called attention to this and noted that the indigenous people, who had since been exterminated or driven out of the area, would have known to eat these fruits, because they had good night vision. Had the children been carrying on the traditions of the local culture, they would have been including these fruits in their meals—they would have eaten them on their own or had recipes that included them—and there would have been no need for the supplements.

A seemingly objective scientific inquiry into the effect of vitamins has so changed the way we think about diet and health that we sometimes forget completely that food and vitamins go together. We think of vitamin A deficiency as a disease to be cured with a capsule, when really it's a problem caused by lack of food or changes in diet. Children on the Polynesian islands of Micronesia never experienced vitamin A deficiency until they shifted away from their traditional diet and replaced it with cheap, imported foods. They started eating imported Cavendish bananas instead of their own local varieties, such as the shorter, fatter, yellow-fleshed and vitamin A–rich Karat banana. The government of Micronesia started a campaign to champion local foods, creating a postage stamp of a toddler eating a Karat banana. Returning to traditional, locally grown varieties of bananas solved the vitamin-deficiency problem in the region.

As part of its Zero Hunger initiative, Brazil has launched school feeding programs in an effort to tackle the dual problems of obesity and malnutrition that plague the children of that country. In 2006, the Brazilian government invested nearly US$800 million to allow schools to buy organic fruit, vegetables, and meat from local sources. The program both improved children's health and provided an economic boost for small farmers. Though it's more work to provide real food for undernourished children than it is to distribute supplements, the results are far more self-sustaining. Zero Hunger addresses micronutrient deficiencies while improving children's health overall with food. It supports local markets and shows people how to grow food, providing benefits that will last well into the future.

For the most part around the world, however, vitamin A deficiencies are still being treated artificially. In addition to the supplementation program, researchers have developed a variety of rice genetically modified to contain a high level of vitamin A. The rice is being planted and introduced into the diet in India and the Philippines, where people have been forced, due to extreme poverty and large industrial farming practices that favor single cash crops, to live almost solely on a diet of rice. The biotech companies see the problem (or perhaps their opportunity) simply as vitamin A deficiency. They acknowledge that it is caused by a poor diet, but they believe that solving the problem with food is unrealistic. (It's funny how the food industry often says it's "unrealistic" for poor people to have access to real food, for parents to prepare real food, or for children to like real food.)

What is so easily forgotten is that children could get the vitamin A they need from a small carrot. Orange and yellow vegetables could do the trick, or some leafy greens, or a little broccoli. A serving of any of these vegetables a day would give them enough vitamin A, not to mention vitamin C, iron, folic acid, and other nutrients. Instead they receive supplements or genetically modified rice that target a single vitamin deficiency and neglect their overall health.

As studies on the effects of particular vitamins or other compounds in food continue, with the results reverently reported in the health pages of newspapers and magazines, it's no surprise that we all start to think in terms of component parts. We don't think about food and we certainly don't think about meals; we think about nutrients. It's this focus that leads us to see children in some parts of the world as vitamin A deficient rather than food deficient, and it's what leads us to think that soft, sweet, candy-like fruit lumps qualify as a healthy snack for a crawling baby.

Michael Pollan, in his book *In Defense of Food*, blames part of our obsession with nutrients over food on the power of lobby groups that have prevented any talk of food in terms of good and bad health. He points to the 1977 Senate Select Committee on Nutrition and Human Needs in the United States, which issued a set of guidelines recommending that Americans cut back their consumption of red meat and dairy products and increase their consumption of plant foods. The guidelines were based on solid nutritional research and offered advice that was easy to understand: eat fewer hamburgers and more salad, less pork and more spinach or barley or oats. But the red meat and dairy industries forced the committee to retract its advice and instead ask the public to "choose" meat, poultry, and fish that would reduce their saturated fat intake. "For with these subtle changes in wording a whole way of thinking about food and health underwent a momentous shift," wrote Pollan. We're no longer talking about food, but about saturated fat, and we're no longer talking about eating less of anything because the food industry needs consumption to increase, not decrease. In his book, Pollan quotes a member of a panel examining the relationship between diet and cancer who said that even though the evidence showed that those with higher cancer rates ate more animal foods and fewer plant foods, the report focused on nutrients instead of food. The simple message that we should favor plant foods over animal foods was lost.

Pollan refers to this focus on nutrients as the "ideology of nutritionism," and it's something that serves the food industry quite well. The industry uses science in its marketing to exploit nutritional knowledge, our fears of deficiency diseases, and our desire to improve our health. It responds to the accusation that its foods are contributing to America's, and the world's, ill health by trying to liberate sodium, fats, and calories from junk food and inject it with vitamins, minerals, and artificial sweetness. Increasingly, the industry markets these foods as healthy choices for children.

Eating by Color

I love food shopping with Nico. When he was a toddler, I would frequently stop in the market to load up his stroller with fresh fruit and vegetables. When he was two years old and really making his food preferences known, I enjoyed letting him choose the fruit and some vegetables for dinner. He loved the rows of bright colors and he quickly learned the Italian names of things: the peaches were *le pesche* and the grapes were *l'uva*. On one early summer day when we were passing through the market looking for white peaches, Nico spotted a big display of ruby red cherries from Sabina, *le ciliegie*, the first of the season. I asked for a kilo of them, and the woman serving us handed two by their stems to Nico. Though I'm sure he had eaten them the year before, that was nearly half his life ago and he didn't remember. This time he was fascinated by them. He loved their alluring red color, he loved plucking the fruit from the stem, and when he took a bite, there was a look of unexpected pleasure on his face. I worried about him choking on the pit, but the fruit vendor shrugged it off and said he would spit it out. We both watched him chew with intense concentration, rolling the cherry around in his mouth, and then, with a messy trickle of red juice running down his chin, he spit the pit onto his lap. We also bought small, bright yellow plums (*le susine*) that day, bright orange apricots (*le albicocche*), and a baby watermelon (*il cocomero*) with the most intense pink flesh. We bought both green and yellow beans (*i fagiolini*); green, red, and yellow peppers (*i peperoni*); and lettuces (*le insalate*) that ranged from pale green through dark purple. These were a lot of words, but they also represented a lot of colors. While he was soaking up the bilingual vocabulary, he was also indulging his innate fascination with the natural colors of food.

James says that when he was a child, his mother used to stress the importance of color in a meal. She didn't talk about the specific vitamins associated with specific colors. Instead she talked about how pleasing it was to look at a plate with many colors of food on it. A plate that had only brown meat, white potatoes, and maybe a green vegetable was dull. She wanted to see yellow, red, and orange, too. My mother also talked about the need for more than one color of vegetable at lunch and dinner. If there was only one color, the plate was lacking. It was wrong. It's easier to think in terms of colors than vitamins, and if we make sure to eat as many colors as we can, we're going to pretty much cover most of our vitamin requirements. If we add to that some whole grains, a little meat and fish, some nuts and seeds, a little dairy, we will have everything we need for a healthy diet. If we're lucky enough to have a market with a lot of seasonal, fresh food, if we have money to buy it, then we can rely on this attraction we feel for all these beautiful colors to lead us to eat what's good for us. In this environment, even a small child can pick out the ingredients for a decent meal. But we don't trust food traditions when it comes to food and health, and we don't trust this folksy wisdom about colors either.

Diets That Lack Nutrients

Part of what is so fascinating (and so anxiety-producing) about food science is that a diet lacking in a single nutrient can make a person extremely sick. People who rely on a single crop or a limited number of foods are particularly vulnerable to vitamin deficiencies, especially when something happens to change their diet. In her fascinating book *Vitamin Discoveries and Disasters,* Dr. Frances Frankenburg tells an interesting story about rice. Before the invention of the milling machine around 1870, rice all over the world was milled by hand, which removed the inedible husk but usually left the brown skin. The steel rollers of the milling machine were able to remove both the husk and the brown skin, leaving polished white rice that was easier to cook and eat. It became popular everywhere. Suddenly beriberi, which is caused by too little thiamine, and which had turned up in various places for centuries, became a more common problem. Beriberi has a few different forms, but generally it makes the legs swell, causes heart problems, and sometimes causes confusion and a loss of memory. Whole grains, nuts, legumes, and yeast are all good sources of thiamine. It turned out that the brown skin on rice contains thiamine, too, so once people who depended on rice as a staple in their diet started eating refined white rice, they became sick. Beriberi had existed before in Southeast Asia and Japan, and its cause had been understood. Many cultures knew that they had to eat beans or meat with their finely milled rice. But when the disease spread again after the invention of the mechanical mill among people who ate mainly rice and little else, they seemed to have forgotten the cause. It wasn't really recognized until well into the twentieth century. But rather than return to a diet of whole-grain rice, many countries fortified the staple food with thiamine instead. The diet was characterized as being thiamine deficient rather than whole-grain deficient.

A researcher on the National Academy of Sciences panel on diet and cancer in the United States told Michael Pollan that he worried about the panel report's focus on single nutrients. He was concerned that the report made it sound as if it was the vitamin C or the beta carotene that seemed to protect against cancer rather than the fruits and vegetables themselves. It could be that there is something else in the fruit or vegetable, or it could be the interaction between more than one element of the fruit or vegetable, that protects against cancer. Focusing on nutrients alone misses the point, and it makes it seem like fortifying unhealthy foods will fix our health problems.

The history of zeroing in on single nutrients shows that scientists and researchers frequently failed to recognize that many cultures already knew how to eat in a way that preserved their health and didn't leave them vulnerable to deficiency diseases. The knowledge had been passed down through generations in the form of specific foods, recipes, rituals, and tastes, though the knowledge was not articulated and parsed out in a way that the scientists would recognize. Nutritional researchers' discoveries often amounted to a rediscovery or a scientific confirmation of some kind of local knowledge. For example, when the Spanish conquistadors brought corn from the New World back to Europe in the sixteenth century, they failed to note the way the Native people grew, cooked, and ate it. The body cannot absorb the niacin in corn when it is cooked and eaten alone. But corn soon became a staple crop in countries like Italy, France, Spain, and Egypt, replacing local, more nutritious grains. Many poor people in these countries, whose diet consisted only of corn (cooked in the form of cornmeal and corn flour), developed pellagra, a disease that made their skin become coarse, scaly, and red wherever it was exposed to the sun. They developed diarrhea and dementia, and they often died from the disease. For a long time, people thought there was something wrong with the corn, that it contained bacteria or a fungus. What they didn't realize is that a diet that relies on corn lacks essential nutrients, and that corn needs to be consumed with other foods for it to release the nutrients it does contain.

Why didn't the Native people in the New World develop pellagra? They had a diverse diet based on local plants, animals, and fish to start with, but they also knew from generations of trial and error how to treat corn so that their bodies could extract the maximum nutrition from it. They prepared the corn with the mineral lime, which is an alkaline substance that softens the kernel and releases the niacin. The Aztecs, the Incas, and the Native Americans didn't suffer from pellagra because their food culture contained this knowledge. They might not have known about the individual nutrients, but they didn't need to know. What was important was the observational knowledge that people didn't get sick when they ate food prepared a certain way. So food grown and prepared this way became a part of their food culture. Yet it wasn't until well into the twentieth century that scientists identified niacin, also known as vitamin B3, and realized that it prevented pellagra.

Even the way Native Americans grew corn reflected a deep understanding of the plant. They practiced a form of agriculture known as the three sisters: they planted corn in the center of a mound and then planted beans and squash around it. The corn plants grew tall and the bean stalks used the corn for support. The beans themselves provided nitrogen to the soil, making it richer, and the squash grew along the ground, which prevented weeds and made it harder for pests to get in. The three plants grew better together this way than they would have if planted separately. When eaten together, the three plants offer a fairly complete array of amino acids and vitamins.

The literature is full of stories about the food and health knowledge of Native people, and even today, pharmaceutical companies try to use and patent the medicinal plant knowledge of these people. In the sixteenth century, when Jacques Cartier was exploring in Canada, he and his men became sick with scurvy after they were forced to spend a winter in Quebec. At the same time, few of the Native people were becoming sick, and those who were seemed to recover, while the French continued to suffer. The Native people gave Cartier and his men an infusion of bark and leaves or needles (possibly from a white cedar, though it's not known for sure) and they recovered quickly.

The Inuit, who traditionally didn't have fresh fruit or vegetables but did eat a diet of raw meat and blubber, also didn't suffer from scurvy. The British who were exploring the Arctic in the nineteenth century did not want to eat as the Inuit did. They brought salted meat with them and tended to boil away the vitamins in anything fresh they might have found. The Royal Navy sent ship after ship into the region looking for the Northwest Passage, and sailor after sailor became sick, many dying and none realizing that the Inuit knew something about preserving their health. Not only did the Inuit not get scurvy, they also did not suffer from cardiovascular disease. Raw meat, blubber, and fresh fish are intensely nutritious, and they contain enough traces of vitamin C to ward off scurvy.

A contemporary traveler might also be repulsed by raw meat, but it's the fat content of the blubber that would likely prevent him from eating it. Though we have become accustomed to demonizing fat as unhealthy, it was a healthy part of the Inuit diet. The Inuit survived because they figured out how to live in that environment, balancing their bodies' needs with what was available. Although whale blubber is high in omega-3 fatty acid, which is being injected into nearly every packaged food on the shelves these days, it's probably only part of the reason for the Inuit people's good health.

Unlike the British, the French Canadian voyageurs, the *coureurs de bois*, did copy the Native people in the seventeenth and eighteenth centuries. They dressed in furs, carried few provisions, and ate what they found around them as the Native people did, and they were able to avoid scurvy. In each of these cases, it was local foods and food knowledge, not nutrient knowledge, that protected people's health.

It was in the early twentieth century when scientists discovered that sunlight could stimulate the body to produce vitamin D, which would cure and prevent rickets. Yet scientists were puzzled by the fact that poor children in the Hebrides in Scotland, who lived in dark, smoky, almost windowless houses and were rarely taken outside and almost never saw sunlight, were not suffering from rickets or any sign of vitamin D deficiency. In fact, these children were quite healthy. The protective factor turned out to be the food culture of the Hebrides. The children were breastfed until they were ready to be weaned to solid foods. Then they were given exactly what the adults ate, which was cod heads stuffed with cod liver, milk, different kinds of fish, turnips, oatmeal, and potatoes. Now that children's foods are fortified with vitamin D, it's hard to imagine encouraging a child who lives in a gloomy climate to eat a cod head stuffed with its own liver. Certainly it's an acquired taste and one that was best developed in childhood.

In recent years, vitamin D has become controversial. The food industry wants to fortify many more of its food products with it because of its purported health benefits. The industry is not talking about rickets anymore but is conducting its own research and calling attention to the possible role of vitamin D in preventing autoimmune diseases, cancer, and heart disease. But a joint review by the Institute of Medicine (IOM) commissioned by the Canadian and US governments found that there was no evidence to support this theory. To the contrary, the IOM warned that vitamin D can be toxic at high levels. Too much of it raises the risk of bone fractures and irreversible kidney damage. Pregnant and lactating women should not take vitamin D supplements or eat vitamin D–fortified foods. The IOM found that most people need no more than about six hundred International Units (IUs) a day, but with what our bodies produce in sunlight and what many of us are getting in foods that are already fortified with vitamin D, like milk and orange juice, many people might already be getting too much. In addition, most supplements contain anywhere from one thousand to five thousand IUs. If we lack sunshine (and the IOM report said we need only low levels of sun to produce enough vitamin D), we can get vitamin D in fatty fish, cod-liver oil, whole eggs, and beef liver. The body processes the vitamin D absorbed from sunlight and food differently and more efficiently than from a supplement.

Vitamin supplements don't act in the body the same way as vitamins derived from food. For example, when diabetics take vitamin B supplements, they increase their risk of heart attack, stroke, and kidney damage. High doses of vitamin C, higher than anyone would be able to ingest through food, seem to cause cataracts. When people take vitamins, there's also the risk that because they think they're covered, they might not be careful about what they're eating; they might not bother to think about whether they're getting most of their calories from fresh (or frozen, in some climates and at certain times of year) fruits and vegetables, or whether they're eating more whole grains and not too much meat. The same is true when it comes to giving vitamin supplements to children. We all worry that our children are not eating enough vegetables or fruit or getting the whole range of nutrients they need to grow. My own pediatrician in Rome recommended against giving my son vitamins because she said I would be more vigilant about his diet if he wasn't taking them. She stressed the importance of training the child to eat properly. She also looked at his diet, checked his weight, height, and other vital signs regularly enough to reassure me that he wasn't going to get scurvy, rickets, pellagra, or beriberi. As Michael Pollan noted, we should strive to be the kind of people who take vitamins—that is, people who look after themselves in numerous ways—and then not take them.

The scientific approach to food is intellectual, whereas traditional diets rely on collective memory and cumulative knowledge passed on through culture. On the surface, the science seems smarter, whereas eating by color and because of happy memories seems positively dippy in this day and age. The science is smart; it's the application of the science that has sometimes been wrong-headed. The scientific approach to nutrition disregards traditional wisdom. It tells us that we can be more than healthy; we can be super-healthy by getting extra vitamins and nutrients, by eating special foods. It tells us to mistrust our sense of smell, taste, and texture, to ignore the visual delight of multicolored fruits and vegetables, and to take supplements and eat fortified foods. The food industry uses the science to promote its products. And it trains children to think this method is not only normal but superior.

SIX

Selling Food to Children

The Stranger with Candy

THE HEALTH CLAIMS on children's breakfast cereals and other food products appeal to a parent's intellect. We want our children to grow up healthy and strong, so we are more likely to choose foods that promise to promote their health and strength. The food product manufacturers need to persuade parents to trust them. But they have an even greater need to influence the tastes of children very early on so that their sense of taste will lead them to these foods throughout their lives, and food products will become their food culture. To do this, they quietly bypass parents and speak directly to the child.

It was clear that we had a problem when, at age three, Nico would ask for a specific type of yogurt by name and for the chocolate bar that you can eat for breakfast and is really very good for you. We had been letting him watch cartoons on Saturday mornings, as James and I had done as children. Though the commercials made me uneasy, I fell back on the assumption that I survived commercials in childhood and certainly he would too. But I noticed that Nico was becoming more agitated after watching television, that he would want to eat things that we didn't have in our refrigerator or cupboards, and that he would recognize children's food products when he saw them in the supermarket or in the hands of one of his little stroller-bound peers.

We tried muting the TV during commercials, but he would still stare at them open-mouthed. We then tried turning the TV off while the commercials were running, but he would go crazy with fury and want them back on. We tried to interest him in videos instead, but he would ask for "real TV," and I realized it was because he was drawn to these ads for food: colorful, happy, fun food meant just for him. He was also drawn to the ads for toys, which worried me, but the food ads worried me more. Maybe I should have put the TV in a box and left it on the curb, since there's no such thing as commercial-free children's television in Italy. But I didn't. I let him watch TV on Saturday mornings because I enjoyed the break. I could sit down beside him on the couch and sip my cappuccino, flip through a magazine, or sometimes watch a full episode of *Manny Tuttofare* (that's *Handy Manny* to the rest of you). We tried to be careful about the cartoons that we chose, but we couldn't do much about the advertisements.

Now I realize that even the cartoons are problematic. Many of them are American shows dubbed into Italian, and I didn't immediately recognize that they portray fast-food culture as the norm. The characters are always eating fast food. In shows like *Ben 10*, the main character is always walking around sipping from a giant soft-drink container and eating in a fast-food restaurant. Much of *SpongeBob SquarePants* takes place in a fast-food joint. Scooby-Doo and Shaggy do little but eat unhealthy snacks and fast food. In fact, the snacks are depicted as so alluring that Shaggy and Scooby are willing to go against their better judgment and chase ghosts and monsters, as long as they can have their tasty treats as a reward. And yes, you can buy Scooby-Doo fruit-flavored snacks by Betty Crocker. It makes a parent long for the days of Popeye and his spinach. These cartoons reinforce fast-food culture in America and help to introduce it to children in other countries. Children from non-American cultures see characters eating this way and assume it is normal, almost a part of their culture, too, especially when they see snack foods and drink containers depicting these same characters.

We tried to limit Nico's exposure to commercial television, but we did let him watch it for about a year. Then we moved to a different house and decided not to bother getting the satellite service at our new place.

Other than the international news on BBC and Saturday morning cartoons, there was nothing to watch anyway. We live in Italy, remember, and television here is unrelentingly awful, unless you like endless variety shows hosted by women in their underwear. Also, around that time, I saw a statistic from the Center for Science in the Public Interest that said that nine out of ten food advertisements shown during Saturday morning cartoons were for foods of poor nutritional value. The study was carried out on major broadcast and cable networks in the United States, but it sounded about right for Italy, too. We saw countless advertisements for sugary cereals, packaged cakes, chocolate bars, cookies, yogurt-like products, and ice cream. They certainly weren't showing children eating bowls of fruit salad or plates of broccoli. James and I both knew our son would be better off without these ads. So we bought lots of DVDs of cartoon shows, movies, and even old TV shows so that we would have something for Nico's Saturday morning viewing.

At first, he asked for "real TV" and was a little annoyed that we no longer had it. But then when he realized we couldn't do anything about it, he forgot about it. He also forgot about the food products he had wanted. He became happier and generally more agreeable. He was content with far less viewing time. In the past, we would have to argue with him about turning off the set. Now he would turn it off himself at the end of a show or movie.

We have to be on guard to protect our children against so many potentially destructive intrusions into their lives, yet food marketing that goes directly to children often slips in at their level where we don't even see it. Even when we do see it, it's astonishing how little we can do about it. If a well-dressed man in the park persistently offered sweets to your child, ignoring your requests for him to stop, I'm sure you would scoop up your child and leave the park. I'm fairly certain everyone in the park would run the man out. Yet there are men and women offering candy and food products to our children all day long. We let them into our houses through the television, radio, Internet, and DVDs we let our children

watch instead of commercial TV. They beckon our children to follow them, they offer them sweet and savory delights, and they promise never to say no the way that grouchy old parents do. These candy and food product pushers are on billboards on our streets, they are in our schools, and they are hidden, like sleeper agents, among our children's friends. They find our children through video games and social networking sites. They pop up, unseen by parents, when children are researching their homework projects online. Our children are under constant bombardment by advertisements for food products in what those in the industry call the "360-degree world"—a world of their creation. Ed Mayo and Agnes Nairn, the authors of a book called *Consumer Kids*, refer to these advertisers as "the child catchers."

Corporate Food Culture

Contrast this environment where food is constantly pushed on children with a healthy food culture in which the man who sells you a slice of pizza is concerned about you ruining your dinner; where children learn from an early age that however alluring those pastries in the shop window might appear, you eat them only after a special dinner; where markets are stocked with a huge array of fresh ingredients and where the shoppers chat with each other about ideas for cooking. Imagine a culture where everyone upholds a certain standard when it comes to food so that you can be sure that the food your child eats at school or his friends' houses will be fresh and healthy rather than packaged. Advertising food products, particularly to children, subverts such a food culture. Though the culture supports healthy habits, marketing exploits your desires and weaknesses and encourages you to do what is bad for you. The traditional food culture incorporates opportunities to take pleasure in food, with feast days for religious, seasonal, or familial reasons. Marketing encourages self-indulgence, and when every day is special, nothing is special. Children have little defense against food marketers, and it doesn't take long before these intruders define the culture to suit their needs.

Though regulators in many countries are struggling to place limits on advertising to our children, for the most part, companies have the right to pursue them throughout their childhoods. In the United States, the food corporations raise their First Amendment right to free speech whenever regulatory agencies threaten to rein them in. Through a series of cases that began in the 1700s, the corporation is now legally defined as a person, which gives it the same rights as a human being. Of course, the First Amendment was not intended to allow corporations to sell food to babies (or to brand baby bottles with their logo as PepsiCo did in the 1990s). It was intended to allow all voices to be heard, so that no one voice would dominate. But with the amplification of marketing, food industry voices are being heard far more clearly than the more sober voices of individual parents. As a result, food corporations have the right to implant the idea that parents don't know what they're talking about when they say no to fast foods or that we only eat potato chips and drink soft drinks at a party, not as a mid-morning snack. This type of marketing has created a toxic food culture for North American children, and now it is decimating healthy food cultures in other countries. Marketing to children is essential for the food industry to ensure its future, to shape children's tastes and their brand loyalty, and to separate them from the culture they live in—the one populated by people who love them and might, therefore, say no to them.

When we first moved to Italy, I thought I had found a place that was less toxic in terms of consumerism generally, but my impression was partly due to the fact that I didn't understand the language very well and could quite easily tune it out. I didn't understand all the chatter around me, and I didn't really notice the advertising because it took effort on my part to pay attention and understand it. It was a blissful, though brief, experience. When you're used to having advertisers whispering in your ear urging you to buy, buy, buy all the time, it's hard to imagine the peace that results in your own head when their voices aren't there. But of course, our son is growing up bilingual, and it didn't take long for me to realize that he was absorbing the same kinds of food messages that his North American peers were receiving.

We made two changes: we no longer took Nico into the processed-food-filled supermarkets and we no longer allowed him to watch commercial TV. Our new approach had an enormously positive effect on his behavior and on our relationship with him. We weren't able to eliminate all the advertising that an almost-four-year-old child sees and hears, but our changes certainly cut down on it. He was more content when he was not being tempted and frustrated by food advertising. He couldn't read, so it was a little easier to limit the influences, but as he gets older, it becomes more and more impossible to shield him.

When I hear the food industry spokespeople argue that all of this advertising has no effect on our children, I know they're wrong. The American Psychological Association warns that children are deeply affected by the commercials they see, they can recall a product name after seeing the commercial once, and they tend to see commercials as authoritative and factual. If it didn't work, why would these companies be spending billions to advertise to children and to defend their right to advertise to them as well?

Space to Dream

In 1957, American journalist Vance Packard wrote that the advertising industry sees us as "bundles of daydreams, misty hidden yearnings, guilt complexes, irrational emotional blockages." Through surveys, the industry had learned that people were quite content with what they had. They didn't mind driving an old car and they didn't need to buy a complete new wardrobe at the change of each season. All this contentment was a problem for an industry with products to sell. So the ad industry set about making us unhappy by playing on our daydreams, our emotions, our yearnings, and our "subconscious," as Packard referred to it, to make us long for those products and the kind of dreamy, perfect world that went with them. It's bad enough that the industry uses our own adult minds against us to convince us to buy cars and clothes that we don't need, but when it plays on children's emotions to make them desire objects and crave foods, it seems our cultural priorities have changed.

The marketing industry regards children as little consumers learning to become big consumers. Sociologist Juliet B. Schor describes in her book *Born to Buy* how industry uses developmental psychology to advertise to children according to their emotional needs. Little ones need love, so ads created for them are soft and adorable. When they get a little older, they need to confront their fears, so ads created for them can be scarier (and can advertise scary products like movies and related tie-ins). As children near puberty, they feel the need to fit in with the group, so ads for them tell them what to buy to be cool. "If you tell them to buy something, they are resistant. But if you tell them that they'll be a dork if they don't, you've got their attention. You open up emotional vulnerabilities and it's very easy to do with kids because they're the most emotionally vulnerable," said the president of the Shalek Agency, in Schor's book.

Yet publicly the marketing industry holds to the position that today's children are savvy, sophisticated, and completely incapable of being manipulated. The food industry is also sticking to the same position. It blames parents for the rise in childhood obesity, saying that parents shouldn't let children eat food that's bad for them. The fact that the industry makes this food and relentlessly bombards children with advertisements for it is, according to the industry, irrelevant. It's incredible, but it really seems to be arguing that its own advertisements do not affect the food choices of children. So, did the fast-food sector spend US$4.2 billion in the United States alone in 2009 to advertise to children for no reason? It's not a public service meant to keep the advertising industry afloat. Of course, the ads work. A child's first request for a specific product usually happens at about age two, usually in a supermarket, and the child typically asks for the product by its brand name, which suggests that advertising to children works remarkably well. The industry would not be as worried as it is about regulations restricting its access to children if advertising didn't work.

Parental responsibility is important. Parents do have to set limits for their children and they do have to say no, but they can't say no all the time without affecting their relationship. It is natural that children should make requests, that they should explore their interests, their likes and dislikes, and it's important that their parents listen to them and allow them to have some influence on family decisions. But when the child is being manipulated by the food industry and the advertising industry to ask for hamburgers that are sold with toys, potato chips that come with popular cartoon action figures, and chemically concocted ice-cream products in the shape of a cat's head, then these companies have inserted themselves between the child and the parents and are trying to use that natural parent-child relationship for profit. If you go along with it, you risk your child's health and eating habits; if you don't, you risk becoming an authoritarian parent nurturing a potentially rebellious child.

A mother tried to test the legality of preying on children in this way. Along with the Center for Science in the Public Interest, Monet Parham, the mother of two small children, filed a class action lawsuit in December 2010 in San Francisco against McDonald's, saying that it had engaged in deceptive advertising by using toys as "bait" to lure small children to the restaurant chain and to detrimentally change their eating habits. Her statement of claim quoted internal McDonald's studies showing that children alone make the decision to visit McDonald's in 53 percent of the cases and that children influence 95 percent of family visits to Mc-Donald's. It also claimed that McDonald's spends $350 million per year on toys to attract children to its restaurants. In a press release, Parham was quoted as saying, "I am concerned about the health of my children and feel that McDonald's should be a very limited part of their diet and their childhood experience. But as other busy, working moms and dads know, we have to say 'no' to our young children so many times, and McDonald's makes that so much harder to do. I object to the fact that McDonald's is getting into my kids' heads without my permission and actually changing what my kids want to eat." The lawsuit claimed that

McDonald's actions amounted to an illegal exploitation of children. If the California State Court had ruled in Ms. Parham's favor, limitations could have been placed on things like toys and cartoon images on children's food. But the judge threw it out in April 2012. Still, her lawsuit opened the door for greater scrutiny of how the industry creates a food culture for children that is based on unwholesome foods. Though McDonald's has since changed its Happy Meal so that the default choice includes apple slices and a smaller package of french fries with a choice of low-fat chocolate milk, regular milk, or a soft drink, it still comes with a toy, and it's still a hamburger and french fries with the addition of three or four slices of apple. It's not exactly a healthy lunch.

Children Are Consumers

In the early part of the twentieth century, most ads for children's foods were aimed at mothers. They talked about the health benefits and the added vitamins in order to convince mothers that certain biscuits and fruit drinks were good for children. This was known as the "gatekeeper model" of advertising. In the 1960s, researcher James McNeal presented the idea that children, more than parents, constituted a market themselves. At the time, few believed McNeal, but it didn't take long for his ideas to take hold and to rule the marketing industry. In 1987, he published an influential book called *Children as Consumers* and has since been a trusted source of studies and insight into the behavior of children and how to sell to them.

Also, by the 1980s, there were children's media outlets, such as the Nickelodeon channel, which offered up large audiences of children sitting in front of their TV sets not only on Saturday mornings but every day. Nickelodeon allowed marketers to sell directly to children without having to worry about their parents. By the 1990s, the practice was becoming more widespread and creative. Soon the industry started incorporating the "nag factor" into its work. Nagging, of course, is what children do when they see something they want. They will drive their parents crazy, pestering them and offering up reasons why they need an advertised product until their parents buy it for them. The nag factor in selling is based on a study by Western Initiative Media that analyzed how children nag and how their parents respond. Researchers found that when children nagged with "importance" (i.e., if you buy me that ice cream with calcium and extra vitamins, my bones will grow stronger) rather than just with "persistence" (i.e., I won't stop whining until you buy me that ice cream), parents were more likely to give into the nagging and buy the product. Around the same time, "anti-adult" advertising also became popular. It was designed to create an alliance between the advertiser or the brand and the child by depicting parents and other authority figures as buffoons and idiots—clueless people who know nothing about the child and his desires. And then there are the ads that show all the cool kids eating a particular kind of yogurt, drinking a particular soft drink, or eating a certain hamburger.

Even though we shield Nico from the commercials on television and the products in the supermarket, many of his friends watch television and they tell him about the food products they've seen. Nico carefully observes what they are eating. Children have a huge influence on each other, and marketers know it. When one ad executive was asked how to reach people who don't like being marketed to, he responded: "Covert messaging. Use their best friend." This means getting the kids to talk up products to their friends. And the tactic has a name that makes it sound far less diabolical than it is: peer-to-peer marketing.

One company in Los Angeles specializes in peer-to-peer marketing. Girls Intelligence Agency (GIA) recruits girls as young as age eight to spread the word about particular products or to deliver information about their friends and the things that interest them. The agency claims to have forty thousand such girls ready and willing to go out and gather intelligence. "The GIA communicates with these influencers daily, seeking out their opinions, ideas, motivations, dreams and goals and translates that information to help hundreds of corporations in the U.S. to strategically reach and connect with the female youth market. GIA uses a variety of means—from texting to sleepovers—to tap into the business of girls," says the description on the GIA website. One of its methods is to have an "agent" host a slumber party and invite ten to twelve friends. The participants share news about a specific product with another ten friends, and those friends share the news with another eight to ten friends. The agent also reports back to the agency relevant information about her friends' food habits and whatever else the client wants to know. Sometimes, GIA films the sleepover so the client can watch it. These girls sound like Stasi agents informing on their neighbors. They are children who are snitching on their friends for the benefit of a market research company. GIA promises to track "the infiltration of your product into the field." Among the clients listed on the GIA website are the food companies Nestlé and Sara Lee, as well as Procter & Gamble, the former manufacturer of Pringles potato chips. In return, the children get to keep some of the products.

All of this influencing of small children is a way of supplying loyal customers in the future. At a screening of the documentary film *Food, Inc.*, which is about the problems with the American food industry, at one of the American universities in Rome, I sat next to an overweight man in his early forties. He said that he took his two young children, who were six and four, to McDonald's restaurants in the New York town where he lives because he had gone there himself as a child. He had fond memories of the food and of the restaurants themselves. They evoked his own happy childhood, and he wanted his children to have the same experiences. He said he knew in one part of his brain that he shouldn't introduce his children to fast food because it wasn't good for them, but that the decision to take them there wasn't intellectual, it was emotional. As well, he said, going to McDonald's is such an accepted part of American culture that it would be harder not to take them there. After watching the film, however, he thought that they wouldn't ever again be visiting any sort of fast-food restaurant.

"It is not only possible but logical for a business to nurture children as future customers so that at some point they see that particular business store, brand, or product in a favorable light, they feel an association with that business, and eventually they view that business as a source of much satisfaction. At any point along this cognitive development path, children can be considered future customers," wrote James McNeal in 1999 in *The Kids Market: Myths and Realities*, a book directed at marketers. The fact that we might not like corporations using our children in this way seems to mean nothing. This is between the food industry and our children.

To Regulate or Not

Since childhood obesity has become such a hot issue and there is now, as a result, pressure on governments to put some restrictions on predatory marketing to children, the food industry has promised to back off a little. Many companies, including McDonald's, PepsiCo, Coca-Cola, Nestlé, and others, have promised to regulate themselves, and they have even made pledges in the United States through the Children's Food and Beverage Advertising Initiative to encourage healthier dietary choices and healthy lifestyles in their advertising. Personally, I wish they wouldn't advertise to children at all. I don't really want PepsiCo, Coca-Cola, and other food companies giving my child health and nutrition advice. The problem is not only what these companies tell children to eat, but how they depict food as entertainment and as something to grab on the run. They promote an industrial food environment over a real food culture.

Even with the pledge, the industry has failed to live up to its own extremely insufficient promises when it comes to advertising. The Rudd Center for Food Policy & Obesity issued its report on the food industry in late 2010 and revealed that the marketing of fast foods to children went up and not down after the pledges were made. The average preschooler in the United States sees three ads for fast food every single day. These are little children who shouldn't even know that fast food exists, let alone see advertisements for it three times a day. "Fast food companies speak to children early, often, and when parents are not looking. Fast food is the most unhealthy food product marketed to children, other than sugar-sweetened beverages, and is relentlessly and aggressively targeted toward children starting as young as age two. Food marketing to children negatively influences the dietary choices and health of society's most vulnerable citizens," says the Rudd Center report *Fast-Food Facts.*

It's not reasonable to expect junk-food and fast-food companies to promote healthy diets and active lifestyles when they are the antithesis of those things. I would prefer if they were honest about their products. It's confusing when they put messages about health in their ads and then show someone drinking a diet soft drink or eating an artificially vitamin-fortified granola bar. Those products aren't part of a healthy diet. They are processed foods, what the Italians call *cibo industriale* (which to me sounds more accurate—and horrible). I do let Nico eat potato chips at parties, and he does eat candy once in a while, but we don't try to fool ourselves into thinking that they are suitable to eat every day.

Once when we went to the fourth birthday party for one of his classmates from the *scuola materna*, Nico stopped in front of a table laden with bowls of potato chips and cheese puffs, trays of *pizzette*, which are bite-sized rounds of pizza with tomato sauce, white buns filled with Nutella, trays of cookies and pastries of all shapes and sizes, and the standard juice, Coke, and Fanta Orange. He stood there, uncertain what to do. He reached for a Nutella sandwich and looked at me to see if I was going to pounce. He knew that I disapproved of something about this food, which tastes so good to him. It's pretty hard to explain to a four year old that some foods are good for you and some are bad. Mostly I try to present him with good options and save sweets for special treats, but we don't live in an isolation tank. I told him to go ahead. It was a party and meant to be fun, so I told him to feel free to eat what he wanted. And he did. He ate everything he wanted and came back to refill his plate as often as he liked. Then he ate a big piece of birthday cake, too. He enjoyed the party and he liked the food, though he said he felt a little sick afterward (probably because he decided to mix Fanta Orange with pear nectar). I can only hope that he recognized that a party is an exceptional circumstance and that the food there was different from the food he should eat every day.

I'm trying to carry on what I saw Italian mothers doing with their babies and toddlers by giving him real, whole, healthy food, to instill in Nico an understanding of how food nourishes his body and how it gives us pleasure, too. The messages from the food industry only confuse him. I don't want him to be judgmental about food and how other people eat, but he needs to know what is healthy and what isn't, and how to fit those things into his diet. He needs treats—we all do—but he needs to see them for what they are. Nico and I make really good cookies at home, and we put butter, chocolate, and sugar in them. They taste incredible, especially when they're warm and the chocolate is still melted, and we know that they are not nutritious. We know that we can eat them only rarely, and their scarcity adds to our enjoyment.

So it makes me fume a little when I see Nestlé promoting its frozen dessert products for children on its Italian website with a headline that says: "Ice cream: A healthy and delicious snack for your child." I know I can't trust the company not to twist the message to its benefit. The web article says it's important for a child to have three meals and two snacks a day. That sounds fine. The article quotes a Nestlé nutritionist who explains why small children need a snack in the morning and one in the afternoon. That sounds fine, too. But then the same nutritionist says that all foods should be allowed in moderation. On the surface, that sounds fine, too. But the article gives the impression that a glucose-filled ice cream product is an appropriate daily snack for a small child. A snack is meant to give small children the extra nutrition they need in a day; it's not the place for a treat like ice cream. Since we're in Italy, if we're going to have an ice cream treat, we ought to go to a *gelateria* and get one that is made with milk, eggs, and fruit, not with glucose, dextrose, and emulsifiers. While the milk in ice cream is, I suppose, nutritious enough, it is also loaded with sugar and fat, even when it's made well. We shouldn't pretend that it's healthy.

So far (and I know this won't last for long), James and I have been luckier than many parents. There is a McDonald's restaurant near where we live in Rome. Since we don't watch commercial TV anymore, Nico has never seen a commercial for McDonald's. The children at his school don't seem to talk about it. So it's never been an issue. We stroll past it regularly and it is a sandwich shop like any other to him. It has no particular significance in his life. He's never heard of Ronald McDonald, has never visited a McDonald's playground or been to a birthday party at McDonald's. He has eaten a hamburger before, but it was one his father made for him. He liked it well enough, but it doesn't have to be a regular part of his diet. I have friends in Canada who don't take their children to McDonald's either, but their children know the restaurant, they recognize the golden arches, and they know Ronald McDonald. It's there in their lives, and for some of them, it is alluring and possibly more so when it is forbidden. I'm so grateful that Nico doesn't know about it and that I don't have to forbid it. I spend too much time as it is forbidding, or at least limiting, the unhealthy snack foods that Nico sees his peers eating.

All of these issues raise an obvious question: Why not ban all food advertising to young children? There is an organization called Campaign for a Commercial-Free Childhood that dreams of doing just that. It coordinates petitions and tries to raise awareness of the constant intrusion of marketing in our children's lives. If the food industry were prevented from advertising to children under age twelve, there is plenty of evidence to show that it could make a difference:

- A study at the University of Liverpool showed that children increased the amount of food they ate, particularly high-fat foods, after watching food ads. The study found that all the children ate more after watching the ads, but that children who were already obese and overweight ate even more and tended to choose the snacks with the highest fat content.
- In 2008, the National Bureau of Economic Research published a study that concluded that a total ban on fast-food advertising during

children's television programming in the United States could reduce childhood obesity in that country by 18 percent.

- In 2010, the WHO issued its global guidelines on marketing to children. It acknowledges the role that advertising plays in persuading children to eat. It called for limiting ads for children for foods with specific ingredients like trans fatty acids, sugars, and salt.

Though it's good that WHO is talking about global guidelines, it's disappointing that it is focusing on ingredients rather than the whole category of packaged, processed, and fast foods. Since the food industry is busy remixing its formulas for packaged foods, these kinds of guidelines won't do much to halt the onslaught of confusing messages being beamed out to children between cartoon episodes.

Advertising for Overconsumption

As with infant formula, there is a market for junk food and fast food, but it ought to be a tiny fraction of what it is right now. Unilever's ice cream managing director for France recently outlined his strategy to get the French to consume more ice cream. "We want to develop the frequency of consumption," he said, and to do that Unilever would have to find more "points of sale" as it calls it, as in gas stations and other places where you might see the ice cream and buy it on impulse. It's clear that the industry encourages overconsumption. Its model is so different from an effective food culture where you would go to an ice cream shop to buy ice cream and the gas station to buy gas.

Advertising in general seems to have a detrimental effect on the psychological and social health of children as well. A study of children in the fifth and sixth grades, conducted by Juliet B. Schor, which she recounts in *Born to Buy*, found that the more children are involved in consumer culture (that is watching TV, surfing the Internet, noticing ads on billboards and in magazines, and so on), the more anxious they are, the lower their self-esteem, and the more psychosomatic complaints they have.

Consumer involvement seems to be a cause of childhood depression, and it worsens the relationship between parents and children. Lest we think that these kids were like this to begin with, the study showed that children who were psychologically healthy began to suffer when they became further enmeshed in consumer culture.

The food industry advertises to persuade more people to eat its products, to encourage everyone to eat more and more of its products, and to reach small children to make them lifelong consumers of its products. It is playing a numbers game, which is to earn more each year than it did the last—to grow. But its growth mirrors our own, particularly the growth of childhood obesity.

SEVEN

The Tragic Results

THE WINTER THAT Nico turned three, we spent a lot of time at the beach at Ostia. It was an easy thirty-minute drive from the center of Rome, and though it wasn't hot enough to swim, the quiet sandy beach was the perfect place to spend a sunny day with a child who wanted to dig. The most wonderful thing about Italian beaches, other than the excellent digging, is that there is always a restaurant and a coffee bar, even in the winter. Our standard routine was to stop at the bar for a cappuccino when we arrived in the morning and then reserve a table for lunch at the restaurant on our way toward the sand.

Lunch at the restaurant was always something to look forward to, especially on a Sunday when large groups of families and friends would take over big tables and order endless platters of food. We had a few favorite seaside dishes. Sometimes we would eat spaghetti with clams; other times we would order some chickpeas with potatoes and octopus to start. Then we would order grilled fish, a very plain green salad, and perhaps a plate of french fries—all of it to share. The french fries were particularly nice, as they had been freshly peeled, fried in boiling oil, and then salted. Nico loved all of it—maybe not the salad so much—but he didn't elevate the french fries over the chickpeas and octopus. The food was all fresh and fairly healthy. We could choose among several vegetable side dishes, and there was always fruit for dessert. We always had a carafe of water on the table, and sometimes James and I had a glass of the house white wine. Ours was a fun routine: dig all morning, break for lunch, dig some more, and go home in time for dinner. We would leave the beach feeling good about the whole day. We would feel happy about what we fed our child and what we ate ourselves.

The following summer, several big water parks opened on the outskirts of Rome, and James, probably even more than Nico, really wanted to go to one of them. I expected the water park to be like the beach, with a coffee bar and restaurant. But it wasn't. The coffee bars were filled with packaged-food products made by Nestlé alongside freezer cases stacked with ice cream bars by Nestlé. Even the *gelateria* served only Nestlé ice cream, which might seem Italian on the surface but is made with industrial ingredients like glucose syrup, vegetable oil, guar gum, carrageenan, and emulsifiers, rather than with the milk, eggs, and sugar of traditional gelato recipes. The restaurant had red plastic tables and chairs with the familiar white script of the Coca-Cola logo, and it had the dreaded children's menu. It offered pasta for a first course, and breaded chicken served with french fries for the second. Another choice was pizza slices served with french fries and a soft drink. There were also hamburgers and hot dogs on the menu. North Americans might not find anything unusual about the choices, but they aren't what Italians eat. These big fun parks have only opened over the last five years, and they have brought with them food that is industrial and unhealthy. The idea of combining children's entertainment and junk food is new to a culture that traditionally doesn't feed children differently from adults. There was no nice place to sit down for lunch, the food was kept in warming trays, and children were drinking Coke with their meals. There was food advertising all over the place. Nestlé had a gigantic wraparound billboard on the top of the biggest water slide to advertise its Motta brand ice cream treats, and throughout the park, there were advertisements for potato chips, supermarkets, and McDonald's.

The water park was meant to entertain children, but it seemed that the point of it was really to sell food to them. Nico ate a hot dog for lunch with some french fries, and later we stood in line with everyone else so he could buy a Nestlé ice cream. For the first time in Italy, I realized we were going to have to be careful about children's entertainment because of the food that accompanies it. It's obvious that this food is bad for children, and I don't want my son to make a habit of eating it, but I didn't want to eat it either. It does nothing but add unwanted inches to my waistline. But there wasn't an alternative at the park.

I wanted Nico to have fun and he did. I was disappointed that there wasn't the usual good, food that I had come to expect at the beach or in the countryside or in any of the places where families might gather. Even at the restaurant in Explora, which is a children's museum that opened in 2001, you can eat really good pasta dishes like ravioli stuffed with gorgonzola and nuts, traditional Roman thin-crust pizzas, and lots of vegetables. It has no children's menu, but it does have a decent wine list. Children love to eat there after a morning at the museum, and so do their parents. It's not as though children can't have fun without hot dogs.

The food culture of Italy wasn't truly represented in the mushy spaghetti served at the water park; in fact, it was entirely missing from the children's entertainment complex, and so were its protective properties. The global diet created by the multinational food companies includes packaged snacks proclaiming their vitamin content, fake gelato, and American-style fast food and soft drinks, and it's becoming the new food culture for Italian children. If we decide to go to the water park, we have to accept the junk food that goes with it, even though there is no reason why it has to be this way.

A Vast Problem

The loss of a beautiful food culture like Italy's is sad in and of itself. But to replace it with something as toxic as the so-called "Western diet"—which is what this fast-food, junk-food diet has come to be known as—seems criminal. Our tastes from childhood ought to lead us to enjoy food, to eat well and be healthy, but this isn't really happening anymore. And we know that everywhere the Western diet goes, dietary misery follows. The consequences of shifting children's tastes in this direction are tragic.

Every year, millions of people die from heart disease, cancer, chronic respiratory disease, and diabetes. Obesity is linked to each of these noncommunicable diseases. Obesity is not the only problem with the Western diet, but it is the most visible, the most discussed, and the hardest on children. Since the 1960s, the obesity rate in North America has been rising. It picked up its pace in Europe and the developing world more recently, but essentially the whole world is now on a fast train to bad health. Being overweight and obese is now the fifth leading risk factor for death in the world, and our life expectancy in the rich Western countries, after many years of increasing, is now decreasing. The hardest of all the statistics to bear is that there are 42 million children under age five who are overweight or obese in the world. It used to take years to put on that much weight, and it was rare to see an obese child. Now it's an ever-growing problem for nursery school children. If something doesn't change, these children will live difficult, unhealthy lives, and many of them will die an early death.

There are more theories floating around for why the obesity rate is rising than I have fingers to count them on. The problem is that we eat too much salt, fat, and sugar; the problem is that some of us are genetically programmed to gain weight; the problem is that pregnant women smoke, or that pregnant women have a bad diet; the problem is that new mothers are not breastfeeding exclusively; the problem is predatory advertising; the problem is that junk food is addictive; the problem is that children are not sleeping or exercising enough; the problem is that families don't eat dinner together; the problem is that parents today don't know how to say no to children; the problem is that we have too much food choice in the supermarket; the problem is that our diet lacks diversity; the problem is that we keep our thermostats set too high.

The fact is that all of these reasons are true, even the thermostat theory (if we're cold, we shiver and burn more calories). And that's partly why it's so hard to do anything about this worldwide epidemic. There's no single fix. No one law, regulation, ingredient change, food, parenting technique, diet, or exercise program will solve this massive problem. As much as I admit to my nostalgia for the big pots of soup and family dinners of my childhood, we can't go back to the past. The problem is really a collective one and not an individual responsibility. When the food culture, which is an integral part of a larger culture, is broken, our health suffers. Look at the case of the Pima and Tohono O'odham Native people in southern Arizona. In 2010, the *New England Journal of Medicine* published a study of this community that assessed the risk of early death for adults who became obese as children. The researchers chose this community because it has much higher rates of obesity and diabetes than the rest of the country, and because the epidemic started much earlier among these people. What happens to them could happen to the rest of us.

In the nineteenth century, the Pima and Tohono O'odham were very lean people with almost no incidence of diabetes. They lived on foods that grew easily in the desert, such as chia (now touted as a weight-loss food), tepary beans, mesquite (which is considered an inedible weed by many people), and prickly pear cactus. They also cultivated land and grew their own crops. But toward the end of the nineteenth century and into the twentieth, the rivers in the area were diverted for other uses in Arizona. Suddenly, many of the foods that were a regular part of their diet could no longer grow. The US government distributed surplus foods to them, such as white flour, sugar, lard, canned and packaged foods, and so on—basically what we now know are the ingredients for diabetes—giving them a jump-start on the health problems the rest of the world is struggling with now.

In the early 1990s, the US government funded a study to see what would happen if these Native people, who were by then overweight and suffering with diabetes, returned to their Native diet. The study found that the people lost weight and got their diabetes under control. One man who weighed 239 pounds dropped to 150 pounds and tamed his diabetes by returning to a traditional, local diet that included things like mesquite meal, tepary beans, cholla buds, and chaparral tea. But unfortunately the damage in that community was already done. The food culture was broken. In fact, when researchers were trying to encourage the community to go back to eating some of the healthful foods of their culture, people would frequently ask whether they'd be able to eat all the hamburgers and ice cream they wanted if they ate some local foods. The study, which tracked thousands of Pima and Tohono O'odham children through to adulthood, found that the heaviest children were more than twice as likely as the lean children to die before the age of fifty-five. The unfortunate circumstances of these people serve as a stark warning of the long-term health consequences of the Western diet.

Children and Obesity

When a child becomes overweight, especially at a very young age, it is unlikely that the child will grow out of it or lose the extra weight and become a normal, healthy-weight adult unless many factors in the child's life change. Of course, we should try to change the child's eating habits because there might be a chance of sidestepping a life of obesity-related ill health. If we do nothing, the child faces a difficult life and, perhaps, an early death. More important, though, is to ensure that entire communities do what they can to support a healthy diet and good food habits to ensure that children don't become overweight or obese.

In the United States, 10 percent of children under two years old are overweight. A two-year-old is still essentially a baby, and these are children with more than a little baby fat. We have to ask ourselves how a baby can become overweight. When my own baby was that age and a little younger, I worried about the opposite problem. Whenever I took Nico to the doctor for his checkups, she found that he was off the charts in terms of height, but that his weight was on the low side. He was, and still is, a tall, skinny boy. The pediatrician I was going to at that time was a Belgian woman with what she described as a very European attitude about the benefits of keeping a child's weight low. She told me not to worry about his weight, that very young children are self-regulating. When their hunger is satiated, they stop eating, so I shouldn't try to force him to eat just one more bite, or we might end up with a different problem. She also said to give him only his three meals and two snacks, and possibly a third small one, per day. She discouraged indiscriminate snacking on the go, because he had to train his stomach to know when it was time to eat. Then his hunger would make him receptive to the nourishing food that was presented to him. She wasn't just giving me medical advice; she was passing along cultural rules.

The fact that there are so many toddlers and preschoolers who are overweight suggests that something has happened to override their natural weight-control mechanism. We give them certain foods because they seem to like them, so there's no fighting or cajoling at the table, and it makes us feel good to see them eat. But foods aimed at children—a grilled cheese with fries on the kid's menu at a restaurant, a fast-food hamburger, a package of cookies, or a granola bar—seem to interfere with their innate sense of hunger and satiety. There is some science to suggest that these foods trigger an addictive response in our brains. A study on rats that ate a diet of processed foods, like bacon, cheesecake, and little packaged cakes that children often take to school for a snack, found that their brains reacted to these foods as they would to heroin. The rats that ate the junk food diet developed compulsive eating habits and became obese, compared to a control group of rats that ate a lower-calorie, higher-nutrient diet. The results confirm something we already know. We talk about chocolate as being "addictive," and we call those who can't resist it "chocoholics." We live in a culture where you can have a chocolate or a junk-food fix any time of day or night, so it's no wonder we lose control.

In his book *The End of Overeating*, David Kessler, a former US Food and Drug Administration (FDA) commissioner, examines the food industry's enormous efforts to make foods that we cannot resist, product labels that make us anticipate the irresistible food, and ads that remind us constantly that those irresistible foods are out there waiting to satisfy us. These foods actually change our brain chemistry and compel us to keep eating. The combination of salt, fat, and sugar doesn't satisfy our hunger;

instead it makes us crave these foods even more. This is all very good for business because it builds a loyal, addicted customer base and ensures high sales. It's not so good for us, though. And it's particularly not good for children who will find it even harder to develop a taste for nutritious food when they are constantly being tempted by such irresistible treats, and when their brains are being conditioned to need them.

A cursory look at the foods that are regularly offered to children can make a parent's stomach drop. Thankfully, beyond the amusement parks in Italy, there aren't many children's menus . . . yet. In most restaurants, Italians still order for children smaller portions of the foods the adults eat. But the *Canadian Medical Association Journal* reported that popular restaurants were serving food on children's menus—chicken fingers, hamburgers, french fries—with sodium levels that were twice the daily recommended amount for a child. Most children consume twice the daily recommended amount of salt every day, which puts them at risk for heart disease and stroke. Obese children are starting to experience kidney stones for this reason. A codirector at the new Kidney Stone Center at Children's Hospital Boston said that in the 1970s and 1980s, the doctors might have seen one child a month with kidney stones and now they see nearly one a week.

A chef I spoke to in Italy chastised me for thinking that I could eat healthy food in any restaurant. The restaurant doesn't really care about our health, he said, it cares only about the food tasting good. So it will always add more fat and salt to food than you would at home. I suppose that's why children's menus don't include stir-fried vegetables and broccoli soup. But restaurants could, perhaps, dispense with the children's menu altogether and offer half-portions of dishes on the regular menu, which are often far less salty and fatty.

Heart disease is becoming a disease of the young. Epidemiologists have warned for some time that the growing obesity problem would lead to more heart disease in children, and it is actually now becoming a recognized pediatric illness. Obese children have been found to have thick artery walls, something that used to happen only to people in middle age. Some have enlarged hearts. Extremely obese children suffer from reflux, which is when the acidic gastric juices come up from the stomach into the esophagus, a condition we used to see only in adults. Reflux can lead to chronic respiratory problems and cancer.

Life is not kind to overweight and obese children. They are commonly bullied and teased more than their peers, they suffer physical limitations, and they become sick. More adolescents are having gastric bypass surgery to help them lose weight and keep it off. In the United States, it's only legal to have the surgery after age thirteen. In 2003, there were eight hundred such surgeries performed on US teens, which was nearly triple the number only three years earlier. A Texas children's hospital reported that it performs one or two gastric bypass surgeries a month on adolescents. There are now "fat farms" for children, where they are sequestered and put on a strict diet and exercise regimen. Though they often lose weight in those environments, away from the temptations and habits of their usual lives, sooner or later they have to return to the culture that created the problem for them in the first place.

Adults and Obesity

Overweight and obese children who don't find a way to lose weight and keep it off simply become overweight and obese adults. These adults have a huge burden to bear. Given the rising obesity statistics and our collective hand-wringing over what to do about it, those carrying extra weight are in the spotlight. They have to listen to all the theories about why they are the way they are and what they ought to do about it. About fifteen to twenty years ago, there was a "fat acceptance" movement that promoted the idea that people should accept themselves the way they are, and that the rest of the community should not stigmatize people for being overweight. That movement has pretty much disappeared now. It has since become acceptable to point the finger at fat people, to be judgmental about them, and to be rude to them. They are blamed for everything from rising health-care costs to climate change. In the United States, where the belief in personal responsibility is very strong, overweight people get little sympathy for their predicament.

Now they're also blamed for the declining life expectancy of Americans. A report by the National Institute on Aging said Americans are about to face their first drop in human life expectancy in the modern era if the rate of overweight and obesity is not reduced. A severely obese adult can expect to die twenty years sooner than his or her normal-weight counterpart. That's a lot of years. That's someone's retirement gone completely. A whole segment of people are going to miss out on getting to know their grandchildren. This is hardly the American dream.

Apart from the significant health problems faced by overweight and obese adults, such as higher rates of various cancers (some UK studies have found obesity to be the cause of up to 20 percent of cancers in European women), heart disease, stroke, and diabetes, heavier people suffer economic hardship, too. Obese Americans spend significantly more money than average-weight Americans on health care, about 42 percent more. At the same time, they earn less money. Adults who have been overweight since high school are more likely to be unemployed or on welfare, and to pursue less education than their normal-weight counterparts. They're also more likely to be single by the time they reach age forty. This is all bad, but it's worse for obese women, who earn less money than non-obese women and even less than obese men.

These statistics paint an unhappy picture of a significant portion of the American population, since nearly two-thirds of American adults are overweight. So many people will find it difficult to achieve a satisfying work life, relationships, financial security, and good health. When I try to coax my son to eat within the Italian food culture, I'm thinking about teaching him to enjoy the food, but I'm also thinking about his future. I want good health for him so that he can participate in all that life has to offer and meet the challenges he will certainly face in adulthood. No one wants to handicap his or her child's future in the way I've been describing.

Losing Weight

If it's so terrible to be overweight, why don't people just lose weight? I always thought that if I ever gained a lot of weight, I would go on a diet and lose it. I thought that losing weight required only willpower. Since having a child, I seem to be about eight pounds heavier than what had been my fairly consistent adult weight up until pregnancy. I have summoned my willpower, planned out my salads, shopped for my grains, and stepped up my exercise, and I have lost that weight several times. The problem is that it comes back without me even noticing it. And it happens quickly. All kinds of depressing research have been done on why I can't lose these eight pounds somewhere where they won't find me again. One theory is that our metabolism slows down when we lose weight, so that our weight loss itself slows down and then we're soon gaining the weight back, even though we're still on a diet. The "set point" theory resonates with me. It suggests that our bodies have a set point and the brain tries to maintain it. It's what gives us the urge to eat a little more to compensate for when we've been eating a little less, though there is some evidence that fat burned through exercise might help to "reset" our set point downward. Many successful diet programs like Weight Watchers and the fat farms work partly because they create an artificial food culture to support weight-loss efforts. I found the following description in a *New York Times* blog by Erik Piepenburg of an overweight man's struggle to lose weight, only to gain it back and more, quite discouraging:

> I lost the most weight in my life around 2003, after spending about a year religiously adhering to Weight Watchers. With the accountability of weekly meetings and weigh-ins, I was motivated enough to reach my goal weight of 177 [pounds], and dipped below that to reach 168 for a few weeks. But then I thought I could do it alone, so I stopped going to meetings and stopped counting points. I went back to a few meetings to restart the program after the weight started returning. But something had changed. The program got boring, maybe. Or the counting got monotonous. I stopped going altogether and, eventually, stopped fitting into my jeans.

Only a few years later, he has gained back all the weight he lost and more, and he's now up to 217 pounds. As we all know, this happens all the time with diets. Many people end up putting on more weight than they lost in the first place. I can relate to his story, even though I have so far been doing battle with only eight pounds. Once you put on weight, losing it and keeping it off seems nearly impossible. We need to teach our children how to prevent excess weight gain from happening in the first place.

Making sure that children never become overweight or obese is a communal challenge; it's the culture and not only the individual that needs to change. Parents can't hand that responsibility over to the food industry. We have to stop worrying about the ingredients of processed foods and their confusing labels. We have to forget about them. Some of them might be perfectly fine, but figuring out which ones are and which ones aren't is time consuming and risky. Trying to decode the labels is a miserable task, and once we break the code, the food companies can change it anyway. So we might as well buy a few whole ingredients and cook something ourselves. It's certainly possible to gain weight on your own cooking, but at least you know what you are putting in your food.

Fixing the Culture to Fix the Problem

Neither scientists nor doctors know why children become obese. Common wisdom says the cause is too much food and too little exercise, but it's more complex than that. Some studies point to the fact that women who are overweight when they are pregnant tend to have overweight children. One theory is that if the mother eats too much fat, her children will be predisposed to like fat, which reminds me of Stephen Babcock's experiment that showed how a mother cow's diet affects the health and physical condition of its offspring. Parental habits also influence what children eat. If mother and father are eating fast food or processed foods, it's likely they're feeding it to their children. Focusing on one aspect of the problem won't help. It's cyclical within families and it's cultural. We have to change the culture in order to break the cycle.

There are numerous things we can do that would help, but being overweight and obese is a problem with many causes, and the cure will be equally complex. The cure will require a collective shift in attitude as much as anything else. A 2010 Organisation for Economic Co-operation and Development (OECD) report on obesity showed that the United States had the highest rate of obesity among the thirty-three OECD countries (the organization represents countries with free-market economies), with Canada close behind. The land of bread and cheese—France, that is—had the lowest rate among the group. But the French are not celebrating this fact because even though they have the lowest rate, there is still more obesity in their country than there used to be. France is facing a rise in obesity statistics, mainly among children, just as in other countries. About 20 percent of French children between ages seven and eleven are either overweight or obese. And in Italy, nearly one in three children is overweight or obese. The report showed that the populations of all OECD countries are seeing increased rates of obesity particularly among children, and it mentioned that these countries need to reexamine "social norms," which I take to be "culture." It said that individuals need to change their behavior and that governments need to enact regulations, but also that we need to look at how "social norms are defined and how they change." We have to ask ourselves how this unhealthy way of eating came to seem normal in our cultures.

Children have to be at the center of any change going forward because they are adaptable. If the cycle of unhealthy diets and habits can be broken with children, then the youngest among us could be the ones to benefit from a new food culture, one that has far more to do with protecting our health, caring for the land so that food can grow safely, and enjoying the pleasures of the table than to do with business and profit making.

Changing a food culture is a slow process. But at least there is more discussion now about issues like agricultural subsidies and how they contribute to the production of junk food, fast food, and processed foods. The restaurateur, school-garden and school-lunch activist Alice Waters, the writer Michael Pollan, and other food activists have been labeled as elitist because they recommend that people turn away from cheap junk foods and instead buy more expensive, organic, and locally produced fresh food. If the subsidies were given to the producers of local, healthy foods rather than to those who produce cash crops for industrial food, the charge of elitism would wither, or at least wilt.

Unless the rich Western countries do something to change the food culture, it will only get worse. The problem might have started in the United States, Canada, and even the United Kingdom, but it now afflicts the world. It's a sickness we have exported to other places, when we really should have been importing some of their ideas of tradition and balance when it comes to food.

EIGHT

Normal Food

Happy Memories and Junky Food

WHEN I GO back to Toronto, after all these years in Rome, I am always struck in the first few days with a terrible case of mixed feelings. I don't know how I feel about Toronto—do I like it? I can't tell. I'm not sure how I feel about Rome—do I miss it? I think so. Every trip back "home" shakes me up. Of course, I miss my family and friends, and it's always good to see them. I'm bothered all the time by the fact that Nico doesn't really know his family, and he can't even remember our closest friends' names. Toronto is where I come from, and I'm always afflicted with a deep longing for its familiar streets.

This uneasiness, this straining to find a place in two worlds makes both James and me want to introduce Nico to the world of our child-hoods. We want him to experience backyards and barbecues. We want him to know what it's like to wake up in the morning in a city where you can hear the chirps of robins instead of the whine of motorbikes. And where he can go to sleep listening to the singular, almost thick sound of giant maple leaves softly slapping in the nighttime breeze, a sound I didn't even know I had heard until I had been away from it for a few years. This sense of place is in our bones, and we would like Nico to have a feeling for it, to recognize its unique qualities, even if it's not where he's growing up. James and I also have the urge to introduce Nico to the foods of our culture. As an adult, I ate all kinds of foods that were both good and bad—from Korean barbecue to fish and chips—but I have to fight the urge to feed him the things I remember eating as a child, foods like sweetened breakfast cereal, instant chicken noodle soup, grilled cheese sandwiches made on sliced white bread, factory-made cookies, and much more. It's hard to unhitch my sense of place and childhood from these foods.

Nico mostly enjoys himself when we go to Canada. The problem is always with the food, with what James and I are both tempted to give him and what we can't avoid. During that same summer of disillusion in Rome with the fast food at the water park, we had an eye-opening jaunt through the world of children's food in Toronto. We set off one morning on the ferry at the city's waterfront, headed for the amusement park at Centre Island. I hadn't been to the island in perhaps a decade or more, and I hadn't been to the amusement park itself since I was a child. Nico was alert and excited on the boat, and I had primed him with stories of an old wooden carousel and boats shaped like swans. Thankfully, they were both still there, plus so much more.

We had packed some fruit and some ten-year-old Canadian white cheddar cheese, which is the one food I still miss from home, but we hadn't brought any lunch. We were meeting our friend Elizabeth and her son, Aiden, who is two days short of a year older than Nico. We had planned to pick up something to eat on the island and to make a sort of picnic of it. I really don't know what I was expecting to find, but what we ended up with were cheesy, sloppy slices of pizza that Nico hated because they were completely unlike the thin-crust, far less cheesy Roman pizza that he's used to eating. If I hadn't told him it was pizza, he probably would have eaten it. We ended up giving him some french fries because it was all we could find that he would eat. We weren't feeding him pizza and fries out of nostalgia, but because there was nothing else available. There was only fast food. It was the sort of food we're told that children love. Unfortunately, when it's all there is to eat in a place where you are having so much fun—like in a water park or an amusement park—it becomes part of the fun.

When it was time to leave, James wanted to get a Popsicle to share with Nico, which was most certainly nostalgia for his own childhood outings with his family. But we couldn't find any. There were people operating freezer carts all over the island that were full of the usual frozen ice cream treats from the multinationals. But there weren't any old-fashioned, simple Popsicles, the kind you break in two to share with your father. There were only the same huge frozen ice treats that were sold in Rome and that are full of sugar, food coloring, and artificial flavoring. Popsicles aren't any better, but at least they're smaller. There was nothing but bad food and all of it in huge sizes. The junk food we remembered as kids was replaced with more, bigger, and sweeter stuff.

All around us people were eating fast food and frozen treats. Toddlers in strollers had their own packages of french fries, hot dogs, and pizza. There were also some very tempting-looking desserts like carrot cake with fluffy cream-cheese icing, and strawberry pie with piles of whipped cream. When you go to a place designed for children, there is an overflowing abundance of exactly the kinds of foods you don't really want your children to eat. If you do pack a lunch, it's impossible to make it tasty enough to compete. At the time, parents were complaining that there were no healthy options available on the island or in other children's amusement centers. Even if there had been, I think young children would end up feeling quite deprived if they had to eat the "healthy" food on offer alongside the junk. Unfortunately, the food choices on Centre Island represented the common food culture that children have in North America. Junk food and fast food is what children eat when they go to a fun place, and any deviation from this pattern is a deviation from the norm, from the culture.

It doesn't have to be this way. Imagine a children's amusement park where vendor licenses were only given to those who could produce meals and snacks made with fresh foods. They could sell sandwiches and salads, or pizza if the dough was made from scratch with natural yeast and if they used less cheese and fresh ingredients. There could be any kind of food from anywhere around the world as long as everything was fresh and not processed. Most amusement parks are open in summer, when fruit production is at its peak, so there could be vendors selling fruit cups, filled with chopped-up melons, peaches, and berries. Vendors interested in selling hamburgers and french fries would be permitted as long as they used fresh, unprocessed ingredients, such as free-range, grass-fed beef, and went to the trouble of peeling potatoes. They might not be able to produce and therefore sell as much food this way, but maybe that would be better for all of us. Of course, if our food-subsidy dollars went to producing this kind of good quality food, it wouldn't have to cost a fortune. And, within this environment, there would be room for some treats, some delicious ice cream, pies, and cakes made from scratch, and even candy apples and cotton candy.

Normal Food Choices

The foods that seem normal to children are the foods they eat regularly and the foods they see others in their community eating. Nico thinks sardines and anchovies are fairly common foods, but I certainly did not grow up thinking so. I once met a woman from Zambia who moved to Rome with her family. The food she most missed from her childhood was dried caterpillars. She asked anyone going to Zambia to bring them back for her whenever possible. Because she seemed to love them so genuinely, I nearly—but not quite—relented and tasted some. She pitied me for my aversion to them.

That summer in Toronto was a bad one because of all the kid food we encountered on children's menus, like chicken fingers, and the packaged kid food that was served by well-meaning friends who invited us for dinner. The following summer, we were back in Toronto again, and we brought some Italian chocolate to a friend with a child who was around six. After the relentless feast of junk food the year before, it hadn't oc-curred to me that someone might be put off by a gift of special hand-made chocolates. Our friend said that she strictly forbade sweets and that her family only ate healthy foods. When I opened her fridge to get out some milk for tea, I saw that it was crammed with antioxidant juices; children's yogurts; some low-fat, high-vitamin biscuits; and packaged dips. I peeked in the freezer and saw frozen low-calorie meals and pizzas. (Okay, you really don't want to leave me alone in your kitchen.) When my friend went to another room to talk on the phone, her daughter crammed three chocolates in her mouth at once and ran to the backyard to eat them in peace.

We're all pretty confused and anxious about how to eat. It's like our whole North American culture has a collective eating disorder. We indulge too often and can't really enjoy anything without feeling guilty. We talk about foods that are "bad" and others that are "good." Ascribing moral value to foods is real eating-disorder behavior. But how else do we cope when we are surrounded by the bad? My friend wants her daughter to make healthy choices, but she doesn't know what that means. She's as horrified as I am by the onslaught of junky foods for kids. She hates the way their choices are limited to onion rings or fries in a restaurant or at an amusement park. But she's a busy woman and needs some help feeding her family, so when the food industry says to buy cereal bars, cookies, crackers, or yogurt because they're organic, don't contain high-fructose corn syrup, and have special nutrients to nourish your child's body and help her brain grow, she wants to believe it.

The Lunch Box

The next year, in 2010, we visited Toronto again, and five-year-old Nico went to a day camp in a park west of downtown. We thought it was a good idea for him to mix and mingle a little with Canadian kids his age, and we hoped he might even make a friend. He was happy to go to the camp—he's a sociable child—but he was really excited that he would have to take his lunch. He's used to having a hot lunch of two courses with vegetables every day at his school. He told everyone he met that he was going to be taking a sandwich for lunch. He was excited because he knew that this is what Canadian children do: they take their lunch to school. But he got tired of his packed lunch pretty quickly (the prosciutto didn't taste right, and neither did the tuna or the eggs), and he actually asked the teenaged camp counselors if they could whip up some pasta. He told them he could help them to make a little *minestra*, which is a vegetable soup with beans and sometimes pasta, and he described the recipe to one of them, who said she would definitely give it a try at home. I'm glad the Ontario blueberries were still in season so that Nico had at least something to look forward to in his lunch box.

I asked the counselors if they could tell me what the other children brought for lunch and snacks. I was interested out of sheer nosiness, but also because I was looking for ideas. Pretty much everyone brought sandwiches (the standard tuna, egg, or salmon with mayo or cold cuts) and fruit, and some brought raw vegetables, too. There was a little bit of junk food like potato chips and candy, but mainly there were food products that the counselors themselves described as healthy snacks—things like tubes of yogurt that contained added vitamins, sweeteners like sugar or high-fructose corn syrup, and thickeners with names like locust bean gum and carrageenan; fruit leather that was high in sugar and corn syrup and low in fruit; or commercial granola bars that contained fiber and omega-3 along with the chocolate and sugars.

Parental concern for the health of the children seemed evident in the products they chose, but whatever the marketing suggested, they were still products rather than real food. Everyone had gotten the message that there was something wrong with the food that children were eating, but in a culture based on industrial foods, the parents still looked to food products to solve the problem.

I can see why. Parents want to teach their children to choose healthy food, but it's hard to do it alone. It's hard to get your child to eat something healthy when the child sitting next to him in a lunchroom is eating something wrapped in an alluring package with his favorite cartoon character on it. It's hard to instill the idea that seasonal fruit is a wonderful snack when the other children define a snack as a chocolate bar or a cake. North Americans lack a common agreement on what is healthy. We lack a functioning food culture, and the food industry has become our health authority.

It's also a lot of work to prepare food every day. That summer Nico needed only a morning snack and lunch, but I found even that difficult to manage. I struggled partly because we were out of our element and I wasn't always sure where to find the ingredients I needed. It's also hard to come up with ideas to keep lunches healthy and interesting. So when you see a box of snacks at the supermarket decorated with banners and flags shouting about their vitamins, nutrients, and fiber, they seem like a helpful solution. And if everyone else buys them, it seems like they can't hurt.

This kind of trust in the experts and faith in product labels take us back to scientific motherhood all over again. Articles in the newspaper, often written by nutritionists, tell us to read labels closely because health claims are often exaggerated or misleading, such as when "whole wheat" crackers are only partly whole grain, have little fiber, and are full of sodium, or when fruit snacks are topped up with lots of sugar. But few, other than a handful of food writers such as Mark Bittman in the *New York Times* and Michael Pollan (who plainly advises in his books to avoid food products that make health claims), ever suggest shunning food that comes in packages. To say that we need to learn to read nutrition labels is to accept that North American food culture can't do better than food supplied in boxes and packages. It's actually quite liberating to realize that we don't need to learn to read nutrition labels or to teach our children to do so. We need to give them real food.

But parents who don't have time to prepare three home-cooked meals plus two homemade nutritious snacks a day need some help. (Who out there has that kind of time?) Perhaps the most important thing that communities, countries, or governments can do is provide a cooked lunch at school and summer camp every day. School lunch isn't only about nutrition, but about teaching children to share a meal together. It's an opportunity for them to see real, satisfying food cooked from whole ingredients as the norm, and the packaged stuff as the deviation. It also gives them a chance to learn some table manners and a little about the art of conversation.

An Advocate for Children

I met with Alice Waters one day in Rome not long after Nico's Toronto summer camp experience, and we talked about the problem of feeding children at school. Waters is one of the best-known food activists in North America. She started her restaurant, Chez Panisse, in 1971 in Berkeley, California, because she wanted to recreate the experience she had had of eating in restaurants in Europe, particularly in France, where the food was locally grown and of very high quality. She was interested in how food tastes and in the creative challenge of coming up with recipes for local produce. Of course, she had great difficulty finding local produce, because foods in California were industrially grown and shipped inside and outside the country. The process of trying to procure food for her restaurant led her to a few unexpected places, like prison gardens, her own backyard (literally), and her friends' gardens. It also led her to become one of the country's first local-food advocates.

Now she travels the United States and Europe advocating for a more just and equitable food system, often on behalf of children. When I met her in Rome, she was returning from the biennial Terra Madre conference organized by Slow Food in northern Italy. She was excited and deeply pleased by the way the Slow Food organization had reached out to small farmers and artisanal food producers around the world to become a bigger voice for changing the system, but also by the fact that there were more young people taking an interest in the traditional foods of their own countries. She connects the problems parents face right now in trying to figure out what to feed their children with the highly industrial food production system that is changing food cultures everywhere.

She told me that she would like to see every child in America receive a tasty, locally grown, nutritious lunch at school every day for free.

"Imagine the economic and enormous psychological relief this would give parents—to know that their children have eaten well at least once that day," she said.

Really, every child from the wealthiest to the poorest would benefit from such a program, because children generally eat better when they eat together and when they are all eating the same thing. If it is a good, solid, nutritious lunch, it's not only one less meal for a busy parent to prepare, but it means the evening meal doesn't have to shoulder such a great burden. It can be something simpler.

In Italy, all the schools, public and private, prepare a two-course lunch with vegetables for all the children. Some schools might offer dessert once a week, but most don't offer it at all. I went to Nico's school, which is a fairly inexpensive private Italian school, to watch the children at lunch one day. Several classes at a time came to the *mensa*. The children sat around a table and each of them set their own place with a placemat, napkin, spoon, fork, and cup that they brought from home. The cook, a young man whom the children adore, rushed out with a big bowl of pasta with *ragù*, which is a tomato sauce with a very little bit of ground meat, for each table. The teachers served the children and then themselves, and sat down to eat with their class. The teachers engaged in casual discussions with the children about whatever the children wanted to talk about. They also helped them to hold their forks properly, insisted that they wipe their hands and faces with their napkins, and required them to stay in their seats throughout the meal. When they were finished eating their pasta, the cook brought a large pan of scrambled eggs with Parmesan and a bowl of green salad to each table. Each child took a plate with a little of each. He also offered them *ortiche* (nettles) that he had picked that morning from their terrace garden and cooked and dressed with olive oil, salt, and lemon, and also some fresh, giant cranberry beans to taste. The beans had come from a parent of a child in the nursery school. She had brought several kilos of the beans in that morning. The nursery school children had shelled them, and the cook had simmered them in water, salt, and fresh herbs. The teachers drizzled on some olive oil, and everyone tried them. (The oil, by the way, comes from an organic olive grove in Sabina owned by a family with children at the school and is supplied in lieu of school fees.) Some of the children asked for more. There were pitchers of water on the table, along with bowls of freshly grated Parmesan. When they were finished, they were offered bread that had been delivered that morning from a nearby bakery.

Bread is served at the end of lunch so the children don't fill up on it first. The food is all cooked in the morning, and all the children eat the same thing. The school does not accommodate picky eaters or vegetarians (because vegetarianism is not part of their food tradition), though it will make allowances for genuine food allergies. There's no dessert, except during cherry season, when a family with a few cherry trees on its property brings in crates of the plump, red fruit for the children to eat after lunch. There are no fruit juices and certainly no soft drinks, and the children don't expect them. When everyone is finished, which is usually after about half an hour to forty minutes, the children clear their places and go outside to play.

The standard form of lunch at this school is a first course of soup, risotto, or pasta and a second course of fish, meat, eggs, or cheese and a vegetable. I've seen the children eat pumpkin risotto; sautéed zucchini flowers; meatballs made with ground chicken, Parmesan, and lemon zest; and fish with tomatoes and capers. Nico tells me that no one can beat the cook's spinach with olive oil and lemon (and then he kisses his fingertips). Tiny children from the nursery school, some of whom are still in high chairs, eat their two courses and vegetables along with everyone else. It's not only the food that is important, but the social skills the children pick up by sitting around the table with their peers and their teachers. They learn to take turns speaking, they learn to share, and they learn to pass the water pitcher. They learn to stay seated until everyone has finished his meal. These are all skills that will make their lives smoother and much more pleasant.

I should add that recently Nico has changed schools. Lunch at the new school is the same except that it always offers fresh, seasonal fruit at the end of the meal. The English schools in Rome, as a contrast, do not serve lunch in this way. Instead, they offer choices. An Italian friend who works at one of the English schools told me that if it offers a choice of bean and vegetable soup, spaghetti Bolognese, or pasta with butter and cheese for the first course, inevitably most children choose the most plain (and least nutritious) option. But if the school only offers the bean and vegetable soup, everyone eats it and enjoys it. She also notes that the lunch program is more expensive, and the school wastes far more food than the Italian schools because of having to prepare several options.

The Italian schools do not manage lunch the way they do because they are particularly enlightened, because they are locavores, or because they are trendy. They do it because it's their cultural tradition to eat this way. It's also part of their culture to get excited about something seasonal like the fresh beans, and to pull the weeds out of the garden and cook them. But there is no reason why this couldn't work in the United States and Canada. It's only our cultural expectations that stop us from trying.

I was at my friend Valeria's house one afternoon (not the midwife, a different Valeria), chatting with her while our children played together after school. By early evening, Valeria started to prepare dinner. She said she never makes a huge dinner on a weeknight, since her son, Luca, has eaten a big lunch at school, and her husband eats pasta every day at lunch and often a second course, too. Valeria is a very busy equine veterinarian and works in various places, treating horses in the countryside around Rome. She said she can usually eat well at lunchtime wherever she's working. So on this night for dinner, she was making a pot of lentils. She poured some olive oil into the pot and sautéed some onions, carrots, celery, and garlic, which is called the *sofritto* and forms the base of so many Italian dishes. Then she threw in the lentils and stirred them around for a minute; added some white wine and let it cook for another minute; added a couple of chopped tomatoes, some water, and salt; and put the lid on and left it to cook for thirty to forty minutes. She wanted the lentils to be "soupy" when they were ready, and she would serve them in their broth. Then she washed some broccoli, which she planned to cook in salted water until barely tender, and pulled some cheese out of the fridge to soften. She said they might have some bread with the cheese. Andrea, her husband, would likely have a glass of wine with dinner, and she might too if she felt like it. It was around seven o'clock. Valeria said they usually eat around eight (Italians let their children stay up late: eight o'clock is a fairly early dinnertime for an Italian family). She said she didn't spend a lot of time cooking: about ten to fifteen minutes to prepare the food, and the rest of the time was how long the lentils would take to cook. Since Luca has always eaten with his parents, there was no need to make anything special for him. If they had all eaten sandwiches for lunch, she might have felt the need to make something more substantial for dinner. A substantial lunch for school children makes life much easier for parents. A culture that doesn't give children their own special foods also makes it easier for a family to eat together.

Having an all-important school lunch program is still a distant ideal in far too many places. Many schools lack a kitchen and provide only a room where children can eat their lunch. Alice Waters's own daughter, Fanny, went to a school that did not have a lunch program, and so Waters had to make her daughter's lunch every day from kindergarten through high school. My first thought was that it must be nice to have Alice Waters pack your lunch. But while this is true, she wasn't making anything that I couldn't do myself. "Mostly I made salads for her, and I would change it every day. There was always some lettuce, something green, but one day I might put in some roasted peppers or shavings of carrot," she said. She started doing this almost from the beginning, she says, even though it's hard to get many young children to eat salad. She also added things from the previous night's dinner. If they had eaten chicken the night before, she would shred some of it on top of the salad, or throw in some of the vegetables from dinner. She packed it all with a cold pack to keep it fresh and put the vinaigrette into a separate small container. Fanny, like many children, preferred to use the vinaigrette as a dip rather than dress the salad with it. From time to time, Waters made garlic toast to go with the salad, or she included some hard-boiled eggs, sometimes stuffing them with herbs, and she might add edible flowers from her own garden to dress the whole lunch up. The idea was to make it look appealing but to keep it simple so that the child could get to know and love the taste of the vegetables.

When Fanny came home from school in the afternoon and needed a snack, Waters might give her a bowl of warm peas, some cherry tomatoes, some fruit, and a piece of cheese, or even some popcorn on occasion. Snacks were always something fresh and nutritious. "I gave her vegetables and fruit at times when she was really hungry, and then I didn't have to worry at dinner if she didn't eat everything, because I knew she had been eating well all day."

What strikes me most about Waters's recollections of feeding her now-grown daughter is the simplicity of the food. She wasn't making complicated meals like slow-roasted duck sandwiches with caramelized onions and honey-orange mustard, nor was she preparing special savory or sweet snacks for her. She was trying to get her daughter used to the taste of fresh, local produce. "Kids don't crave salt and sugar. The idea that they are craving these things all the time isn't true. We feed them these things because we think that will make them happy. They will also be happy with savory foods. I never used much salt or sugar when my daughter was growing up, and later when she tasted store-bought foods, she found them too salty and sugary."

Waters always included a linen napkin and some utensils with her daughter's lunch, which is a small civilizing gesture in what can be a chaotic time of day for many children. Fanny has said that far from being teased, her friends were all envious of her delicious, fresh lunches.

Though it is possible to pack a nutritious lunch for a child every day, even Waters concedes that it takes effort. She said she couldn't get out of bed in the morning and try to figure out what to make for Fanny's lunch. She had to plan it out ahead of time and make sure she had everything she needed the day before. She knows how time consuming it is to make a good lunch, and that's why she presses for universal lunch programs across the country.

To prove how effective they can be, Waters funds school gardens and healthy lunch programs through her Chez Panisse Foundation. Her Edible Schoolyard Project—the original was carried out at a school in Berkeley—enables children to plant a vegetable garden in their schoolyard, harvest the food, and cook and eat it together. In her book about starting that first project, she recounts a story about how the cook who had been hired to work with the children was worried they wouldn't eat the first crop that was available, which was kale. But she got the children to sauté the kale in olive oil and garlic, and had them toast some bread. The children arranged the greens on the toast and made up platters for sharing. Then they all stared at it. "After a long time, this girl finally took a piece of toast with greens and passed the platter. The next kid . . . did the same thing," Waters wrote. Before long, all the kids were eating the kale and toast.

I've noticed the same pattern in Italy: when children eat together, especially when they are eating a shared meal rather than different things they've all brought from home, they are more likely to influence each other. If one child is brave enough to try the kale, the others will try it too. The lunchroom can be a place where children learn from each other to eat good, healthy foods. There is no amount of parental coaxing and cajoling that can equal the experience of seeing another child eat a green vegetable and survive. When children eat this way together, they redefine normal food to include fresh vegetables and sautéed kale on toast.

Since the first Edible Schoolyard started in 1995, Waters has replicated the project in several places in the United States such as San Francisco; Brooklyn, New York; and New Orleans. Now there are similar unaffiliated projects popping up in schoolyards all over the world, some inspired by Waters and some by those who came independently to the same conclusions about the need to feed schoolchildren well at lunchtime. These are much needed initiatives, but they are still a tiny minority.

One Important Meal

The United States has a program to feed children—the National School Lunch Program—but it has not exactly been the help to parents that Waters envisioned. The program was meant to provide a nutritionally balanced and low-cost meal for children in public and nonprofit private schools. That sounds perfect except that the schools really became the dumping ground for agricultural surpluses, and somehow french fries became listed as a vegetable serving.

Canada doesn't have a national or even a provincial school lunch program, and given the American experience, that might be a blessing. But there are individual schools working with outside organizations to create programs that serve food to children that defy even their parents' expectations. After talking with Waters about the broad benefits of school lunch, and after recognizing how much Nico's school lunch saves me time and influences his eating habits, I became convinced that lunch is the factor that could change a food culture for the better. Generally I think everyone agrees that fresh foods—meaning fruits and vegetables—are the best foods we and our children can eat. If, as scientific parents, we need confirmation of the beneficial effects of a diet high in fresh produce, there are numerous health studies that can supply it. The biggest complaint is that no one has time to prepare this produce, and it's hard to get children to eat it. If you have to send your child's lunch to school, you have the double challenge of trying to come up with something that can both survive the trip and still be fresh and appetizing. Providing children with a cooked meal in the middle of the day could be a way of gently encouraging a food culture to emerge. If children become interested in what they're eating, how it's prepared, and sitting around a table together to share the same food, the experience gives them something in common.

Though fresh ingredients are more expensive, the overall cost can be offset if the school prepares just one meal without options. Many Americans find this unimaginable, yet I've seen American children come into the Italian school system, sit down to lunch with their Italian peers, and tuck into their pumpkin risotto with great pleasure. It's easier, of course, to start with young children because their habits are not as entrenched.

In Toronto, an organization called Real Food For Real Kids provides lunch to nursery schools across the city. In spite of the multicultural mix of children, Real Food provides just one choice between a vegetarian dish or one with meat or fish, or sometimes just one meatless meal that the children are expected to share. It's always made fresh, from high-quality ingredients, and includes many dishes most of us wouldn't imagine North American preschoolers eating, such as Madagaskar Chicken, chick pea chowder, or red and black bean chili. The children love the food and so do their parents. Preschoolers who have been learning to eat this way would have no trouble moving on to schools with a simplified though nonprocessed and fresh-food-oriented lunch program.

The Challenge of School Lunch

I made a visit to Toronto on my own, without Nico and James, to visit a few schools. But first I stopped in to see my friend Elizabeth again. She had been worrying about Aiden. He had just started the first grade and was finding the lunch hour to be an ordeal, so we were going to pick him up after he had eaten and take him out for a walk. Elizabeth and I walked toward the school through the lovely neighborhood in the city center where they live, while Aiden's little sister slept comfortably in her stroller. It was late fall and starting to get cold, though the sun was bright that day. I hadn't been in Toronto at that time of year in nearly a decade, and I was enjoying watching Elizabeth's neighbors raking piles of leaves, all oranges, yellows, and reds. It seemed like a paradise: that blue sky, the fall colors, the air beginning to turn cold, those big houses and gardens, and friendly neighbors saying hello to us as we passed.

We arrived at the school, which is a really attractive, well-maintained, red-brick public school with a great playground. It's physically a million times better than the schools in Rome, which are all old (not in a good way), ruined (also not in a good way), and usually without a playground at all. The lucky ones have a few square meters of asphalt, and the teachers have to stagger outdoor time carefully because they can't squeeze too many students in the yard at once.

Aiden's school, lovely as it is, has no school lunch program. The children are given twenty minutes in a crowded, noisy room to wolf down whatever their parents have packed for them. Elizabeth said that Aiden finds it stressful, so whenever it's possible for her to do so, she brings him home for lunch or at least tries to check on him. I watched the other children as Elizabeth went to find her son. I saw a girl with a Thermos full of soup and a bag of Cheezies; a boy with a bottle of water, a ham and cheese sandwich on a white bun, and a small container of Pringles chips; and another boy eating a slice of cold pizza. There were lots of juice boxes, chocolate milk, and yogurt drinks. I saw two girls around seven or eight years old drinking Diet Coke, and a boy with a can of Sprite. Another boy had a processed cheese sandwich on whole wheat and a silver bag that he sucked at with a straw. I saw a few apples and one banana and quite a bit of fruit leather. I was surprised to see a girl eating spaghetti with tomato sauce from a Thermos and another eating a takeout Caesar salad in a clear, plastic container with a bottle of vitamin water. The children sat at long tables, some together and others trying to eat alone. There were two adult monitors trying to keep things from getting out of control, but the room was incredibly noisy and most of the children wouldn't sit down. They were running around with their food, and some left their lunches untouched. When their twenty minutes were up, the monitors rang a bell, which was their signal to pack up and go outside, whether they were finished eating or not.

There was no coherence to the food, since all the children brought their own. Some of it was healthy-ish, but there were a lot of food products and loads of actual junk food. But what bothered Elizabeth the most was that the children were so unruly; there was no one to tell them to behave. They were fighting, yelling, and picking on each other. Aiden sat down to eat a bagel that his mother had packed for him, but he complained that another child was trying to take his lunch bag and yet another kept kicking him while he was eating. As we left, Elizabeth said that the rowdiness that day was quite mild: "You should see it on pizza day."

The next day I went to see a high school in Scarborough, a suburb east of Toronto. Bendale is a technical high school. It's not a place that young people aspire to go to, but where some of them end up. Many of the students are unlikely to move on to a postsecondary school education, but at least here they can learn a trade—acquire a skill like carpentry, plumbing, or even cooking or horticulture—and with luck they can get a job when they graduate.

Physically the school is much like the place where I went to high school. It was built in the early 1960s and has long corridors lined with lockers painted pale yellow. Groups of teenaged boys in baggy pants and baseball caps stood around speaking in streams of amazing profanity. The students had that universal bored look, as if they were enduring the day and everyone around them while they waited for their lives to start.

The Toronto nonprofit group FoodShare saw Bendale as an ideal place to try out an idea it had about school gardens. FoodShare has created numerous gardens in Toronto schools, but at Bendale, it wanted to create a working farm. It put a young man, Ian Aley, in charge of the project. Though Aley is twenty-five, he looks even younger, as young as the high school students, but he is more neatly dressed. He and I squelched around in the rain and the muck in front of the school to look at the garden beds, which were still producing food in November. There were huge red cabbages and rows of enormous, leafy green bok choy and kale still coming up. He and the students had already harvested some of the cabbages, bok choy, and kale as well as a Japanese mustard green called mizuna, arugula, lettuce, tomatoes, carrots, lima beans, corn, squash, cucumbers, peas, callaloo (a Caribbean green), and some heritage varieties of beans.

They grew bitter melon and had planted fruit trees of numerous kinds. If it stopped raining later in the week, they were going to plant garlic, which they expected to harvest in roughly ten months. In their first season, they harvested 1,800 pounds of food—almost a ton.

Aley explained that a technical school was the ideal place to try out the farm idea, because the students were learning some very practical skills. The horticulture students built the cedar beds, rain collection barrels, and compost bins. A wide range of students helped to plant, tend, and harvest the vegetables and fruit, and the culinary arts students started cooking. "The food is pretty standard in the cafeteria," explained Aley. "Lots of hamburgers and other high-fat, salty, and sweet things." But the student cooks and their teachers were game to try doing something with the produce. They started incorporating the vegetables and salads into the menu when they could.

Of course, the school year and the growing season don't coincide so well, and the bulk of the crops were ready during the summer holiday. FoodShare hired a few students to keep working on the gardens over the summer, and the students set up their own farmers' market table on the sidewalk in front of the school.

I talked to a student, Kurtiz Coady, who did some weeding and harvesting and sometimes worked the market table. He was sixteen, tall, and quite a big boy. He was one of the sullen-looking students I had seen when I first arrived (though the longer I hung around, the less sullen they became). I was surprised by how open he was, how enthusiastic he was about the garden, and his genuine affection and respect for Aley. He was not a tough kid at all. He wasn't the least bit jaded. Aley said that a lot of the kids had ended up in a technical school because people had underestimated them. The kids had become defensive and sometimes hard to reach. But he found that all the students he worked with in the garden were eager to learn and to try the food.

Coady said he really liked working the market and watching people stop their cars and come to look at the produce. He was surprised when people looked over the Swiss chard and kale and asked him how to cook it. "I was even more surprised when I started telling them how," he said. Before working in the school's gardens, Coady hadn't been much inclined to eat many of the vegetables there, but having had the experience of growing them, he actually wanted to try them. He really liked the carrots and the peas, both raw and cooked, and he found the Swiss chard surprisingly good. He took vegetables home, as did many of the students, and his mother had to figure out how to cook them. He even started a small vegetable garden of his own at home in his suburban backyard.

Coady is studying horticulture and landscape architecture, and said he would really like to grow things. "I love flowers," he said. "I want to be a horticulturalist, and I really want to grow flowers." He was sitting beside his friend Shane Young, who nodded in agreement about the flowers, though he said he was more interested in the design and building aspect of landscaping. I wondered for a minute if they were kidding, these two young men in oversized clothing, but they were sincere. They are sweet boys who like to garden. "If I ever have a nice house someday, I'll make sure the garden is full of food," said Young.

I was a little shocked by my encounter with the students at Bendale. I hadn't expected them to genuinely like the vegetables so much. I thought they might enjoy gardening, but I expected that they'd see the vegetables as an evil intrusion on the fast-food outlets surrounding their school. Aley said that after harvesting carrots, he brushed the dirt off one and started eating it while carrying several bunches to the kitchen. By the time he got there, he had no carrots left because so many students had wanted one and he'd handed them all out. Both Coady and Young said they went out for fast food sometimes but less often now that they'd been thinking about it. They also like to eat their vegetables, and it's become less of an either-or world for them.

The gardens were such a success after the first year that the school has been willing to give FoodShare more space to grow more food and involve more students. The money earned from the market stand was used to buy more supplies for the following year, but Aley said they were going to have to come up with an effective strategy to use up or sell all the food they were going to be able to grow with more garden beds.

Bendale sits on thirty-six acres of great growing land, and its current garden uses only a tiny fraction of it. Debbie Field, the executive director of FoodShare, says the land is typical of Toronto schools. They have huge lush fields—so much potential farmland. They could all have a working farm if they wanted and still have lots of space for sports and other activities. They could supply their cafeterias with fresh food for part of the year, and sell the extra produce to make money for special activities (and maybe get rid of those vending machines full of junk food) or give it to the students to take home to their families.

The FoodShare office is in an old school building in the west end of Toronto. Through a series of coincidences, a French school in the city center had to relocate, and the seventh- and eighth-grade students ended up sharing the same school where FoodShare has its office and warehouse. Some parents approached Field about creating a cafeteria in the school that would serve decent food rather than the usual fast-food options. Though the students are all French-speaking, they come from many different cultural backgrounds, so finding common ground with the menu would be an interesting experiment. The day after seeing Bendale, Field invited me to join a small group of people interested in seeing FoodShare's cafeteria, which is called the Good Food Café.

We stood in the cafeteria, out of the way, as the cook, Alvin Rebick, got the food in place. Then we heard the rapid-fire pounding of feet as dozens of students came running down the stairs and flying through the cafeteria doors with an explosion of chatter and laughter. The kids quickly grabbed their plates of whole-grain spaghetti with meat sauce, salad on the side, whole-grain garlic toast, and a plate of red grapes and honeydew melon. They poured water from pitchers (there is no juice or soft drinks, though they can buy milk if they want) and sat together in groups of six. The food costs $4 a day per child and includes dessert (things like whole-grain zucchini bread) twice a week. "There's no childhood obesity here," said Field. I looked around the room and realized that she was right. There were roughly seventy kids in the room and none of them were overweight. She pointed out a couple of children who were drinking from juice boxes and one who had a can of Coke, and she gave a deep sigh of resignation. "The only unhealthy things in the room are what the parents send with them."

Rebick then prepared plates for our small group, and we took them to another room to continue talking while we ate. I twirled the spaghetti and sauce around my fork. It smelled great. I tasted it, and then I got up and ran back to the kitchen to see Rebick before he left. I had to know what was in the sauce. Because it was red, I had expected it to be a to- mato and meat sauce, but its flavor was more complicated.

"First, there's no salt and no sugar," he said. I was with him about the sugar, but I argued about the salt. If you're not eating processed foods and fast foods, both of which are loaded with salt, you can use a little salt in your cooking. It's so essential to Italian food, I can't imagine cooking without it. He agreed with me that a little salt can add something to the flavor, but because people are so worked up about salt levels these days, he thought it was better to cook without it. Also, he said, who knows what they're eating outside of school. To make the sauce, he cooked red pepper, carrots, celery, and onions in a saucepan with chopped tomatoes, and then puréed the mixture smooth, giving it an almost creamy texture. The beef came from a farm that used to grow tobacco but is now raising organic, grass-fed cattle. He crumbled the meat into a pan and cooked it, removed the excess fat and then added the sauce. The vegetables blended together, and the earthiness of the carrots, onions, and celery balanced the sweetness of the peppers and tomatoes (though I still think it would have been even better with a pinch of salt). When you consider the spa- ghetti sauce, the salad, the fruit, and the zucchini bread for dessert, it seemed as if Rebick was trying to get the entire day's recommended fruit and vegetable servings into a single meal. But it was very good, and the students ate it up without complaint. I asked some of them about the food, and they said, in that flat-toned, use-as-few-words-as-possible way that early teens have, that it was good. I was told by one of the more chatty students that I should taste Rebick's baked fish.

Two college students who were among our group cleaned their plates and complimented the chef. They were making a film about alternatives to the fast-food model their college uses in its food services. Field encouraged them to work hard on their film, to get people talking, and to go to those in charge and tell them that they want some good food options. They smiled at her with shining, hopeful faces. She told them not to expect great changes right away. The college has contracts with the multinationals that it has to adhere to, but if enough people want the food to change, it will, but not before these two unhappy eaters graduate. "Just think of it as a good deed you are doing for future students," Field told them.

Good Role Models

There are now numerous—too numerous to ignore—successful models for feeding children a healthy school lunch. School gardens themselves have become extremely fashionable. A school nowadays seems a little dowdy, a little out of touch, if it doesn't have at least a few bean stalks growing from a pot or a few herbs in the windows of classrooms.

Alice Waters's Edible Schoolyard, Debbie Field's Good Food Café, and the Bendale school farm show that children and young adults will actually eat good, healthy food as long as the emphasis is on the *good*. The college students making their film demonstrate that it's a crime not to give children and young people who want to eat better food the option to do so. Young children are quite open to eating nutritious lunches if they are involved in the process in some way, such as helping to grow or cook the food where possible, or having some say on the menus. The rest are details—annoying, pain-in-the-neck details like teaching the staff to cook rather than fry, creating proper kitchen facilities, and that sort of thing.

The cost is an issue, though FoodShare's French school experiment managed to stay within the same budgets that schools with standard industrial-fare school cafeterias use. There are good ways of cutting costs, from growing some of the food to limiting the meal options. Personally, I like the Italian school method where there is one meal and everyone eats it. It reinforces the sense of community and cuts back on food waste.

A school lunch program really ought to be designed with the students' best interests in mind. Currently, it is designed for the benefit of the food industry both from the money the industry makes selling its food in schools and in the way that a processed, junk-food lunch shapes children's tastes.

Of course, if I'm going to mull over the merits of a good school lunch, I have to think about Jamie Oliver. I have to admit (though I would never admit it to an Italian) that I frequently use, along with Marcella Hazan's books, Jamie Oliver's cookbook *Jamie's Italy* when trying to decide what to make for dinner. His recipes are very Italian; he hasn't twisted them into a strange English-Italian hybrid. But I also like his offhand manner, the way he says to pour a "glug" of olive oil into the pan instead of two tablespoons. Italians glug their olive oil; they don't measure it with a spoon. When Oliver went to America's most overweight city, Huntington, West Virginia, to see what he could do about its school lunches, as part of his TV series, I had to watch.

His goal was to wean the school from its dependence on processed foods and give the kids real food cooked from scratch. He didn't remake the menu so much as change the ingredients. Instead of allowing the cafeteria to make macaroni and cheese with powdered or canned cheese, he assigned someone the job of grating real cheese. Instead of reheating chicken nuggets, he made barbecued chicken with his own homemade barbecue sauce. He wanted the kids at the school to learn to taste real food. "I'm not doing healthy hippy stuff, just proper cooking," he said. Along with using real food ingredients, he worked on getting more vegetables into the kids' diet by replacing french fries (which the West Virginia Department of Education's Office of Child Nutrition actually said counted as a vegetable) with salads and broccoli.

Oliver's show starts out by scaring us with shots of children eating gooey, cheesy pizza at the school breakfast; drinking sugary chocolate and strawberry milk; and mistaking tomatoes for potatoes because they have no idea which is which. As the show progresses, we learn that the children are not the problem. The children will change their habits and tastes. Oliver learns quickly that he can't be a dictator; he can't take away their french fries. But if he offers an alternative and appeals to their intellect, at least with the older children, they will try the real food. Many of them will actually like it and come to prefer it. There is a wonderful scene in the first season where Oliver is fuming because after he removed chocolate and strawberry milk from the school, the Office of Child Nutrition insisted that they be offered along with white milk, even though they contain more sugar than soft drinks. The Office of Child Nutrition believed it was more important that the children get calcium than to worry about the sugar, and that they would choose to drink nothing rather than drink white milk. Oliver watches as several small children—they look about five or six years old—choose either chocolate or strawberry milk, but then suddenly child after child starts choosing plain milk. It turns out their teacher told them to choose the plain milk because it was better for them—and they did.

It's as Alice Waters told me: We assume children want salty, fatty, sweet foods, but they will also like real, whole, unadulterated food if we give them the option. They might not like it the first time, but as Waters said, we're the grown-ups and it's up to us to teach children to like the food that is good for them.

Children aren't the problem; adults are. In Huntington, the processed food and fast-food culture was entrenched. It wasn't only the children who were eating badly, but whole families. One of the school's kitchen cooks resisted Oliver's every move to change the food; she didn't think his ideas would work, and she didn't want to have to change the way she works either. And the bureaucracy was against Oliver. The school had contracts with suppliers for tons of frozen, processed foods.

But the school did change. A year after Oliver filmed in Huntington, in spite of the bureaucratic and cultural resistance, the school was still cooking from scratch and incorporating more fresh foods into the meals. It was making rotisserie chicken and chicken parmigiana instead of fried chicken nuggets (though it said it still served the nuggets once a month because the children were nostalgic for them). It was serving vegetables and salads and homemade soups. One of the cooks told a local newspaper that it's important to keep the kids in the lunch program because it's always much healthier than the stuff their parents send with them.

Just as every school must now have a garden, it seems every celebrity chef must have a program for children. Mario Batali, the chef and owner of Babbo (which is what Tuscan children call their fathers) in New York and cookbook author, has started a foundation aimed at promoting literacy among children but also encouraging them to eat well. He's involved in community gardens and has funded a community cooking project for low-income parents and teens in New York City. Generally I find trends empty and irritating, but I like this one, and I hope it represents a permanent shift in attitude.

All of these examples acknowledge something the food industry figured out a long time ago: that it is children who can change the future, if only adults will give them some guidance. The food industry tries to replace the concerned adult with marketing for guidance. Now that the grown-ups are starting to realize this, the food industry is working even harder to retain ownership of children's tastes.

NINE

An Industrial View

Food of Another World

I'M SITTING IN an office at PepsiCo's headquarters in Purchase, New York—the drab sort of office that greets corporate executives all around the world. There's a desk to work at and a table for holding small meetings. But the window of this office looks out on a garden where sculptures by some of the giants of twentieth-century art such as Joan Miró, Henry Moore, and Max Ernst are displayed on an expanse of lawn and intermingled with highly manicured hedges and trees. It is not a wild garden. Here, nature has been flattened, domesticated, and totally reshaped. Many of the sculptures come from that fascinatingly hubristic period of Modernism that didn't seek a mere break with the past, but its complete annihilation. The sculptures are powerful symbols of a new world, and the fact that they dot the lawns of one of the world's big industrial food companies seems appropriate.

For me, the juxtaposition of the bland office and the distracting garden calls up countless parallels: the utopian dreams of globalization; the destruction of traditional agriculture in favor of a clean, efficient system of chemically grown, high-yielding monocrops; pyramids of perfectly formed glossy fruit, unbruised and unblemished; biscuits, cereals, and crackers made with a tasteless grain (the blank canvas of food), then plumped up with flavor enhancers and fortified with nutrients. The food industry's creations are amazing as works of art and feats of technology, but rather terrible as food. They bring to mind the Italian futurist Filippo

Tommaso Marinetti's 1930s futurist cookbook that advocated the eradication of ordinary foods. He wanted Italians to consume vitamin pills and eat food sculptures solely for their sensory and aesthetic appeal. Marinetti would have fit in well here at PepsiCo's headquarters, and I wonder if I were to search hard enough, if I might find a copy of *La Cucina Futurista* on someone's shelf.

I have come here not to marvel at the art work so much as to hear PepsiCo's story of how it and other giant food companies can help fix the nutrition crisis that is manifesting itself in both hunger and obesity in children around the globe. Derek Yach, PepsiCo's director of global health policy, is sitting across from me. I imagine that if anyone truly believes that the food industry can do something constructive, it is he. He came to PepsiCo after working with WHO—where he did effective and influential work on public health issues such as obesity and tobacco—because he believed that PepsiCo could actually be a positive force for nutrition in the world. Well, first he tried to be that force himself when he was with the WHO by suggesting the food industry adhere to regulations and cut the amount of salt, sugar, and unhealthy fats in its products. This made him rather unpopular with the food industry for some time.

WHO, he explains, can illuminate the path and advocate for certain health policies and corporate action, but it cannot take action itself. While it can publish statistics and reports, it can't really do anything about the problems it sees. After leaving the slow-moving world of international health policy, Yach worked for private foundations. But then he was offered a job with PepsiCo and told to go ahead and make those changes he was talking about at WHO. "Here we reach over a billion consumers every day with products in over 170 markets. We've got the scale and we've got the diversity to have an impact," he says. "I think for me this is the right place to be."

Even when Yach was at WHO, it's clear that he believed that industry could make changes to solve or at least help with the problem of obesity. So his move from health advocate and industry critic to industry insider isn't as unlikely as it first appears. But still it is a big leap. Besides manufacturing Pepsi and 7Up, the company makes Lay's potato chips and Cheetos. It also makes Quaker granola bars and Cap'n Crunch. Given that the company makes soft drinks, junk food, and snack foods that are less unhealthy than the junk food, I ask Yach what he thinks PepsiCo could possibly do for children's nutrition?

In answer, he grabs a box called Planet Lunch, which contains a processed food lunch for children to take to school, a product PepsiCo has already launched in the United Kingdom. "It has three components," he explains. "First is this sort of squeezable fruitlike thing [i.e., juice in a pouch], which is 100 percent juice, no additives put in; the second is a fruit and grain bar that meets the [UK] Food Standards [Agency's] sugar, fat, and salt levels and are all very low with modest calorie intake. And the third is a sort of bread thing. It's not a chip, it's made from bread. But the size is carefully thought through."

The lunch is three separately packaged, processed food items packed together in a box. It is meant to meet a child's nutritional requirements while keeping calories down. In a world where processed foods are the norm and where people think of nutrients instead of food, I suppose this piece of surreal food processing might in fact be an improvement over a baloney sandwich on white bread with a soft drink and a bag of potato chips. But the compass seems to be a little off. This might genuinely be the best the food industry can come up with for lunch, but it's not the best option for a child's lunch.

Carlos Monteiro, the Brazilian nutritionist who believes that processing is more of a problem than the actual ingredients, is extremely bothered by the trend toward "healthy" processed foods. In an article he published in the *Journal of the World Public Health Nutrition Association*, he wrote, "This is now a colossal worldwide business, which is—ironically—fuelled by concerns about disabilities and diseases in part caused by food supplies and dietary patterns increasingly composed of ultraprocessed products . . . They are a large part of the global public health problem, and such products that make health claims may well make the problem worse." He finds that these foods, rather than being genuinely healthy, are usually just less unhealthy than other processed foods.

Yach seems to see the food debate as between the pragmatists, of which he is clearly one, and the dreamers (here I am). At one time, I might have been as pragmatic as Yach, but when I moved to Rome, I realized that what I saw as realistic was just habit. Rome, of course, has different ideas about food than New York or London or Toronto, and that's how it should be. But it's our cultural expectations that prevent school children everywhere from eating fresh, whole foods. Projects like the Edible Schoolyard in the United States, the Good Food Café in Toronto, and, of course, Jamie Oliver's school lunch program in London and his famous Huntington experiment are all testaments to the fact that kids will eat and enjoy good food when it's offered to them.

Children might well find Planet Lunch to be fun. Children do love those squeezable juice pouches, but they're not really an adequate replacement for fruit. The fruit and grain bar and the processed bread might not be harmful, but a decent sandwich on non–industrially produced whole-grain bread with a peach on the side would be preferable in many ways, even taking into account the purported nutritional content of the futuristic food. The contents of Planet Lunch seem like nonfood to me. They have a lot in common with the processed snack foods that are made especially for toddlers; now we have special food for school-aged children. While it is convenient to grab a prepackaged box off the shelf and throw it in a backpack, it doesn't address the social aspect of lunch, the lack of cohesion and community. A packed lunch made with fresh, whole foods by a parent is at least a little more personal; and a high-quality school lunch program has the added social benefit of gathering children together to sit down and share food.

I ask Yach if creating food products and fortifying others to technically meet nutritional requirements are an unhelpful distraction to parents who are trying to figure out what and how to feed their children. "The desirable goal for any community is to eat fresh, whole foods of the most diversified nature," he says. I nod enthusiastically; on this, we agree. Yach continues, "The question is how realistic is it in a world where we're constrained by massive urbanization, food supply turnover, vulnerability to food prices? All of that means that the processed food world remains, I think, the cornerstone of assuring long-term food security where fresh, of course, is desirable [but not always possible]. I think we've all read [Michael] Pollan's books. I've met him a couple of times and I admire him enormously. He would have us go out and shoot a boar, put it in our fridge, and slice off bits as time goes by and grow our vegetable gardens." Yach then describes an unsuccessful attempt he made with his seven-year-old son to plant a garden. He says it was fun and his son really enjoyed it, but all they ended up with at the end of the season was a pumpkin.

I suggest that perhaps he only needs to work on his gardening skills a little. "Everybody could get better," he laughs. "But think about these hurly-burly cities like São Paolo, Beijing. It's a bit of an elitist phenomenon to think that it's going to be realistic—"

We are interrupted by the sound of a very loud cricket chirping, which turns out to be his cell phone. While he deals with the call, I ponder his use of the words "elitist" and "realistic" together. The elitism charge is often invoked in North America because whole foods, particularly organic foods, are sometimes more expensive than mass-produced processed and fast foods. It's cheaper to drink juice than it is to eat fresh fruit. You can fill stomachs much more economically on McDonald's hamburgers and french fries than with a beef and broccoli stir-fry made at home. My husband recently grumbled over the fact that the less food processors do to the food, the more it costs. But there's nothing elitist about whole foods; the difference in prices is simply the result of food policies that have totally reshaped agriculture around the world to suit the needs of the food processing industry. Now the industry says it's not realistic to expect people worldwide to eat whole, unprocessed foods. Rather than talk about "elitist" foods, we might do better to throw the word "unjust" around.

PepsiCo and other food companies have been discussing the idea of fortifying junk foods and soft drinks as a way of relieving malnutrition in poor countries. It would be so much easier, not to mention profitable, to simply give the world a Pepsi fortified with vitamins and minerals than it would be to ensure that people in poor countries have access to real food. Yach says it is sad that anyone would stand in the way of such an initiative. But Carlos Monteiro, who happens to live in that "hurly-burly" city of São Paolo in Brazil, where Yach says that fresh, whole foods are unrealistic, has condemned the industry-led campaign to sell fortified junk foods to children as a blatant attempt to "teach the world to snack" and to increase food companies' market share. He pointed out that the poorest, most malnourished people cannot afford the price of a soft drink, and that only those who are slightly better off, the ones who do have a little money to spend on fresh food, would instead end up buying fortified junk food for their children in the belief that it's good for them.

"If we can increase fresh, if we can get closer to fresh, that's all good, but that's not the business we are particularly good at," says Yach. I nod enthusiastically once more since he's hit on another point of agreement. Providing healthy food is not what these companies are good at, unless they want to give up food processing and become a collective of small organic farmers. So maybe they shouldn't try to do it. Maybe they should stick to making soft drinks, potato chips, and the beloved Cheetos, which alone brought in more than US$3 billion in worldwide sales in a single year. The food companies could be honest about their products, admit that they are high calorie, are not nutritious, and might contain some chemical ingredients, but that they're fun, taste good, and are okay to eat on rare occasions. Maybe the companies could limit the places where their products are sold, so that young children, who can't be expected to truly understand nutrition and who have little self-control, would not be confronted and tempted by them everywhere they go. That would be a big help to parents and a socially responsible thing to do.

But such restraint would limit the size of the companies. The world economy as it is now depends on growth. Like any other publicly traded company, PepsiCo has to sell more stuff this year than it did last year. Why none of us realized that mixing food and free-market capitalism would cause havoc is a mystery for future generations to mull over. But as it is now, a company like PepsiCo (which is already the second-biggest processed food company in the world after Nestlé) has no choice but to expand either by selling more junk food or by taking advantage of the growing demand for healthy foods by creating processed health-food products. Either the companies grow or their shareholders abandon them for another company that will. They are not bad companies run by bad people. Yach and PepsiCo CEO Indra Nooyi have practically turned themselves inside out trying to reconcile the world's food needs with the food PepsiCo is capable of producing, but they have no choice but to seek growth.

Since publicly traded, multinational food companies have pretty much saturated the market in North America—and, in some cases, are seeing shrinking sales—they are working hard to get Europeans to eat more processed foods and to drink more soft drinks, and they are look-ing to the developing world for growth. Essentially, this means that they are encouraging people who have fairly healthy diets and eating habits to eat junk food. And they are trying to convince people of limited means to spend their money—money they could be using to buy fresh, whole foods—on processed, fortified foods instead.

PepsiCo does give the impression that it cares. Its executives listen to the critics and they try to respond. The food industry is charged with favoring single crop varieties for its products, which contributes substan-tially to a loss of biodiversity. Farmers try to grow the type of potatoes that PepsiCo needs to make its Lay's chips, for example, and abandon nu-merous other varieties that are not so good for making potato chips. So, in Peru, PepsiCo actually pays small farmers to grow eight rare varieties of potatoes that were in danger of disappearing, and it uses them to make a premium potato chip called Frito-Lay's Andina. Yes, they're still potato chips, but in making them, PepsiCo is doing less damage to biodiversity. And yes, Andina is still only a drop in the bucket toward offsetting the loss of biodiversity that the other potato chips contribute to. Andina is a good thing in itself, but as long as it's only a token gesture, it's not enough.

Nooyi, PepsiCo's charismatic CEO, championed the company's Pepsi Refresh campaign, which was a fund of about US$20 million to give to projects that could change the world. Pepsi Refresh handed out $5,000 to fund a prom at a high school in Springfield, New Jersey, and $250,000 to fund research into a rare genetic disorder, Sanfilippo syndrome, that affects children. The campaign funded numerous projects that were good for communities, including playgrounds and homeless shelters. It did exactly what it said it was setting out to do. But in an article in the *New Yorker* magazine, Nooyi characterized the campaign as a failure because sales of Pepsi went down in the United States. She had wanted to tie the projects funded to Pepsi, but the campaign didn't make people drink more Pepsi. And selling more Pepsi, not the good work of the campaign, was the point of Pepsi Refresh.

PepsiCo has also responded to the criticisms leveled at the industry about ingredients. The company is trying to use more whole grains and fewer preservatives, unnatural flavors, and colors, and trying to find salt substitutes and sweeteners. But it is primarily a snack-food company, and the food still has to be tasty or no one is going to buy it. PepsiCo has figured out that if most people should be eating around two thousand calories a day, snacks should only take up about 15 to 20 percent of those calories. So the company is reformulating its products in an effort to lower levels of salt, sugar, and calories. The only way for the company to grow richer and bigger without making people grow fatter is to lower the calories. The message is sell more packages but fewer calories.

The reformulations have more to do with saving bottom lines than with improving nutrition for children. The food companies know that they'd be in trouble if everyone started to eat more local foods, cook more often, and reduce their intake of fast food and junk food to a minimum. The more that people follow their traditional diet, the less room there will be for processed food products, and the food companies will suffer. Vitamin fortification and "healthy" processed foods are PepsiCo's way of making itself seem necessary.

I went to PepsiCo mainly to ask how the company can promote the increased consumption of its products without also promoting childhood obesity. The answer was through science—by lowering calories and using salt substitutes. Fresh food has no part in its approach because that's not what it does. It's not a fresh-food company. So maybe we should stop looking to the food companies to solve our health problems. The solution lies in moving away from industrial food, not in creating more technically acceptable versions of it. You can't ask these corporations to come up with a solution when the only real answer means that they will lose business.

The Corporate World

Corporations defend themselves with a practice known as corporate social responsibility. PepsiCo calls it "Performance with Purpose," which is a philosophy of sustainable growth. "At PepsiCo we believe that what is good for society and what is good for business can and should be the same thing. We believe in 'Performance with Purpose' and we act on this daily, delivering sustainable growth while investing in a healthier future. This is our promise and our mission." This quote comes from the inside cover of PepsiCo's 2009 Corporate Citizenship Report. It sounds nice, but it rests on the premise that what is good for society and what is good for business is the same thing. What if they are not the same thing? PepsiCo's statement echoes Milton Friedman, the economist who influenced an entire generation of economists and industrialists. In a 1970 article entitled "The Social Responsibility of Business Is to Increase Its Profits," Friedman wrote: "The businessmen [who talk about social responsibility] believe that they are defending free enterprise when they declaim that business is not concerned 'merely' with profit but also with promoting desirable 'social' ends; that business has a 'social conscience' and takes seriously its responsibilities for providing employment, eliminating discrimination, avoiding pollution and whatever else may be the catchwords of the contemporary crop of reformers. In fact they are—or would be if they or anyone else took them seriously—preaching pure and unadulterated socialism." Friedman thought that a corporation seeking profit for its shareholders would naturally produce good in its wake. Some years later, in an interview with Joel Bakan, author of the book *The Corporation*, Friedman said there is one exception when business should proclaim social responsibility, and that is when the business is insincere. When the appearance of going along with the whole corporate responsibility narrative will boost the company's bottom line, it's fine. "It's like putting a good-looking girl in front of an automobile to sell an automobile," he said. "That's not in order to promote pulchritude. That's in order to sell cars."

Corporations were originally given charters by governments to perform public services. For centuries, they were considered benign and, in fact, quite helpful. "Corporations were not originally created to 'maximize profits to stockholders,'" wrote Ralph Estes in his book *Tyranny of the Bottom Line*. "From their creation until well into the 1800s, that notion would have seemed bizarre; a person proposing it would have risked being seen as a bit 'off.'" Their original purpose was to offer goods and services that the community needed. If you think about it in terms of a food business, it makes a certain amount of sense. A bakery can bake bread using whole ingredients as you would at home. It can save you time and even offer you more variety than if you had to do it yourself. A dairy saves you from having to keep your own cow and make your own cheese. When a food company's primary function is to serve the customer, it will use the best ingredients and it won't compromise your safety.

But the corporation's primary function has clearly changed. In his book, Estes described numerous instances where a corporation's single-minded pursuit of the bottom line hurt its customers. He wrote about women who suffered and died from using the Dalkon Shield intrauterine birth control device. The corporation knew about its dangers but continued to sell it to protect its profits. When the primary purpose of a food-producing company is to maximize profits for shareholders, it's more likely to use cheap ingredients and find cheap, chemical ways to mask the taste. It's going to cut costs and try to increase consumption. Considering the Dalkon Shield example, we have no way to be sure that a profit-maximizing food company will be good for anyone's health.

Look at the example of ConAgra Foods, the makers of Chef Boyardee pasta in a can, Kid Cuisine frozen meals, and Peter Pan peanut butter. An unknown person from inside the company leaked information to the FDA that the company had found salmonella in the peanut butter at its processing plant in Georgia in 2004. But the company didn't make an announcement, and it did not recall the peanut butter. The FDA made an inquiry but didn't pursue the issue aggressively. ConAgra didn't alert its customers to the potential danger. Three years later, after hundreds of people had become sick from salmonella in the peanut butter, the FDA finally demanded that the company turn over its records. They showed that the salmonella had been detected three years earlier. Though much of the criticism fell on the government agency and inspection process, the fact is that the company knew there was a problem with the food and continued to sell it for children to eat.

The rise of giant multinational corporations is a relatively recent phenomenon, and when Estes was writing his book, he felt that people were recognizing the threats they posed and were looking for ways to constrain them. What's depressing is that Estes published the book in 1996, and the situation shows little sign of changing. We've known for some time that the corporation's best interest is not always the same as our best interest. Bakan, who is a legal scholar, looked at the corporation's legal status as a person and found it to be a psychopath. "Corporate social responsibility is their new creed, a self-conscious corrective to earlier greed-inspired visions of the corporation. Despite this shift, the corporation itself has not changed. It remains, as it was at the time of its origins as a modern business institution in the middle of the nineteenth century, a legally designated 'person' designed to valorize self-interest and invalidate moral concern. Most people would find its 'personality' abhorrent, even psychopathic, in a human being, yet curiously we accept it in society's most powerful institution," wrote Bakan in *The Corporation*. This revealing book was written in 2004, and the companion documentary film of the same name was released around the same time worldwide, winning awards and accolades. Like Estes, Bakan documented numerous misdeeds of corporations, including an analysis done by General Motors in the 1970s that showed that it was more cost effective for the company not to fix a problem it was having with fuel-fed fires and instead to pay the legal damages that resulted when people were killed and injured by the fires. Per automobile, it would have cost $8.59 to fix the problem but only $2.40 to pay the legal damages. The company opted not to fix the problem. It was more profitable for the company to allow people to be killed and maimed by its faulty automobiles than it was to produce safer cars.

Bovine spongiform encephalopathy (BSE), more commonly known as mad cow disease, is an example of how profit overrides pretty much everything else. Cows are meant to eat grass. When they are allowed to graze outdoors as they please, they are generally healthy and don't produce horrific strains of E. coli. When they are slaughtered properly, their meat is nourishing to us, as long as we don't eat too much of it. The problem is that grazing cows need space, and you can't squeeze too many of them into one place. It's expensive to raise cattle safely. But if cows are fed grain, they can be crowded together, which is what started to happen around the middle of the last century. When they are crowded, they don't work their own manure into the ground and bury the significant carbon dioxide they produce. Since there are now so many of them, it's a real environmental problem. But the big meat producers didn't stop with crowded pens and feeding cattle grain. After mad cow disease appeared in Britain in 1986, researchers discovered that it was being caused by cows, which were meant to eat grass and could more or less handle grain, eating animals, particularly other cows. The cows were becoming sick and passing the disease on to humans in the form of Creutzfeldt-Jakob disease.

In *Fast Food Nation*, the book that showed the world what was in our fast-food hamburgers, Eric Schlosser described how cows are crowded together in filthy lots where they have to stand in their own manure and drink dirty water. And until 1997, they were still being fed other animals, including dead cattle, pigs, horses, and chickens that had previously fed on cattle. Some cows were also fed the remains of dead dogs and cats from animal shelters. If that isn't bad enough, cattle were also fed waste products from poultry plants, including sawdust, newspaper that had been used as litter, and chicken poop. Then human beings ate the cattle. It makes one think, rather sickeningly, of the phrase "we are what we eat." In 2008, the FDA banned certain "cattle materials" from animal feed, such as cattle tissues that have the highest risk of carrying the agent thought to cause BSE. That woefully inadequate development occurred twenty-two years after BSE first appeared.

If the goal of the corporations that allowed these practices to flourish was to serve their customers, there would be far fewer cows in the world, they would be grazing on grass or at worst grain, there would be much less meat being produced, and what was produced would be safe to eat. We couldn't be farther from this situation.

A food corporation needs to convince us to consume as much of its food as we can hold down and then some. It profits mostly from providing packaged foods with a long shelf life, while we need to consume mostly fresh foods. It relies on monocrops, while we need to diversify our diets. The activist nutritionist Marion Nestle told the *New Yorker* magazine that the only way PepsiCo could contribute toward better nutrition would be if it went out of business.

I believe that Derek Yach is sincere. I met other nice people at Pepsi-Co, and they seem to believe in what they are doing. They see fortified food products as a quick fix in countries with malnourishment. They see the reformulations as improvements, but they're not really thinking about what would be the best situation. They can't think about it because the best situation is something that could potentially put them out of business. So they have to convince us that the best solution is unrealistic.

Yach is well read in the area of food politics. During our interview, he quoted Marion Nestle; Paul Roberts, who wrote *The End of Food*; and Michael Pollan. (Even so, he presented a caricature of Pollan's views on what we should eat. In *The Omnivore's Dilemma*, Pollan went so far as to hunt and kill a boar to illustrate that it is an animal, not just a product in the supermarket. He wasn't saying that we all have to kill one.) Yach complained that these writers all have much to say about the problems in the food system but little to say about what to do about them. That's not true; but the solutions don't involve the food industry. Pollan's slogan—eat food, not too much, mostly plants—is about as clear and concise a solution as possible. Yach suggests that the critics want to live in the past, but they don't. Most talk about the past in order to remind people that for most of human history, it's been quite possible to live without a lot of industrially produced foods. Until I moved to Italy, I might have thought it would be unrealistic to imagine myself cooking from scratch for my family every day. It's all a matter of habit, perspective, and the expectations of the culture in which you live.

An Industrial Food World

In a sense, Derek Yach's view is also nostalgic—another sort of yearning for the past. Industrial food got a big boost in the 1960s with the Green Revolution, which was a political effort by the US government to prevent hunger from giving rise to left-wing protests and socialist ideas in poor countries. It promoted a system of agriculture that was heavily dependent on irrigation and fossil fuels, with chemical fertilizers and pesticides. While the system increased food production in India, Pakistan, the Philippines, and countries in South America, hunger remained ever present. At the time, the increased production suggested to many that technology was the answer to feeding the world. But the cracks in that theory have since become apparent. Fertilizers and pesticides are expensive, over time they deplete the nutrients in the soil necessary for growing food, and they contribute to greenhouse gas emissions. High-yielding seeds displaced local biodiversity, which provided micronutrients to the local populations. Irrigation has depleted groundwater and left salt deposits in the soil that make it unsuitable for growing anything.

Even now, economists talk about how much grain yields will need to increase to feed the world in 2050. But people can't really live on grain. People need a varied diet. When I mentioned this to a nutritionist at the UN Food and Agriculture Organization (FAO), she quipped that the food and pharmaceutical industries would very much like us to live on grain made into therapeutic foods with a few vitamins mixed in. The food industry needs grain for processed foods and livestock. Less than half the grain the world produces goes to feed humans; the rest is used to feed livestock, to create biofuels, and to make starches and plastics. We need grain, of course, but grain yields are not a true measure of whether or not the world can produce enough food to feed a growing population. In fact, small farms produce more food per acre than large industrial farms. Small farmers intercrop different plants, because some of those plants nourish the soil, while others provide the necessary shade for certain plants to thrive. Many plants act as natural pesticides, while chemical pesticides breed resistance and often create more crop loss. Small farmers are able to watch their crops and weed by hand, unlike farmers with massive fields of single crops. If the small farmers have animals, they can use manure instead of chemical fertilizer and thus tend to use far less oil and water to produce their crops. The world's current problem with hunger is not caused by a lack of food. It is a political problem. As Brazil has shown with its Zero Hunger initiative—a multifaceted program of school and community gardens plus grants to schools and families to purchase food from local organic farmers that has ensured access to real food for about 24 million people who did not have it before—positive changes happen when there is political will to deal with hunger directly. While Yach says the food activists are unrealistic and elitist, there's nothing elitist about eating fruits and vegetables or learning to cook and maybe trying to be a little creative with your lunch. There is certainly something unjust about putting those things out of reach of people with lower incomes, or saying that poor people should be satisfied with less. I once attended a conference on the human right to food, where an Indian human rights lawyer asked the audience why they thought it was acceptable that their children (meaning those of us in the richer countries) could eat real food while Indian children were expected to make do with micronutrient-fortified lollipops.

Despite PepsiCo's agenda, Yach's pragmatic views still had an effect on me. Maybe he's right that many children will not receive an adequate lunch, so a processed food lunch that is less unhealthy is an improvement. As for North America, he's right that eating industrially produced foods for meals and snacks is the norm. It has become the food culture. No one expects french fries to be made from freshly peeled potatoes anymore. In this culture, making packaged food a little less unhealthy seems sensible. From the viewpoint of PepsiCo's suburban office building, my life in Italy—that world of fresh food markets; abundant, seasonal foods; and the simple yet deep pleasure of the table—might as well be on the moon.

Planet New York

After visiting PepsiCo, I took the train back to Manhattan. I had been staying with Brenda—my old and dear friend who had made the cultural mistake of eating a pastry on the street in Rome—and I wanted to make dinner for her. We had both been very busy and had been eating out, along with the rest of the city. I love New York, but it's exhausting. Even if you don't have anything to do, you feel this frantic energy that makes you want to shovel down your lunch and power walk to the subway. New York has always been known for its great restaurants, for expensive food, new trends, and exciting chefs, but not so much for regular cooking at home. In fact, I had no idea what people ate at home. Brenda said, "Takeout Chinese," when I asked her about it, and suggested we get some, which we did. In New York, you can eat anything at any time of day; you can order any combination of foods and no one looks twice at you. A friend of Brenda's with a young daughter said they order takeout several times a week because that's just what you do. Otherwise, how would you eat? She was implying that you can't possibly cook every day.

I hadn't been to New York since we moved to Italy nearly ten years earlier, and Brenda wanted to reintroduce me to the particular standards of New York fare. So one night we ate tiny hamburgers and drank expensive wine at the Algonquin Hotel, which is more famous for its literary history than for its food. Another night we met a friend of Brenda's who had an adorable little girl named Violet, and for dinner we ate grilled-cheese sandwiches with french fries and ketchup at a diner. One afternoon for lunch, we had a perfect, crisply roasted chicken with a green salad at a friend's downtown bistro. We had elegant, ordinary, and in-between. At one point, we were on the subway, completely absorbed in conversation, when Brenda casually reached around me and brushed lettuce and tomato off my jacket. I turned to look and realized that the well-groomed woman in her early fifties next to me was eating a tuna-salad sandwich. It was an overstuffed kind of sandwich, with filling squishing out with every bite, and she had the plastic container that she'd bought it in resting on her lap. But bits of loose tuna and mayonnaise-coated lettuce and tomato chunks were falling here and there. She wasn't the only one eating or drinking on the crowded train. Everyone was in danger of being dripped on by the guy standing up and eating a slice of cheesy pizza, or by people with soft drinks, iced tea, juice, and, of course, the ubiquitous coffee. I used to be one of them—I was a habitual subway-riding *caffe latte* drinker—but I had forgotten. We were only a few hours by plane away from a place where people only drink *caffe latte* and cappuccino in the morning for breakfast, and where they certainly don't drink it or eat on public transportation. It's funny that in Rome, people commonly drive through red lights, cheat on their taxes, and overcharge foreigners for meals in restaurants, but they won't drink a cappuccino after noon or eat a sandwich on the bus. Some rules you don't break.

At first, I found the contrast between the ritualized respect for mealtimes in Italy and the all-day buffet on New York public transportation to be stark and extremely off-putting. It stopped bothering me soon enough, probably because I come from this sort of culture. By the third day, I was going to the Starbucks on the corner to get a takeout cappuccino (complaining endlessly, and likely quite annoyingly, to Brenda about how weak and bitter it tasted) and drinking it on the subway.

To suggest that people shouldn't eat while commuting is like suggesting they stop breathing. In big American and Canadian cities, it is completely acceptable to consume food while you're doing something else, either because you are busy or because you are bored. If everyone around you is doing it, you do it too.

In fact, before I went to PepsiCo that morning, I stopped at the Starbucks on the corner to buy coffee. When I saw the case filled with cakes and muffins, I considered getting something to eat, even though I had eaten breakfast only half an hour earlier. But then I noticed the posted calorie counts: banana walnut bread, 490; lemon pound cake, 490; raspberry scone, 490; and glazed old-fashioned donut, 420. I got the coffee and carried on. But when I arrived at Grand Central, I had time to kill before my train to White Plains was due to leave. There was no place to sit, so I wandered around. Eventually, an appetizing smell of toasting bread led me to a bagel shop, and before I could stop myself, I was eating a giant, toasted, sesame-seed bagel spread with thick, white cream cheese. It was really good, but I had bought it completely on impulse; I wasn't even hungry until I smelled it. I ate it while leaning against a wall. I felt pathetic and out of control, but every bite was very, very good. Afterward I felt full, and my feelings of guilt lingered all day.

So after too much easily accessible food on the go, I felt a longing to get out a knife and start chopping. Before I had left for PepsiCo that morning, Brenda had said, "There's a chicken in the fridge and we better cook it soon." I thought today would be my chance to cook. I was heading toward a Whole Foods store near the Fourteenth Street subway station that I had noticed earlier in the week, when I saw a fresh food market, like a mirage in the desert, right there on the pavement in Union Square: the Union Square Greenmarket. It was a place that until then I had only heard stories of—a mythical place of freshly picked produce on a busy Manhattan street corner. It was late afternoon in the middle of the week and the place was crowded with people. I walked around the stalls, taking in the fantastic display of fresh food. I picked up a huge bunch of very curly kale and, out of habit, asked how to cook it. It was completely different from the kind of kale, the *cavolo nero*, I'm used to buying in Rome. It looked different even from the variety grown by the students at Bendale. To my great and everlasting delight, the woman who was selling it told me that the best way is to simply drop it in a big pot of salted water and let it cook for a few minutes, then drain it well and dress it with a little olive or canola oil and lemon juice or red wine vinegar. A woman standing next to me then told me that I could also cut it roughly into ribbons, toss it with some kind of oil and salt, and then "roast" it in the oven until it became crispy. She said her children eat it like this for a snack. I had some radishes in my hand, big, plump red ones, and the woman who told me to roast the kale asked what I was going to do with those. I said, "I'm likely going to boil the kale, but now that we're talking about roasting vegetables, I might toss the radishes in oil and salt and put them in the oven until they caramelize a little, and then throw them into a salad." She bought some radishes and said she would try that too. This was the same kind of conversation I have in my Roman markets, except that I didn't have to watch my verb tenses and worry about my vocabulary.

In farmers' markets, people who have spent their lives immersed in or at least surrounded by a fast-food, processed-food world are slowly creating an example, parallel to the one put forward by the food industry, of how to feed ourselves and our families. The markets are places where you can shop with children and feel confident about indulging them with some fall apples or freshly baked bread.

Though I had been missing James and Nico while in New York, as I wandered around the market, I found I missed them even more. I wondered what Nico would have made of the small, sour apples, of the weirdly shaped gourds and the orange pumpkins, which are so different from the more grayish-orange, wide-ridged variety we buy in Rome.

I took my haul back to Brenda's place and got to work on the chicken in her tiny galley kitchen. I rubbed it all over with olive oil, stuffed it with lemon, rosemary, and garlic, sprinkled garlic and chopped rosemary on the skin, and put it in the oven with a separate pan of potatoes with rosemary to roast. Then I cut some whole-wheat, sourdough bread that I had bought at the market. It was dense and a little chewy and had that nice acrid smell from the natural yeast. It was really good and a pleasant change from my beloved, crusty, wood-oven-baked bread in Rome. I put the bread on a plate along with some chicken liver pâté and goat's-milk cheddar cheese—both of which had been made by the people from whom I bought them at the market—and some slices of apple.

Brenda and I poured ourselves a glass of wine and nibbled the cheese and pâté while the chicken and potatoes were roasting in the oven. Then I prepared the vegetables—all of them from the market—and we sat down in the living room, put our feet up, and chatted about our day while the meal cooked.

Brenda jokes that she has the palate of a child, and by that she means she doesn't really like vegetables. She and I both grew up in Toronto eating the same kind of unpleasant mixed frozen vegetables and canned green beans. I reminded her that she's a grown-up now and ought to eat her greens without being told to do so. (Ever since having a child, I have a tendency to insist that everyone eat his or her vegetables.) She smiled uncertainly at me and without directly looking at the kale, put a small portion of it on her plate and then dutifully ate it. She later admitted that it wasn't too bad. We ate by candlelight and listened to old jazz CDs—Duke Ellington, Cab Calloway, and Ella Fitzgerald. We both felt much better.

Food Islands

The next morning, we ate leftover potatoes and kale with scrambled eggs and toasted sourdough. Since returning to Rome, I sometimes think about the delicious kale I had in New York. It had a deep, mineral flavor and a sturdy texture, without the thick spine up the leaves like the *cavolo nero*, that makes it stand up well to being cooked in water one day and then sautéed with garlic and olive oil the next morning. I like knowing that it is different from what I'm eating in Italy. I like the fact that foods, and not just cooking styles, are not the same everywhere.

When I was in Toronto a few weeks earlier, I stayed with my friend Lorraine Johnson, who writes about gardens and urban agriculture. Staying with Lorraine meant that I was eating very well. Lorraine has been known to invite you for dinner, then ride her bike to a local public park just before you arrive to pick flowers and wild herbs for a salad. One night during my visit, she invited a group of good friends over for dinner. Around noon, she browned some chicken pieces and then simmered them with reconstituted dried mushrooms. She left it on the stove all afternoon while she worked in her office upstairs. One or the other of us would pass by the pot every now and then and give it a stir. When it was nearly time for the guests to arrive, she tossed a salad and roasted some parsnips from her garden. Parsnips are something we never see in Italy. But they are a distinct taste from my childhood. I remember not liking parsnips, but when I tasted them this time, their flavor was so comfortingly familiar, I ate a second serving. One of the guests brought some cheese from a cheese maker in her Toronto neighborhood. Another brought cupcakes for dessert. I made two kinds of crostini: one with mashed cannellini beans drizzled with olive oil, garlic, and rosemary; the other with broccoli steamed until soft and then mashed in a hot pan with olive oil, garlic, and dried chilies, and with curls of shaved Parmesan on top. (I brought Lorraine some fresh, green oil from olives that only a week earlier had been on the trees at my Roman wine merchant's country house in Umbria; I think I used most of it up before I left.) I sprinkled the crostini a little with the forbidden salt. It was all really simple food; the ingredients were good quality, mostly local where possible and uncomplicated. I wished Nico had been there with us. After all the bad food experiences he had had in Toronto, he would really have enjoyed this dinner, I think.

In New York and Toronto, it seems as if there is a burgeoning food culture. In fact, it's happening everywhere. Organic farming is now the fastest-growing segment of agriculture in the United States, where farmers' markets grew by 16 percent between 2009 and 2010. Cities all over the world are seeing an increase in demand for local and traditional foods. With the growth of farmers' markets, home gardens, small artisanal cheese makers, and butchers sourcing hormone- and antibiotic-free meat from small farms outside the cities, ingredients are getting better and better. North American markets are starting to look more and more like the ones in Europe that we used to fantasize about, and North Americans are behaving like those know-it-all Europeans who used to irritate us. They are cooking and sharing recipes in the markets. The structure of eating is still a problem in North America: people don't seem to adhere to set mealtimes or refrain from snacking in between. But slowly, along with the amazing food, rituals will, I imagine, emerge to help us enjoy it without overdoing it.

Just when it seemed that food couldn't get much worse in terms of factory farming and industrial food products, in many places food suddenly got a lot better. Many people have greater access to locally grown food. What the food industry tells us is unrealistic is actually happening in places where we least expect it. Small farmers markets open midweek in city neighborhoods, making it easier for busy families to cook something fresh. And the US Department of Agriculture (USDA) has even helped farmers markets install the wireless technology they need so that shoppers with electronic benefit cards (like food stamps) can buy fresh food. Local fresh foods have not replaced processed and fast foods, but we are starting to have some real choices about what to eat, at least in the richer parts of the world.

TEN

Natural Food Cultures

The Significance of Memory

SOMETIMES I LOOK at Nico sitting in his favorite chair in the kitchen, a tall chair that raises him to the level of the counter, his long legs dangling in the air, and I can't believe how quickly time passes. He's grown so tall. Two years ago, I had to lift him onto that chair and then keep an eye on him to be sure he didn't fall off. Even a year ago, he wasn't so steady. Now that he's six, he climbs up on his own so he can help me prepare dinner (he shells peas, snaps the ends off asparagus, measures rice, pits cherries whether they need it or not, and so on) or tell me about his day. If I ask him a direct question, he rarely answers. But here in the kitchen while we're both busy working together, he tells me stories about what Giulio said to Giovanni, and how Johann organized them into battalions to fight the forces of evil (which turned out to be the girls). He has even introduced me to some Roman slang words, which worries me a little because I'm not sure if they are rude. When James comes home from work, he usually lends a hand with the chopping, and they both set the table and keep me company while I stir the risotto or pasta sauce.

The kitchen is our own little cocoon of domesticity where we entertain each other with stories and relax after our busy day. It's not always tranquil; sometimes we argue, or I feel stressed out because I've decided to make something too complicated, or whatever I put in the oven is taking too long to cook. Sometimes we get home a little late from soccer

143

practice and I haven't thought out what I'm going to make for dinner. I've even started fires by forgetting the pine nuts I'm supposed to be lightly toasting under the broiler, but Nico actually thinks that's pretty exciting. The hassle and pleasure of feeding ourselves at the end of the day is just normal life, but it's the normal moments in childhood that shape us, that build our habits and inform our preferences.

I am so aware of the need to protect Nico from the food industry, but I also need to give him the resources to look after himself. I think that's partly what we are doing here. We're making dinner, tending to our daily need to eat, but we're also enjoying ourselves. He will ask me what's for dinner, and I know if it happens to be a summer night when the basil has been flourishing and I can say *Pesto alla Genovese* (though I make it with our Roman basil), he will be happy. He'll help tear up the basil leaves, measure out some pine nuts, throw in some garlic, drizzle in the olive oil, and press the button on the food processor. If I say *Cotoletta alla Milanese* (more recently, we've started calling it "chicken schnitzel" because Nico likes the word), he will also be happy. He's far less happy when I say we're having farro risotto with spinach and a salad or lentil soup with broccoli to follow. I feel like I've let him down on those nights when dinner is less exciting.

Like many parents, I have resorted to frozen fish sticks to cheer him up, though I think I shouldn't give in so easily. I know the odd bit of processed food isn't going to kill him, but I want him to prefer real food. My friend Sarah struggles with her son, Dylan, who only wants to eat spaghetti with tomato sauce. She feels guilty when she caves in and lets him have it instead of the soup, fish, or vegetables she cooked. She makes the tomato sauce herself, so it's not a processed food, but she worries that Dylan isn't learning to love all the other great foods available to him. We all have our crutch, and sometimes, for our own sanity, it's necessary to lean on it. But if I feel like being lazy, I try to think of Alice Waters telling me to be a grown-up and insist he eat what's good for him. I'm hoping that by doing exactly that, when he's older he will choose to eat real food because it tastes good to him and brings him pleasure, and not only because he *thinks* it's good for him.

I'm also hoping he will eat real food because of the happy memories associated with it. While the marketers try to tap into his deep yearnings, his desire to be part of the group, and to associate those feelings with their factory foods, I'm trying to help him associate his happy childhood with real food that tastes good. He might sigh with displeasure over the lentil soup, but he eats it. He'll sometimes eat two bowls of it. He rarely asks for broccoli, but when it's on his plate, he eats it without question. And while we're eating our dinner, we're talking. James usually puts on some music while we eat. Nico has been learning about the Beatles, Bill Evans, Billie Holiday, and Duke Ellington over dinner. He's been soaking up music from our adopted culture, too, with songs by Luigi Tenco and Fabrizio De André along with his lentils, crusty bread, and vegetables. If it's winter, we eat by candlelight; if it's summer, we eat on our balcony surrounded by vines and flowers.

Dinner is often a nice time of day for all of us. I hope the ordinary happiness of these meals becomes firmly attached to the smell and taste of the food. I hope the food culture will continue to support its traditional preferences so that the other children his age will be eating similar foods and building similar memories, and they can share these foods and that their yearning to be part of the group will lead them to their own happy memories of being part of this great culture.

Native Foods

Food has a way of evoking our own past and reminding us of who we are. Whether the food tastes good to us or not is connected with our memories. I think this partly explains why some people want to hold on to Happy Meals and powdered orange macaroni and cheese. Those tastes are tied so firmly to people's pasts that wrenching them away or demonizing them can be devastating. The memories that go with the food are more important than the food itself. This is why food marketers feel such urgency about reaching children early.

I think the experiences of Native North Americans who were forced to assimilate into American and Canadian society illustrate the connection

145

between food and identity. When Native children were forced into residential schools in the nineteenth century, they were robbed not only of their family and religion, but of their diet, too. They were cut off from their foods and flavors, and from the rituals of collecting, preparing, and eating them. They were given "civilized" and "European" food to eat: mostly refined food and some meat, very little of it fresh. The children who went to the residential schools left records of their longing for the foods of their families and communities: the roast moose, the fresh fish in the frying pan, the warm bannock, and the berries. Those foods connected them to their communities and their past—to all the generations before them. The tastes of their traditional foods and the happy memories associated with them would have naturally led them to eat what was good for them. Now, as the past recedes even further and the continuity of Native food ways has broken off, not only are most indigenous people disconnected from their traditions, but they are sick as well. Before 1940, the Inuit in Canada's far northern territories didn't suffer from diabetes. Now it's a disease borne by more than 70 percent of the community.

We argue endlessly about why the world's children are becoming overweight and sick. Yet when we look closely at the diet and health of indigenous people, we have some pretty clear before-and-after stories that point directly to processed foods. The study discussed in chapter 7, of the Pima and Tohono O'odham people in Arizona, was a good example of the way a change in diet altered the health of an indigenous community. For centuries, indigenous people lived much the way our bodies have evolved to live: they ate the foods that grew around them; they hunted and fished; they expended energy finding, growing, and preparing food; and they shared it with their community. They passed their food knowledge to their children just by feeding them, linking the food to their traditions, and building memories connected to the food. But in every case when indigenous people started to eat processed foods, obesity and its related illnesses increased, especially in children.

The closer indigenous people stay to their traditional diets, the better their health. The more "market food" (that is, food they buy in a store, usually processed or imported—nonlocal food, in other words) they eat, the worse their health. The reasons why each community eats more market food varies, but the effect on people's health is the same. For instance, Mand, a village on the island of Pohnpei, one of the Federated States of Micronesia, is blessed with great biodiversity: 55 varieties of bananas, 133 varieties of breadfruit, 1,196 species of edible fish, and a list of traditional foods that could go on for pages. What amazingly rich resources the people there have to draw from for their own indigenous cuisine. In Mand, they ate cheesy-textured bread made from breadfruit that had been buried in a pit and left to ferment for several months until its doughy, puffy mass could be kneaded and baked. They also ate papaya, citrus fruits, passion fruit, pineapple, guava, mountain apple, chaya leaves, pumpkin tips, taro leaves, and spinach. Imagine the children becoming increasingly more excited as summer approached and mango season was beginning. Imagine the taste of a mango allowed to ripen on the tree. Yet in the last twenty years, nutrition-related chronic diseases have become an epidemic in Mand. Micronesia itself is one of the top-five most obese countries in the world, with 90 percent of its population considered to be overweight. In the late 1940s, there was no obesity on Pohnpei and little malnutrition either. By 2005, more than half the children were vitamin A deficient and a third were anemic. Stunted growth in children is now a common problem. Until recently, the people in the community ate the most micronutrient-dense variety of foods in the world. Now three-quarters of their diet comes from imported fruits and vegetables and food products. Children have it even worse; 84 percent of their food comes from the international market. Infant formula has become common, along with imported baby food, bread, soup, donuts, ramen noodles, and biscuits.

Researchers carried out a campaign to persuade people to eat their traditional, local foods to improve their health. The solution to their health problems grew all around them, but already parents were losing the skill to recognize it, and their children had no memory of it. People didn't necessarily make the connection between their increasingly bad health and the change in their diet. They exported some of their traditional foods, but mostly the cheap imports were killing their own markets and making their own food culture less available and certainly less visible. Researchers set up cooking classes for adults and children, and activities for children related to local foods. They held workshops on farming techniques and published collections of recipes that used local foods. By 2007, the people of Pohnpei were eating more local foods, particularly more of the local varieties of banana and taro fruit (this is where the government campaign, mentioned earlier, to cure vitamin A deficiencies in children with local banana varieties took place). But they were still eating the imported food, too. The market food was easier for them to find than local foods. But unlike in many other indigenous communities, there are still enough of their traditional foods available that they could, if they wanted, return to a more traditional diet. The market food isn't going away unless people stop eating it.

The experience in Pohnpei shows that returning to the local diet becomes harder as time passes. People lack the happy recollections from childhood that might steer them to seek out their traditional foods. So every year, people from the Federated States of Micronesia gather at the Guam Micronesia Island Fair (GMIF) to meet and share their cultural traditions and to try to keep them going. People wear traditional costumes, perform traditional dances and songs, and share food. In 2010, the theme of the fair was food—"Celebrating the Tastes of Micronesia"—which sounds great until you realize that one of the official sponsors was PepsiCo. The general manager of Pepsi Guam Bottling Gold said the company was proud to be a sponsor once again. "We are the exclusive beverage for the GMIF so that means that we get lots of people consuming our products . . . that's always a good thing," he said in an article about the fair. "The Pepsi brand is No. 1 in Guam and in the islands of Micronesia, and the GMIF helps us to reinforce that position."

The story of the people of Pohnpei is a story that repeats itself all over the globe. The Gwich'in people, who are part of the Dene Nation and live on the Peel River in Canada's Northwest Territories, were once nomadic and lived as hunters, gatherers, and fishers, until they later became fur traders with fixed trading posts. They continued to have an ancient food tradition based on an intimate knowledge of the foods that grow near the river. They also have a tradition of eating every part of the animal, fish, or plant, and of sharing their food. Even in the interior subarctic climate in which they live, they were able to eat extremely well. But now they get most of their nutrients from market food (adults get 60 percent of their nutrients from market food and children get 90 percent) and suffer from the usual accompanying assortment of health problems.

The same story can be told about the Nuxalk, who have lived for thousands of years on the Bella Coola River in British Columbia. Traditionally, they lived on a diet of wild meat and fish supplemented by berries, wild greens, roots, bulbs, nuts, and seeds. They made grease from smelt called *ooligan*. Their food system required physical work, which helped them keep fit. They shared what they had, wasted nothing, and considered food sacred. But as processed foods were introduced into the community, the food culture changed. By the 1980s, they were suffering from alcoholism, dental problems, obesity, and diabetes—problems that were new to the community. While their nutrient deficiencies could be corrected by eating more traditional foods, the less of them they ate, the more they lost the taste for them. *Ooligan* is extremely healthy, and traditionally the Nuxalk loved it. But you have to grow up eating it in order to like it. It's hard to keep eating it if you only do so because you know it's good for you, rather than because it links you to your past in a visceral way and because its taste is a pleasure that is part of your very being. Interestingly Nuxalk grandmothers interviewed in the 1980s could identify many foods they used to eat, such as grey currants, red elderberries, and high bush cranberries. The taste of the food was part of the memory itself. You can bring back the foods and say, "Here, eat this, it's your culture," but when the memory dies, you have lost the link between the food and the cultural identity of the people who eat it.

A follow-up study in 2006 found that the Nuxalk were eating more of their traditional foods, but not enough to offset the damage being done to them by the processed market foods. Rates of obesity and diabetes were going up. It was getting harder to use some of the traditional foods they had relied on because of environmental changes. There were no longer enough smelt to make *ooligan*, sockeye salmon had become rare, and fishing abalone had been banned because a commercial fish harvester had opened nearby and rapidly depleted the stocks. So in a sense, where the old tradition is lost, a new one has to be found. The more traditional and wild foods people can find and eat the better, but otherwise they have to turn to the market. If they can buy whole foods and fresh foods, even if they are not traditional, a new and healthier food culture can begin.

It's the same in a Karen community in Sanephong, a small, extremely isolated community in western Thailand. In good weather, you can reach the community on motorcycle or with a four-wheel-drive vehicle; in bad weather, the only way in or out is by trekking along the mountainous and muddy trail. The people in this village are extremely poor. Yet their isolated little community of 661 people has seven grocery shops that sell processed foods, crispy snacks, candy, beverages, and an orange-flavored syrup popular among the village children.

While the children here are eating more traditional foods than in many indigenous cultures today, about one-third of their diet still comes from packaged foods bought in those seven shops. Parents reported that children over age six asked their mothers to buy them snack foods like crackers and potato chips, and they tended to prefer fried and stir-fried food over fresh.

Across the world, the UN has found example after example of the damage that market food has done to aboriginal people. Barbara Burlingame, a senior nutritionist at the FAO who was involved in a study of indigenous food systems around the world, says the overriding cause of food-related health problems in indigenous communities is globalization. It's the aggressive marketing of the same products worldwide. "They get deliveries of cheap processed foods," she says. "And they're just as happy to eat a frozen pizza as to eat their traditional food—happier in fact because it's just more accessible and available. And the poor kids don't have a food culture anymore . . . so they don't know what they're missing."

I've met people who have worked with indigenous communities, and they have told me that indigenous people will quite happily use a food product over local foods because it is easier and usually tasty. The food industry has not forced these foods on people. Indigenous people, like my mother in the 1970s, have been willing to accept something that makes their lives easier. But the cost of such choices has been ruinous.

In places where they can return to traditional diets, says Burlingame, the UN is encouraging people to do so, or to at least incorporate as much traditional food as they can into their diet. Otherwise, they can turn to fresh foods from nearby agriculture and imported fresh produce where necessary to supplement their diet. Traditional and local are best, but the second-best choice is fresh over processed. If people eat less processed food, they might improve their health, but when the environment has been degraded and the food people once relied on has dwindled or become extinct, they have lost an important aspect of their culture. They can find a way to eat that might be healthier, but the culture that supported both their health and the environment is gone.

ELEVEN

How the World Eats

The Global Diet

INDIGENOUS CULTURES, WHICH exist within both developed and developing countries, are not the only ones that have been changed by the globalization of food; the whole developing world has. James's job takes him to rural areas around the world. He's a journalist by profession and not a development expert. He makes documentary films about people who, for the most part, work in agriculture. These are some of the poorest people in the world. After Nico was born, James always found his trips, where he would see families with small children struggling to live and work and trying to give their children a better future, to be particularly poignant. He would be stern when Nico was being picky about eating his vegetables, and he would tell Nico about the children he saw in Ethiopia sharing a porridge made of chewy grains with their family; they ate the same thing at each meal. He would describe how the children were grateful for what they had and ate it without complaint. He sounds like all parents admonishing their children to clean their plates because of the starving people in Africa, only he does so with more authenticity and authority.

James doesn't work in emergency relief, but his work has taken him through refugee camps in Sri Lanka and in Burundi on the border with Tanzania. He's talked to jumpy children holding automatic weapons, and he filmed a family of very young children in Mozambique who were trying to figure out how to grow food on the small plot of land that had been their family farm before both their parents died of AIDS. He's been to places where there is drought and famine, and yet at the end of the day he can walk into a restaurant and order a meal and a bottle of mineral water. He has been to places where people are slowly starving, but where shops are full of packaged foods and bottles of water and soft drinks available to anyone with the money to buy them. Neither of us believes that governments should just provide handouts and that people should become dependent on aid. But something doesn't seem right in these places. Something isn't working. Amartya Sen, the Nobel Prize–winning Indian economist, has pointed out that people don't starve because of a lack of food. He examined data on famines and discovered that, in many cases, food production increased while people were starving. They starve because they don't have either the land to grow their own food or the money to buy it from someone else.

The food products on the shelves of supermarkets in the developing world, many of which are fortified and aimed at children, do not reach the hungry, who have no money to buy them. Instead, they are sold to people who can afford them and who can also afford to buy better-quality, fresh foods, but who are anxious about malnutrition and quite likely to see these foods as a better bet.

Food products have made their way into pretty much every corner of the world. Just as there is no longer anywhere you can go where you're not reachable by phone or e-mail, there's almost no place too poor or too remote for processed foods for children. Early one summer, James went to Mongolia to make a film about a kindergarten that allowed children in nomadic herding families deep in the countryside to meet, socialize, and have fun together. Though the people were poor by Western standards, they were healthy and had enough to eat. Their problem was to figure out how to socialize children when their families moved around so much. Many of the children who met at the kindergarten had never played with another child.

When James landed in the capital, Ulaanbaatar, he went into a supermarket and saw rows of junk foods, soft drinks, candy, juices, and packaged cakes, all targeting children. His "fixer" on the ground was a local woman who complained to him that the children beg for these foods and are all getting fat.

The next day, he started on a two-day drive to meet the herders and their families at their summer pasture. James spent some time with the herders, sitting up at night listening to their stories, sleeping in a yurt (or *ger*, as the Mongolian people call it), and following the progress of the children as they prepared to perform a series of Mongolian dances.

The performance was held on the children's last day together. Afterward, their families would pack up and head off in separate directions in search of new pastures for their herds. The teachers wanted to give their young students a present before they left. James expected to see them pass out any number of handcrafted objects that Mongolia is famous for producing. He had already bought some for Nico: beautiful, sturdy woolen slippers with turned-up pointed toes; a warm, fleecy jacket with elaborate fasteners and a Mandarin collar; and a black hat with a long red tassel on the top, which looked as if it should have been worn by a little Mongolian prince. The teachers might have passed out hand-knitted woolen mittens or socks for the coming winter. Instead, in an otherwise deserted plateau, surrounded by yaks and horses, far from the capital city, the teachers presented the children with packaged children's foods made by multinational companies.

I started out by thinking about the problem of food products as it relates to Nico. It would be easy to see it as a problem we can fix in our own homes. Make healthier food and insist your children eat it. But when you look around and realize the pervasive pressures on our children to eat bad food, it's obvious that this approach is too weak. When you dig even further, you realize that nearly every parent in the most remote corners of the world struggles to keep children from being lured by a diet that will ruin their lives. And when parents are told that these processed foods will actually nourish their children, that's when you realize that this is a big, big, big systemic problem.

Food products are everywhere. A friend of mine recently visited Ka-
zakhstan, where she saw giant supermarkets full of processed foods and
bleak shopping malls selling fast-food tacos and hamburgers. A friend in
Nairobi sent me photographs of the rows of processed foods and sugary
cereals available in his local supermarket.

The year before Nico was born, I spent a week in Albania on assign-
ment for a magazine. I found the food in the restaurants to be very heavy
on meat and light on vegetables, so I thought I would cook. But I couldn't
find fresh fruits and vegetables in the shops, other than a few bruised
apples and some wilted lettuce. All the stores had were imported packaged foods, frozen meals, and packages of dubious-looking meat. I was
interviewing parents about an experimental news program their children
were involved in creating, and many of them invited me into their homes.
Albanians are famously hospitable people, and I was warned that I should
arrive with an appetite. I looked forward to trying some of the local food.
But in every home I was offered soft drinks, potato chips, store-bought
cakes, candy, and chocolates. When I arranged to interview some teenagers involved in the project, they suggested we meet for hamburgers and
french fries. I had to struggle to fit into my clothes by the end of the week.

It would be easy to see the food and health problems we are grap-
pling with as the peculiar difficulties of the rich world, where we are
surrounded by so much food and fancy packaging that we can't help ourselves. Representatives of the food industry frequently depict the obesity
crisis as a problem of personal responsibility: we need to learn some self-
control and we need to get off the couch and take a walk once in a while.
There is a little truth in that, but once you consider the global scope of
the obesity crisis, the shocking inadequacy of that approach is obvious.
The developed world started showing signs of obesity as processed and
fast foods took over our diet. Then, in the 1990s, when developing countries were persuaded to liberalize their trade policies and open themselves
to foreign markets, the same thing started happening to them. There
are now around 2 billion people lacking adequate food (almost 1 billion

are chronically hungry and another billion are malnourished) and about 1 billion people suffering from overweight and obesity. That's 3 billion people in the world with serious food issues, and there are only 7 billion of us living on the planet right now! Clearly, the global food system is off balance, and it's no wonder that people are worrying about how we're going to feed a projected 9.1 billion people by 2050.

Food and Trade

Marion Nestle, the nutritionist and writer, told a group of nutritionists and economists at the FAO that there is an elephant running amok in their offices that no one wants to acknowledge: capitalism. She told them that they would not be able to fix the problems of soaring food prices, hunger, and obesity without changing how our economies function.

Global free trade was supposed to bring prosperity, not increase starvation, malnutrition, and obesity. It was supposed to help economies diversify so that they weren't overly reliant on agriculture and so that people would have jobs and therefore money to buy the food on supermarket shelves. The basic idea was that poorer countries would see their economies grow, their GDP (gross domestic product) rise, and their citizens thrive. In the words of the Harvard University economist and critic of globalization Dani Rodrik, it was supposed to "lift all the boats." In the 1990s, the infamous Washington Consensus held that poor countries remained poor because they relied on their small domestic markets, which operated inefficiently because of their government's restrictions on trade. If they opened themselves to international trade and investment, they would prosper. "What was at stake was no longer some relatively minor efficiency gains—the standard argument for gains from trade—but a rapid convergence with the standards of living in the rich countries," says Rodrik. Free trade was supposed to wipe out poverty and eradicate hunger and malnutrition in the world.

The problem is that it's not working. Rodrik—who, I should add, still supports globalization but with reformed trade policies that respect broader social goals—writes that economics has to date been "two parts wonder drug and one part snake oil." There is money being made, but it's flowing upward and not down to the poorest people who need it. The notion of bringing about the well-being of others through globalization has been lost, and now globalization itself has become the goal, regardless of what it does to cultures, the planet, and actual flesh-and-blood people. Rodrik is one of a growing number of prominent economists (joined by Joseph Stiglitz, Amartya Sen, and Tim Jackson, to name a few) who advocate a broader, more nuanced approach to economics with less reliance on GDP as the sole measure of prosperity. GDP is supposed to be a measure of our well-being, but really it's only a measure of the market value of all goods and services produced in a country. It tells us something important about our economies but not everything. It doesn't tell us about the *quality* of our lives. It binds us to the need for growth, which is a problem in a finite world. In fact, many factors that damage the quality of our lives add to GDP. A *Washington Post* article explains how overweight people are contributing to the economy. The writer, Michael Rosenwald, who admitted to carrying about sixty extra pounds himself, quotes numerous experts on how obesity is just a "side effect" of a good economy, meaning that we don't have to work as hard physically anymore or spend as much time cooking or spend as much money on food. Since all of these developments are good, we shouldn't worry too much about the harm. He also wrote that what he calls the "obesity industry" will make billions and billions of dollars in the United States from the sale of fast food, diet products, diet books, medical interventions, and oversized caskets. While the article was somewhat tongue-in-cheek, it wasn't a joke. The economy can do very well by something that is harmful to people.

Changing Trade, Changing Diet

In 2008, when world food prices were rising and there were food riots in many countries, the UN acknowledged that the change in trade policies had not helped but had hurt the poor: "Agricultural trade liberalization was meant to help developing nations generate export earnings, increase the market share for their small farmers and make food cheaper for consumers . . . Cheap and subsidized farm imports from developed countries have made subsistence farming in the developing world uncompetitive and unsustainable." When import barriers were taken away from foods being brought into various countries, those countries could not control what or how much was coming in. They were flooded with cheap food from developed countries, which made it impossible for them to find markets, either inside their own countries or globally, for the foods their small farmers were growing.

At the same time, huge multinational supermarkets were able to set up shop to sell these cheap foods to the ever-growing urban populations. Small local markets that might once have been adequate could no longer cope with the demand in these growing cities. In some countries, such as India and Kenya, there were more people earning more money, so they could afford to buy processed foods from the supermarket. There seems to be a pattern that when the poorest of the poor come into a little more money, they tend to buy better food—meaning they buy some vegetables and a little meat to add to the grains that barely sustain them—and their health improves. But when they earn just a little more again so that they're still poor but not so desperately poor, they buy processed foods. They do so for many reasons: it's considered modern to eat and drink brand-name Western foods; they're a status symbol because you need to have a little money to buy them; and with their fat, salt, and sugar content, they're tasty; also, many food products are marketed as healthy foods. Suddenly, throughout the developing world, you see great big supermarkets stocked full of convenience foods, refrigerators by the side of the road stocked with soft drinks, and fast-food kiosks making processed foods much more accessible than local foods. At first, the appearance of supermarkets in these regions was reported as a positive trend. They represented the modernization of poorer parts of the world and were evidence of the growing prosperity that globalization can bring.

But large supermarkets have centralized procurement, meaning they buy their products or produce at the best price on the global market. Their goal is to keep costs to the consumer down. It's a matter of efficiency, a business decision. If local producers want to sell their produce to the supermarkets, they have to compete on price and comply with the super-markets' standards for quality, hygiene, and so on. While such standards are supposed to inspire confidence in consumers and are sometimes good for producers, they require investments that most small farmers cannot make and can end competition from small producers and retailers. Once the supermarkets had killed off the local markets, subsistence farmers, who barely grew enough to eat and to sell to a local market, couldn't sell their produce. In the world of global trade, markets are amoral; the farmers who had to sell their crops below cost or sell their land to indus-trial farms were wiped away. Large, foreign supermarkets took over the retailing of the food and influenced how food in developing countries is produced and consumed. Even if local retailers had wanted to create larger supermarkets, they would not have been able to get credit, which is available much more cheaply to the multinationals.

Who Wins?

Since these free trade policies took effect in many developing countries, the GDP has indeed been rising. But whether or not people's lives have improved is questionable. India is now the type 2 diabetes capital of the world; in Kenya, about one-quarter of the children are now diabetic; and in Mexico, one-third of the children are overweight or obese.

In 2004, the FAO, which is usually concerned with the number of hungry people in the world, started talking about the global spread of obesity. It also acknowledged that there was a greater concentration of the food industry and a convergence of dietary patterns and preferences. The culprit, it noted, was globalization and trade policies that make it easy for industrial foods to cross borders. Basically, this means we're all eat-ing the same things, no matter where we live. If a processed-food diet has not been good for us in the developed world, it looks even worse for those who have been poor and malnourished for most of their lives and are now "emerging," as they say, from poverty. If people were able to eat a greater variety of the traditional, unprocessed foods from their regions as they emerged, they would not likely suffer so much. But now they are eating high-calorie snack foods that are making them both obese *and* malnourished.

In India, dietary change started when the country opened its economy in 1991 in reaction to a severe financial crisis. India went through the usual liberalization process of privatization, removing import duties and inviting in foreign investment. India is often heralded as a success story because of its rising GDP. At first, researchers monitoring the situation expected that those who were earning more income would become healthier. City dwellers would be able to buy fruit, vegetables, eggs, milk, meat, and pulses such as lentils and beans from the supermarkets—items that have always been a part of Indian food culture. But this didn't happen. Instead, Indians used their increased wealth to buy tea, biscuits, salted snacks, prepared sweets, edible oils, and sugar, and their consumption of fruit and vegetables went down. As incomes rose in urban areas, so did the consumption of processed and ready-to-eat foods. Now higher-earning Indians consume about one thousand calories a day in sweets and prepared snacks such as soft drinks, pizza, and potato chips. Companies like Coca-Cola, PepsiCo, McDonald's, and Pizza Hut have all established themselves in India since trade was liberalized. The market is flooded with these well-known brands as well as unbranded prepared and fast foods from smaller companies imitating the big guys. In fact, the unbranded producers sell their food products even more cheaply in order to attract those with less income. India was awarded the distinction of being the diabetes capital of the world in 2007. Many of those afflicted with type 2 diabetes are children, which was not the case before 1991.

Eighty percent of people with diabetes live in low- and middle-income countries. Type 2 diabetes in children used to be rare, but now half of newly diagnosed cases are children and adolescents. Even WHO, which emphasizes that the diabetes epidemic is new and directly related to diet, links it to lack of exercise. The organization never blames multinational companies for flooding these countries with cheap food products or acknowledges that changing these countries' economies results in migration to cities, where people get less exercise as a result. WHO makes the spike in diabetes sound like a worldwide epidemic of laziness and bad choices rather than a worldwide systemic change in the foods that are available and the way people live: "There is an emerging global epidemic of diabetes that can be traced back to rapid increases in overweight, obesity and physical inactivity." It never traces the overweight, obesity, and physical inactivity back to market liberalization and the rapid change in food cultures.

Relaxing restrictions on trade was supposed to benefit consumers with lower-cost imported food and benefit farmers by giving them access to global markets. As it turned out, few farmers in developing countries can compete in the global marketplace. Those who have managed to do so have found that their health has suffered as a result. Globalization has pushed larger, more industrial production of single crops and encouraged people to eat foods that are not native to their culture. As a result, quinoa is no longer affordable for many people in Bolivia. Bolivians, who once relied on the nutritious grain, have been shipping it to health-conscious Americans and Europeans who are willing to pay a better price for it than Bolivian farmers can get at home. They use the little money that they make from the sale of the food that used to sustain them to buy processed and fast foods.

I'm not an economist—I'm just Nico's mom—but the world looks like a trade-induced dietary mess to me. So I called up the World Trade Organization (WTO) in Geneva to see what it thinks. In some ways, the WTO started the whole process. It was the WTO that pressured countries, particularly in Europe, to drop barriers to trade in food products. The WTO made agriculture a development issue, putting pressure on

Europe to accept hormone-treated beef and genetically modified organisms (GMOs). If the European Union refused to accept the products of a poorer country because of these issues, it looked as if it were standing in the way of the poorer country's economic development rather than upholding the demands of the European people for safe food.

Mike Moore, the former director general of the WTO, wrote in 2003: "Throughout the developed and developing world packaged food of every exotic sort is available just about anywhere, from tinned lychees to cubes of sugar. In lonely desert outposts in the midst of political chaos a working refrigerator selling Coca-Cola can stand as a temple to consumerism, choice, global integration and corporate organization. That such variety should be within reach of so many would have stunned the ancient emperors of Rome." He saw the changes as a good thing.

I suppose the worldwide obesity epidemic was not making headlines in 2003 as it does today. "People of just a few generations ago would be amazed if they could see the range of products available; they would also be staggered that we have such faith in food not grown by ourselves or trusted village neighbors. It is proof of the power of global markets and the confidence most of us now have in domestic and global regulators for food safety," writes Moore.

Rhetoric aside, that faith is rapidly being eroded by contaminated foods that are traced back to industrial farming. Even the 2011 case of E. coli O104:H4, which erupted in sprouts throughout Europe, eroded confidence in the system because it was nearly impossible to tell where the food came from or where the problem originated. Was it something to do with the seeds of the contaminated sprouts themselves? Was it the industrial manure used to fertilize these otherwise organic sprouts? Were they grown in Germany or did they come from Spain? At least I can take comfort in the fact that if I get sick from eating salad greens, I can go to my local market and yell at Loredanna or Carlo.

Choice is supposed to be the cornerstone of free-market economies, but it's becoming evident that the global market gives us only the illusion of choice. Only a handful of supermarket chains sell us our food, and only a few giant food-processing companies make those alluring packages. At the same time, we are losing one breed of livestock every month. Plant biodiversity continues to shrink as farmers breed for durability and travel, and neglect the rest. In the past hundred years, we have lost 75 percent of the world's crop diversity. This is how everyone on the planet ends up with those Cavendish bananas sliced into their cornflakes, while the far more nutrient-dense and tasty varieties that bruise too easily for travel are disappearing from even their local markets. It's why we see the same four or five varieties of apples—Granny Smith, Golden Delicious, Royal Gala, and Fuji—in markets worldwide but rarely see the pear apple, Crawley Beauty, Etter's Gold, or Kandil Sinap.

So biodiversity goes down, obesity goes up, noncommunicable diseases like cancer and diabetes go up, hunger goes up, life spans for overweight people go down, traditional diets disappear, ancient knowledge from the beginning of time is lost, and cultures are subsumed into the globalized mix. Even the ubiquitous Cavendish banana is at risk of extinction because of a tropical fungus that has already destroyed numerous plantations on tropical islands.

The UN, the one-time champion of globalization, now sees its flaws. Yet when I call the WTO to ask whether there are any plans in the works to rethink the globalized trade in food products, it tells me no. Other than a few isolated incidents, countries are not complaining to the WTO about trade in food. Even though there is so much discussion about health and diet issues, countries are not talking about pulling back or reforming trade practices. My highly placed (but reluctant) informant asks not to be quoted. I ask whether people who work at the WTO talk together informally about trade in food over coffee or at lunch. Apparently not.

Although the UN does criticize the effects of globalization, it has committed itself to an ideology championed by the WTO that holds that countries should grow what they grow best (fields and fields of rice in Asia, coffee in Africa) and import what they need from other countries.

But UN researchers are continually publishing papers that make it clear that this system is not helping the poorest people, that it is not best for agricultural production, and that it is ruining children's health. Food sovereignty—which is when a country looks after most of its own food needs—is considered a form of protectionism. I'm all for it if it means protecting health, biodiversity, cultural diversity, and a future for the world's children. But the WTO insists on leaving the market to work out any problems.

TWELVE

The Global Market

Feeding the World's Children

WHAT IS A market anyway except a place where goods are bought and sold? I've described throughout this book the pleasures of shopping in fresh produce markets. But market-led solutions seem to favor the opposite of this model: the industrial model. On the surface, the system sounds fine: you have a need and someone steps forward with a product to fill that need. But the industrial model doesn't ensure the best solution for communities or countries. In the developing world, the two basic problems are that people need food, and small farmers need places to sell their crops, milk, and meat. The global market does nothing to help them, in part because producing good quality, local food and getting it to local markets do not produce the profit margins that industrial food and commodity crops do.

Jean Anthelme Brillat-Savarin, the French food philosopher, asked the question, "What is meant by food?" and offered two answers: "*Popular reply:* Food is everything that nourishes. *Scientific reply:* Food is all those substances which, submitted to the action of the stomach, can be assimilated or changed into life by digestion, and can thus repair the losses which the human body suffers through the act of living." The people who live in developing countries—diverse places with extremely different cultures and food traditions—are the same as people in developed countries. They are mainly trying to figure out what to feed their children so they will grow to their full potential, but many of them are trying to do this with

165

very few resources. They, like us, are encountering an increasingly larger array of food products claiming to fix all their children's needs. They, like us, are increasingly being treated like so many units requiring a scientific concoction consisting of X number of calories as fuel, calibrated carefully with a dose of vitamins and minerals. This careful, scientific balancing of nutrients sounds far more intelligent than just eating fresh food in a variety of colors or eating "everything that nourishes."

Even if fortifying processed foods worked terrifically well, there would still be issues of culture and tradition at stake. There is an intense debate going on now over the future of supplementation programs, such as the vitamin A programs, largely because they have failed to deliver on their promise to eradicate micronutrient deficiencies. Many researchers are looking at ways of using local foods and cultural knowledge to solve the micronutrient problem, as they did with the local bananas on the islands of Micronesia. Brian Thompson, a senior nutritionist at the FAO at the UN, went to an international conference on malnutrition in Istanbul in 2007. He looked at hundreds of posters and presentations about treating micronutrient deficiencies, but something struck Thompson as strange about these posters: they were pretty much entirely about fortification, supplements, and biofortification (that is, genetically modified foods), with next to no mention of real food and traditional diets. At this time, hardly anyone talked about food when they talked about treating micronutrient deficiencies.

There were others who felt uncomfortable about the approach, and they started to ask, "Where's the food?" Thompson sent out a call for papers to assess what was the best option in specific locations. The answers to the micronutrient deficiency problems in most places could be found in the foods that were already growing around the communities or could be grown around them. As shown by the earlier example of those children in Brazil who were being treated with vitamin A capsules when they could have been eating the vitamin A–rich fruit that grew in their area, malnourishment is seen as an illness. In Malawi, a project to promote small-animal husbandry—in other words, to help families keep a goat or some rabbits or chickens—would solve its micronutrient deficiencies. In parts of South Africa where vitamin A deficiencies among children were high in spite of long-standing supplementation programs, the solution lay in promoting home gardens. When food instead of supplements is used as a solution, it tends to make people healthier overall, because goat milk, eggs, rabbit meat, pumpkins, carrots, spinach, and other foods have many nutrients, not just one targeted to a specific deficiency. In the gardens project in South Africa, mothers were delighted to see their children eating and enjoying the vegetables they grew and were empowered by the idea that they themselves could grow food or buy some from neighbors who grew extra. The project put the basic and essential knowledge about what a child needs to eat in order to grow up healthy back into the hands of parents, rather than in the sweaty palms of the food industry.

Around the same time that Thompson's group at the UN was preparing to publish the studies and to declare that real food was really the best way to treat micronutrient deficiencies, Lisa Fleige, a food scientist at PepsiCo, wrote a blog post on the company site about the need for the food industry to use fortified food products to fight the terrible scourge of micronutrient deficiencies and to assist the UN in its goal of eradicating poverty and hunger. The food industry acts as though micronutrient deficiencies are a disease that people need to be cured of, rather than something that happens to you when you don't have enough to eat. Fleige wrote that "a group of leading economists" ranked providing micronutrients as one of the best opportunities for fighting malnutrition. *Economists* decided this?

The Need to Grow

Food companies have been quite open about seeking growth in the developing world. Nestlé documents even refer to the people of Africa as "emerging consumers." Are they not also human beings with needs and desires, hopes and dreams, with history and culture? Nope. They're consumers. Unilever talks about the enormous growth opportunities for its company in emerging markets. Coca-Cola's marketing chief has said that the company's plan to expand its share of the market around the world is to target teenagers: "There was a time [a decade ago] when we walked away from teen recruitment and probably lost a generation of drinkers . . . Parts of the world lost confidence in cola as the engine of growth. We've gotten that back in a big way." PepsiCo also counts on the global market for 45 percent of its revenues, with 30 percent coming from "emerging markets" where "we have tremendous growth opportunities." As these companies target emerging markets, their corporate websites begin to look eerily more like those of development agencies. Some of them even post the UN's Millennium Development Goals, such as "Eradicate Extreme Poverty and Hunger," "Improve Maternal Health," and "Ensure Environmental Sustainability," as if achieving these goals was their reason for being in these countries.

In 2010, the *American Journal of Public Health* published an article entitled, "Can the Food Industry Help Tackle the Growing Global Burden of Undernutrition," which I thought at first was going to be an actual examination of the question. But then I realized that all four authors, Derek Yach, Zoë A. Feldman, Dondeena G. Bradley, and Mehmood Khan, were employees and consultants of PepsiCo. In other words, the article was not an exploration of this question but rather an argument for it written by people with a vested interest in it.

The article begins by describing the effects of malnourishment and then discusses how to solve the problem by investing in agriculture, using the food company's distribution networks to distribute food aid, and creating fortified foods and healthy weaning food products for children under age two. The article also encourages big food companies to create social businesses to invent new fortified food products for children, with profits going back into the company. The options it suggests would increase the food companies' halo of corporate social responsibility while positioning themselves as the only solution to the problem of global malnutrition.

In the same issue of the journal, there is an article by three nutrition-ists in Brazil entitled "The Snack Attack," which outlines their reasons for not being in favor of the food companies' approach. The three au-thors—Carlos A. Monteiro, Fabio S. Gomes, and Geoffrey Cannon—point out that the PepsiCo article talks about the importance of using novel, enriched food products without mentioning the importance of local foods or placing malnutrition in its context. Malnourished children lack not only food but a secure local food system, access to water, sani-tation, health care, and an appreciation for food preparation and family meals. Most importantly, these children need their mothers and other caretakers to be empowered, they need better wealth distribution, and they need access to strong public health services.

The authors argue that weaning foods contribute to mothers aban-doning breastfeeding too soon, and that what they really need is support for breastfeeding complemented, after six months of age, by locally avail-able, affordable, nutritious, real food. The authors express their concern that ready-to-use therapeutic foods(vitamin- and mineral-enriched food products used in severe cases of malnutrition) branded with the names of big food companies would be advertisements for their less healthy offer-ings. And the nutritionists are disturbed by a project by Nestlé, already in place in Brazil, that offers what it calls "popularly positioned products," which are biscuits, instant chocolate milk powder, instant baby food, and instant soups and noodles that have been fortified "especially to cover nutritional deficiencies." The products are sold in train and subway sta-tions in big cities, in small shops, and door to door. The solution to the complex problem of micronutrient deficiencies, the article says, should be solved by governments, international bodies, civil society, and others who are more interested in the public good than in corporate profits.

The industry retorts again and again that real food systems are not re-alistic in poor countries and in sprawling, rapidly growing cities. It turns fortified and processed foods into a moral issue, as the WTO did with free trade in agricultural products, so that if you are against them, you sound as if you are in favor of allowing children to suffer the ravages of malnutrition. If you are against industrialized agriculture, you are against helping the poorest people in the world. You would think from listening to the industry that there is no realistic solution to poverty and childhood malnourishment other than chemicals and food products. It frequently refers to scientific solutions because of our long history of relying on science over culture in food matters, but also because it's easy to dismiss detractors as people who don't understand the complexity of technology.

Unheard Voices

In 2009, I went to the World Summit on Food Security and related presentations at the FAO in Rome. I sat in on discussions that were billed as "high-level" and "expert" (which included representatives from the GMO industries and food products industries as well as academics, agronomists, and representatives from NGOs) on how to feed a projected 9 billion people in 2050. One delegate pointed out that the estimates of how much food needed to be produced assumed that everyone would be eating processed and fast foods and much more meat than is good for them. She also pointed out that the world's diet did not have to take this path. But no one wanted to talk about that. The idea that this food product diet is inevitable for "emerging economies" is entrenched. Some people in the room had an interest in the world continuing to eat this way.

At lunchtime on another day of the summit, I ran over to my favorite organic food market for a quick bite and inadvertently met a group of pastoralists from Ethiopia, Sudan, India, and Palestine, a farmer from Sri Lanka, and a shepherd from the Abruzzo. Almost all of them had come to Rome with the help of various nonprofit groups in the hopes that their voices could be heard at the high-level food meetings. After lunch, I took the subway back to the summit with them—many of them wearing the traditional clothing of animal herders in their countries and some of them barefoot. As we emerged from the Metro at the Colosseo stop, they turned more heads marching through the streets of Rome than the men dressed as gladiators milling about the Colosseum. When we finally reached the summit, the pastoralists weren't allowed inside the building because of security, so they waited outside, willing to talk to anyone who would listen. Two worlds were represented: the one allowed inside the building was populated by government representatives, food industry representatives, international bureaucrats, and journalists; the one outside was made up of food-justice activists, environmentalists, and an international mix of farmers and herders.

The group I met was an eloquent rebuke to the industrial option. Industrial farming is ruining their lives, they explained, not enriching them. They are representatives of some of the poorest people in the world in monetary terms, and they have no money for fortified food bars. They need some help, certainly, but they don't want to become Western-style industrial farmers. They have herds of animals and they move with them to allow them to graze. They live in mountains and in deserts and have for centuries fit into the ecosystem in which they live. They told me that they want to carry on their traditions, not leave them behind. But there are obstacles. Industrial agriculture and the privatization of common lands for development have left them with less space for grazing. They are affected by wars, drought, and environmental degradation, and some of them have had to feed their families on food aid. At the summit, they only wanted to ask that their right to exist as herders be taken into account during the discussions; they wanted their right to pass on their tradition to their children to be respected.

Unrealistic Food

Since the food industry pushes the idea that the Western diet is an inevitable aspect of economic development, and that expecting to feed the world with real food is unrealistic, it's useful to take stock of those who are forging ahead without industrial solutions.

There are farmers in Latin America using green manure and cover crops to simultaneously grow food and replenish the soil in places where soil quality has been deteriorating. They grow plants that produce nitrogen-rich legumes. The beans are harvested and eaten, adding a source of protein to their diet, and the plants are left to rot in the fields, rather than cut down and cleared away, to nourish the soil. The earthworms and termites get to work burying the organic matter, saving the farmer the trouble of doing it himself.

The Kingdom of Bhutan has pledged to become the world's first completely organic nation by 2022. The country doesn't bother with GDP as a measure of its success and instead tries to evaluate its progress through "Gross National Happiness."

Nigeria has also announced ambitious targets to stop importing most of its food, as it does now, and to become as self-sufficient in its food production as possible. The country's minister of agriculture, Akinwumi Adesina, pledged that by 2015 Nigeria will produce 20 million metric tons of food for its own domestic use.

In Nairobi, a huge, sprawling, and rapidly growing city where the urban poor spend about 80 percent of their income on food, there is a thriving informal system of urban agriculture. People grow food in containers, in public lots, or wherever they can find a little space. The food improves their health and for some even offers an income that in certain cities is about ten times the minimum wage.

One of the vice presidents of Slow Food International is a dynamic young man of twenty-four who comes from a small farm in Kenya. John Kariuki told me that his family had 1.5 acres of land on which they grew maize, potatoes, beans, millet, bananas, and other fruits and raised some animals, such as cows and sheep. Kariuki saw how difficult life was for his parents and how they were affected by industrialization and globalization. Sometimes they would have to sell their crops below cost because of the pressure from international markets. After finishing high school, Kariuki found out about Slow Food, which had by then established a university in northern Italy. He was interested in the political issues around local foods and wanted to learn what he could in order to help farmers like his parents and preserve their food culture. He encouraged his parents to grow some vegetables that were disappearing—amaranth, black nightshade, and spider weed—and worked on some community garden projects. He also encouraged some hotels to start using more traditional vegetables. When I spoke to him, he was heading off to meet some like-minded young people from other African countries to organize a Slow Food project to plant a thousand gardens across Africa that would be filled with traditional vegetables. They planned to involve older people to help them remember recipes and to come up with some new ones, and to involve children in harvesting, cooking, and eating the foods. "It's becoming popular now to eat traditional foods [in Kenya]," he explained. "We're seeing people dying from the bad food and the bad diet that has been imported to us, and so slowly we're returning to our own foods."

The World of the Fully Emerged Consumer

The evidence is overwhelmingly clear that what human beings need to eat are fresh, unprocessed foods, that children need to learn to know and love these foods early on, and that the best way to access these foods is through a diet based on locally available produce. As the toll of a few decades of a processed and fast-food diet has become painfully obvious, we're looking for solutions. The food industry is acutely aware of this. "Health-conscious consumers who seek more wholesome food and beverage choices are increasingly a large and powerful force in the marketplace," says PepsiCo's 2010 Annual Report. What the food companies do not want is for those consumers to take their money and head off to their local greengrocer to buy spinach. They want them to buy their "healthy" products. PepsiCo estimates the "global packaged nutrition market" to be $500 billion and growing.

So while PepsiCo continues to sell potato chips and sugary soft drinks, it also offers a line of foods it calls "good for you," such as Quaker granola bars and instant oatmeal and Tropicana juices, which are still processed food products. Its long-standing cola rival, Coca-Cola, makes Minute Maid juice, which has a big "reduce cholesterol" banner on the package, and chocolate soymilk. Unilever's website has a nutrition information section with pictures of fresh vegetables that does, in fact, urge consumers to eat local, organic food, while promoting its own products with added "functional" ingredients, and lets you know that it also owns Slim-Fast, the weight-loss system, in case you've overdone it.

Nestlé, the biggest of all the food processing companies, has branded itself a "nutrition, health and wellness company." As part of its nutrition division, it has created an educational kit for children worldwide called Healthy Kids Global Programme. Nestlé sends out packages of teaching materials to schools everywhere to explain nutrition to children aged six and over. I met with Maria Letizia Balducci, a Nestlé representative of this program, for a quick lunch one day in Rome. She was in town for an industry conference on agricultural resources, and we met before she had to catch a train back to Milan.

The kit, she explained, is called Nutrikids in Italy. Why not *Nutriragazzi* or something Italian-ish? She gave me that charming shrug that Italians do when they think the answer to your question cannot possibly be known: shoulders up, palms half upturned, eyes heavenward. So okay, it's called "Nutrikids," a melding of two English words. It's not really Italian specifically, she explained, but it's based on the Mediterranean food pyramid, the healthiest diet in the world. I don't imagine that Greek fishermen, who were the original proponents of the Mediterranean diet, were eating foods from packages.

A booklet from the kit depicts a food pyramid with liquids forming the base. The picture includes a drink with a slice of lemon and a straw, a glass of what appears to be water, a bottle that looks like a wine bottle—but I can't imagine that's what it's supposed to be—a bowl of soup with a spoon, and a teapot with a cup of steaming hot tea beside it. In the next level up in the food pyramid, there are fruits and vegetables with a banana depicted quite prominently. Bananas are part of the Mediterranean diet?

In the next level are grains and carbohydrates represented by bread, rice, pasta, and potatoes. Next are milk and cheese, fish and meat. Then nuts and possibly peanut butter—it's hard to tell—and at the very top is a picture of an ice cream cone, a piece of cake, and a bar of chocolate. Though the kit doesn't promote Nestlé's products, the company's logo is on the front cover of all the materials and on the first inside page of the booklet.

Balducci said the company produces the kit as a service to address the worldwide nutrition crisis. It offers the kit to schools free of charge. The problem in Italy, she said, is that most schools don't want it because they don't trust the motives of the company. I asked her what the company's motives are. "It's in our interest that people go on buying our products but use them in the right way," she said. She emphasized that you can eat whatever you want to eat, but you can't eat the fattening things all the time. The company is trying to get across the idea of balance. She felt it is the responsibility of a big food company to educate people on nutrition, because if people misuse its food products, by eating too many sugary treats for example, they might blame the company. By producing the kit, the company can say, hey, we told you not to do that. And being seen as an expert on nutrition can't hurt either.

What Balducci said to me all sounded fine, more or less, until I walked into the supermarket to reacquaint myself with the products Nestlé makes for children. Where does Chocapic cereal ("Whole grain! Eight important vitamins! Plus a rich chocolate taste that kids love") fit in the pyramid? Kids would assume it goes in the middle with the bread and the grains, but I would put it on the top with the sugary stuff that you should rarely eat.

What about Nesquik in powder, syrup, or ready-to-drink form? ("You can't buy happiness, but you can drink it!") Nestlé emphasizes the pleasure of indulgence with its candy, such as Kit Kat chocolate bars, but when it comes to the ice cream, yogurt, and sugary cereals, Nestlé suggests that they are healthy. I think it would actually be better if Nestlé did refer to its own products in the Nutrikids kit to show children that pretty much all of them belong in that tiny apex at the top of the pyramid.

Tiny as that space is at the top of the pyramid, it might need to shrink, because the Harvard School of Public Health released the results of its ambitious, large-scale study of foods associated with weight gain. The study showed that certain foods, such as potato chips, sweetened beverages (including 100 percent juice), and other obvious junk foods, are associated with weight gain, while foods such as plain yogurt, whole fruits, raw nuts, whole grains, and whole vegetables are not. The researchers found that when people ate more fruit, vegetables, and plain yogurt, they lost weight. The researchers noted that it is dietary *quality* that appears to matter and not *quantity* of calories so much. When a company that makes junk foods for children calls itself a nutrition, health, and wellness company and puts out nutritional guidance information for children, it's difficult for parents and children to know what to make of its products. It's confusing.

Balducci and I talked about Nestlé's concern for childhood nutrition while sitting in a sort of expanded coffee bar. There are a number of places like this in Rome that serve coffee and pastries in the morning and then offer quick lunches in the afternoon. Their food is heartbreakingly awful in a country renowned for its great food. They offer pasta, but it's a frozen, packaged meal that has to be microwaved, and salad that comes straight out of a bag still smelling slightly of disinfectant. We both ordered the "toast," which was really a grilled cheese with ham on white bread, and freshly squeezed orange juice. The juice was nice, but everything else on the menu was horrible. Of course, this wasn't Nestlé's fault, but as I sat there, I blamed it all on companies like it. They tell us that we're always in a hurry and don't have time to prepare real food; apparently we don't have time to eat it either. Balducci and I were in a restaurant eating lunch presumably because we didn't have time to make it ourselves, so why was the restaurant giving us packaged food? Is the restaurant so busy that it doesn't have time to cook for us either?

"What's going on here in Italy?" I asked her. "Why are the food habits here changing so much?" She gave me the usual story about busy working mothers. She is one herself: she has a full-time job at Nestlé, two school-aged children, and a husband who also has a busy career. She talked about the recent influx of immigrants and how they were bringing different habits to Italy and throwing the food culture out of whack, none of which has anything to do with why processed foods are finding their way into restaurants and coffee bars as well as the homes of Italians.

Balducci talked a little bit about growing up in Florence and how her mother cooked for her. She remembers it fondly. She also remembers when McDonald's started spreading throughout Italy in the late 1980s; she was in university by then. Now that she has children, she can see that fast-food restaurants have brought a different approach to food to Italy. "It's the concept of eating that kind of food, in that way in a hurry with chips and sugar and Coke. I've seen that children have started to drink something different from water during meals, but when I was young it was only water," she said. "There's more Fanta and Coke for the children. It wasn't like this before." When she said this, she was clearly not speaking as the official representative of Nestlé but as a concerned parent and as an Italian. When I pressed her to see whether she saw that food products were eroding the food culture, she looked at me through narrowed, suspicious eyes and clammed right up.

THIRTEEN

Changing Eating Habits in Europe

The Illusion Revealed

AMERICAN SOFT DRINKS have been available in Italy for a long time. There are some Italian versions too, but Italians didn't drink them with meals until recently. From what people tell me, they would drink them at *aperitivo* hour if they didn't want an alcoholic drink. A variety of non-alcoholic *aperitivi* such as Gingerino, Sanbittèr Rosso, and Crodino come in small bottles that hold about half a glass of liquid, and you can order them at a bar in the afternoon instead of having a glass of Prosecco or Franciacorta (though it's beyond me why you would ever want to have something instead of Prosecco or Franciacorta). They are bitter and slightly sweet, and they are meant for adults, not children.

But in the summer of 2011 at one of our favorite pizzerias, I was surprised when the waiter asked Nico if he wanted a Coca-Cola with his pizza. Nico said yes and I said no (I said it much louder, so I won). It never would have occurred to him to order a soft drink; he's used to drinking water with meals, as other Italian children did until very recently. Until the waiter offered the possibility of something sweet, he had been content with water. But now I had an angry child on my hands, and the only way to win back his attention over dinner was to promise that he could have sugar and lemon on the bowl of fresh strawberries that he intended to order for dessert. Later, I asked the waiter why he offered a soft drink to a child. I wondered if it was some kind of promotion, but he said no, that he'd noticed that more children were asking for Coke with their pizza and that they seemed to like it. Italians really like to see children enjoy their meals.

Coca-Cola actually had a campaign in the summer of 2011 to encourage Italians to drink Coke with their meals. It wasn't specifically targeted at children, but the campaign was so omnipresent that no one of any age group could have missed it. In the coffee bars, there were special menu deals offering a sandwich with a Coke, or a salad with a Coke, or a slice of pizza with a Coke, or a bowl of prepackaged, microwaved spaghetti with a Coke. In Rome, some ads were designed to look as if they were from the 1950s and showed people sitting at a table drinking Coke with their food, a view of the Colosseum behind them. You were more than likely to sit on chairs with the Coca-Cola script across their back and at tables with it written on the tabletop. The napkin dispensers were all red with the Coca-Cola logo.

In North America, everyone is talking about the link between soft drinks and obesity, but you don't hear much about it in Europe. There's an innocence here when it comes to these sugary drinks that reminds me of North America in the 1970s. Families arrive at the beach lugging giant bottles of cola and orange and lemon soda. I saw a woman at the beach pouring Coca-Cola into her baby's bottle—the baby wasn't even walking yet. I can only imagine that she had no idea why she shouldn't give a sugar-loaded, caffeinated soft drink to a baby. In Italy, soft drinks are perceived as children's drinks, and there's an implicit trust that no one would make something for children that was actually bad for them. One of Nico's former classmates—a six-year-old boy—drinks three or four cans of Coke a day. At every birthday party, there are soft drinks and potato chips. The only time we don't see these things is at birthday parties for American children. In fact, at one late-spring birthday party, the American parents who were hosting it had laid out a bowl of fresh fava beans in their pods with some Pecorino Romano, fresh fruit, their own homemade bread, cheese, olives, water, and juice. The birthday boy's mother even made the birthday cake herself. The children, most of whom were Italian, ate and enjoyed themselves and didn't seem to notice the absence of junk food and soft drinks.

One morning after dropping our children off at school, my friend Marie and I stopped at a bar for a cappuccino. She's from California and her husband is an Italian American. We were swapping ideas for snacks. Because it was spring, she was giving her children fresh, raw peas and strawberries. I was trying out crisp, thin, raw green beans on Nico, as well as fresh cranberry beans cooked and tossed with olive oil and herbs. She said she was surprised at how much sugar Italian children eat, and that the sugary snacks are promoted as sources of quick energy. "Don't they get it?" she shouted at me. "And the refined white flour products! Why does no one question it here?" She said her daughter, Giulia, had never tasted Coca-Cola before they moved to Italy. "Aren't they looking at us [Americans]? They could see where this is going to lead them."

Marie's husband, Giovanni, is a chef, and they used to come to Italy, before they had children, to eat in great restaurants. Giovanni would also go out to the market to buy good-quality ingredients and cook something wonderful with them. Not until they brought their children for a two-year stay in Rome did they notice the way the culture is leaning heavily toward fast food, junk food, and food products. Marie had been looking forward to having her children immersed in this place that takes food very seriously—and it still does—but she hadn't expected that she would have to fight off the food industry's advances on her children to this degree.

I think the reason why Marie and I are so surprised by Italians' acceptance of junk food is because we both relate to the other parents in so many ways. They are all working professionals, moderately middle class, and fairly well educated. But their North American equivalents are now more cautious about obvious junk food and refined food products. The harm caused by these foods is much more a part of their discussions these days. In Italy, there is a kind of naïveté about junk food. In many conversations I've had with parents, they say that of course they know the children shouldn't eat potato chips and drink soft drinks all the time, but that the products are fun. They're a little treat once in a while. Unfortunately, they seem to be becoming the default option for a snack away from home. When I first came to Rome, I would sometimes see old men selling green olives and lupini beans as snacks in the parks, though even then that tradition was dying off with the old men. They would take a piece of thick brown paper, roll it into a cone, and fill it with a scoop of either the olives or the beans. In winter, they would roast chestnuts. Those men are all gone now. There are a few chestnut roasters in the more touristic areas of the city around Christmas time, but otherwise the snacks are all chocolate bars, cereal bars, potato chips, and soft drinks.

Italy wasn't a snacking culture, but it's becoming one rather quickly. A number of us from the school were taking our children to a swimming pool for intensive swimming lessons every day for an hour after school. The children, all between ages four and six, would come out of the water at 6 p.m., completely exhausted and hungry. The first thing they would see on their way out of the dressing room was a row of vending machines full of snack foods, chocolate bars, potato chips, juice, water, and soft drinks. The sports facility didn't even have a water fountain. Every one of the children got a drink and a snack from the machines five afternoons a week. Some got two snacks (a sweet one and a salty one). It was extremely difficult being the one parent who said no. I brought water from home, fruit, and sometimes bread with prosciutto or even peanut butter. But Nico felt so left out and so annoyed with me that I relented and said he could also have something from the machines on Fridays. The other parents thought I was too extreme and restrictive and that the snacks were just harmless fun. The only other parent who felt as I did was an American woman whose child joined the lessons a little later. We watched the Italian children ravenously down sugar, fat, and salt after their hour of vigorous exercise every day, while our own children glowered at us as though the sweet peaches and apricots we brought for them were sour lemons.

I see articles about the obesity crisis in Italian newspapers, but I think parents have been slow to relate junk food to the problem. I asked my friend Raffaella, who is an editor at one of Italy's national newspapers, as well as the mother of two little boys, about it and she confirmed my observation. She said the paper runs stories about childhood obesity all the time, as well as about the way children's diets have changed and the negative effects of junk food. There have been campaigns by schools and pediatricians about the harm of these foods, but parents don't seem to be listening. Raffaella described the birthday parties her sons go to as orgies of junk food. Even government and schools don't know what to do. The ministry of health has just started a pilot project in Tuscany to install vending machines filled with fresh fruit and "healthy" packaged snacks in schools. It's unfortunate that the ministry isn't looking to its own culture for solutions but is instead encouraging processed foods that food companies say are healthy.

I doubt there is much the Italian government can do to change the new eating habits. One of the charming (and frequently exasperating) characteristics of Italians is that they never seem to listen to authorities. Everyone breaks the rules. Even the former prime minister, Silvio Berlusconi, told people to cheat on their taxes if they thought the tax rate was too high—a tactic that was seen as more practical than actually reforming taxation. Benito Mussolini, the Fascist dictator who ruled Italy from 1922 until he was killed in 1945, complained that the Italian people were ungovernable. So any kind of government, school, or medical campaign that tells people what to eat for their health is likely to go nowhere. The beneficial health effects of the food culture came from tradition—from people following their love for the food and the richness of the shared memories attached to it. They didn't come from an intellectual understanding of what constituted a healthy diet.

Politics at various times throughout Italian history affected the availability of certain foods. Subsidized bread, meat, milk, and fresh produce got the Italians through World War I. Though I'm sure no one would want to praise him as a locavore, Mussolini tried to encourage Italians to reject foreign foods and eat locally as a means of economic self-sufficiency. Historian Carol Helstosky writes in her book *Garlic & Oil* about the lengths Mussolini went to in order to shape the nation's appetites to its politics. He tried to create the ideal Fascist diet based on grains, rounded out with fresh fruit and vegetables, legumes, olive oil, and wine, with very little meat. The diet was already the basis of most Italian meals, but he defined it and made it virtuous. He even tried to encourage Italians to eat whole-wheat bread rather than refined white. His motivations were political—he was trying to stretch the wheat supply—but the reason he gave was health. Mussolini-inspired nutritionists blamed white bread for everything from tuberculosis to cavities and claimed that whole wheat was linked to higher levels of civilization and would boost fertility levels, too. Since whole grains were also associated with poverty, those with enough money would buy the more expensive, more refined, more palatable white bread, forcing the Fascists to continue importing wheat from other countries. The Italians! They never listen.

In spite of the political meddling and the wars, Italians have eaten much the same food, with minor differences, for generations. They ate what was available. It was just luck that most of it was fairly healthy and that there was enough variety, most of the time (when there wasn't enough variety, it was because of politics).

The diet in Italy differs regionally. The south is known for its fresh fruit, vegetables, and fish, all cooked very simply; toward the north, in Emilia-Romagna, the dishes are more complex and contain more meat and fatty salamis; it's the home of mortadella, after all. But the whole country used to adhere to the Catholic rules of fasting. Italy traditionally had roughly two hundred days a year when people were expected to go without meat. Italians being Italians, they tried to get around the rules by making exceptions for just a little pancetta, which, you know, could hardly be considered meat. There are many traditional recipes that are based almost entirely on vegetables and grains but call for a little piece of pancetta for flavor. Religious rules likely held down Italian meat consumption considerably, despite the concessions Italians allowed themselves.

The peasant diet that became known as *la cucina povera* usually contained very little meat. It was based more on greens and grains, often supplemented with sardines and anchovies, and sometimes with beans and lentils, with the occasional piece of meat or broth made with a bone with a few scraps still clinging to it.

During the Fascist years, Marinetti, the futurist who recommended vitamin pills over food, tried to encourage Italians to give up pasta and bread. He urged Italians to eat foods that made them dynamic: "Spaghetti and all such foods induce torpor, pessimism and skepticism." But the Italian people stubbornly refused to adhere to Marinetti's aesthetic and dietary concerns and continued to slurp up their pasta. They did pretty much what they wanted with whatever food was available. Of course, World War II caused serious deprivation, and many Italians didn't have enough to eat until well into the 1950s. Apart from that exception, however, the diet remained fairly consistently based on locally available, fairly healthy foods.

Trying to Remember

Alice Waters told me that Americans need to reinvent their food culture and that they are in fact doing it. North America has been so corrupted by industrialized food, and people have been told for so long that they don't have time for cooking or eating together, that no one really remembers a time when the food culture was different. Industrialized food is new to Europe. Europeans, Waters thought, just needed to be reminded of their food culture.

The rich food world I experienced when I first moved to Italy nearly ten years ago still exists, but it is threatened by the fact that children are increasingly left out of it. So many Italian children are now eating the salty, fat, and sweet offerings of the packaged-food world that they're not developing a taste for the foods of their own culture, and they're not carrying on the traditions either.

Industrial food is often marketed in Italy as traditional, local, and part of the culture. Mulino Bianco uses bucolic imagery of perfect rolling hills and farmland to sell processed foods and snack cakes. Its parent company, Barilla, even runs the Academia Barilla to "defend and safeguard Italian food products." The company talks about the diversity and richness of Italian products and offers cooking classes to educate people in the art of Italian gastronomy using its own processed foods.

McDonald's launched its own version of local food with the controversial McItaly burger in 2010. The company promises that the ingredients are all Italian, including the beef. Somehow it managed to get the ministry of agriculture to endorse its American-style, fast-food hamburger dressed with an all-Italian artichoke spread and Asiago cheese, and present it as part of Italy's great food traditions. The agriculture minister posed for photographs wearing a McDonald's apron and holding up a beef patty. It's disturbing to see an Italian government official talking about hamburgers as though they were part of Italian food culture. The ministry backed McDonald's venture, he said, because it wanted to defend the "Made in Italy" trademark and promote the taste of Italy, particularly to young people. "We want to give an imprint of Italian flavors to our youngsters," the minister said at a press conference. The founder of Slow Food, Carlo Petrini, denounced the venture in an open letter published in *La Repubblica* pointing out that trying to reduce Italian flavors into a "taste" for globalization does not promote Italian food traditions; instead it standardizes and homogenizes the taste. He also expressed concerns about how this would further industrialize food production in Italy, as the chain had already created a much larger demand for ground hamburger meat and would also require large quantities of standardized crops.

The fast-food model encourages Italians to consume more meat when everyone should be consuming less. And it puts pressure on Italian cattle farmers to raise more animals than ever, which means that more land will be used to grow cattle feed rather than crops for human consumption. As well, standards could be compromised as cattle farmers try to find ways to meet the demand, which will have an effect on the quality of beef in the country in general and not just in fast-food restaurants.

In European countries with amazingly diverse food cultures, children are eating the same industrial foods and suffering the same problems. For Italians, as for other cultures, the solution is all around them in the fresh fruit and vegetables that are so abundantly grown here. And the traditional recipes are so appealing that it seems a shame not to look to them, rather than to food products and hamburgers, to form the basis of any new Italian gastronomy.

For a while, one news item had Italians thinking a little more about their eating habits. Josef Schmidhuber, an economist at the FAO, analyzed the diet of the Mediterranean region from 1962 to 2002 and found that it had "decayed into a moribund state." He had known there were problems with the diet in these countries before he started his study, but he wanted to know whether Europe's common agricultural policy was contributing to them. He found that people in the Mediterranean countries were eating about 30 percent more calories by 2002 than they had been forty years earlier. He also found that the richness and distinctness of the diets were disappearing as people consumed mostly salt, fat, sugar, and refined carbohydrates. They were eating too much meat and too many processed foods. The situation was the worst in Greece, but Schmidhuber's study indicated that at least half the Italian population was overweight. He didn't, as so many economists do, base the increase solely on the fact that incomes had been rising in these areas, allowing people to buy more food. Instead he pointed at the growth in supermarkets, changes in the way food was distributed, and the facts that more women were working, people were eating in restaurants more often, and people were getting less exercise overall.

After the study was published, there was a flurry of news items about overweight children and their clueless parents who innocently fed them fast-food and ice cream snacks. People began to talk about choosing healthy snacks for their children, but more often than not, those snacks came wrapped in packaging bearing claims of being natural, wholesome, and even traditional. Though Nico had lunch prepared for him at school, he had to take his own food for the *merenda*, which is what Italians call the morning or afternoon snack. I was looking forward to finding out what wonderful foods Italian parents prepare for their school-aged children. I was really disappointed to learn that for the most part they send their kids to school with all kinds of processed snack cakes and special children's yogurts. When I complained about it to a Canadian friend in Paris, she sent me the menu from her daughter's nursery school so I could see in writing—because otherwise I might not have believed it—that this French school gave the children cornflakes with chocolate milk for a snack.

I started asking people what children used to take for the *merenda* before processed foods came along, and I inadvertently stirred up wistful memories among adults of the snacks they ate as children, things like rustic bread drizzled in fruity olive oil and sprinkled with a little salt and eaten along with a piece of fruit, of garlic- and oil-infused vegetables left over from the previous night's dinner and mashed between two chunks of bread, and of frittata sandwiches made from eggs and whatever else was left over from dinner. For a sweet treat, children would sometimes be given thick slices of bread spread with jam or, to be really decadent, butter with sugar sprinkled on top.

Mulino Bianco, the manufacturer of many *merenda* cakes, published a small hardcover book called *Buona Merenda: Una sana abitudine*, which roughly translates as "The Good Snack: A Healthy Habit." It talks about the carbohydrates, fiber, protein, vitamins, and minerals in Mulino Bianco's products. It even compares some traditional, homemade *merende* such as bread with prosciutto, bread with chocolate nut spread (something like Nutella), or bread with butter and jam with its products to show that the traditional foods are higher in calories. But the company's snack cakes are made with refined white flour, refined sugar, glucose-fructose syrup, and emulsifiers, among other things. The company doesn't even try to dazzle you with whole grains or any of that; instead its book shows pictures of the fruit that might be in the jam center of one cake, and pictures of the chocolate that is in the chocolate centers. There is nothing healthy about these foods. Mostly, the company depicts its products as wholesome and tied in some way to Italian traditions. In 2012, though, the European Union objected to one of the company's ads showing two children eating a snack cake while one says to the other, "Non lo mangio perchè è buono; lo mangio perchè è sano" ("I don't eat it because it's good; I eat it because it's healthy").

A ritual that was once practical and mostly healthy has become a daily opportunity for children to eat sugar and chemicals. At one time, children ate vegetables and frittatas for the *merenda*, and now they fill up on something with pretty much no nutritional value. In the past, a jam tart or a piece of cake was a special and infrequent treat. Now children eat factory-made cake every day—sometimes twice a day—and they expect it. Italian parents and grandparents have nostalgic feelings for their wonderful homemade snacks, but children growing up in Rome today would likely find a square of last night's polenta in their *merenda* box to be a big disappointment.

Having a child here completely changed my perspective on Italian culture. I started to see that the markets were pretty much only being used by me and the little old ladies. There is an entire generation of adults who don't really cook much anymore. They buy everything in the supermarket and feed their children frozen pasta dishes and soups made with powdered bouillon. Even worse, many of the markets themselves—in their search for the cheapest products—sell produce from large industrial farms and from outside the country. The cherries often come from Spain and the pine nuts from Turkey, when cherries and pine nuts are falling off the trees all around us in Italy. Some of the markets even sell the industrially produced snack cakes and packages of sliced bread.

Cookbook writer Diane Seed, who has lived in Rome since the 1960s, told me that there used to be people who went around the countryside gathering up all kinds of wild greens—various dandelion greens, wild asparagus, and other uncultivated treasures—to sell in the markets in Rome. She used to buy these wild vegetables from an old, bent-over woman in the Testaccio market. But they are long gone now. There are still a few stands with farmers selling their own food, and some of them offer a springtime mixture of weedy, rough-looking greens, but few of them come to the market every day anymore. Last winter, I saw a stack of *cardi*, which are cardoons, a vegetable that looks like rough, dry, fibrous celery and grows in Umbria. I'd seen it before, but I'd never tried it, and I asked the young vendor how to cook it. He didn't know. He said he didn't cook and that he had never actually eaten *cardi* himself. Selling vegetables was just a job for him.

I wanted to believe that Italy was more sophisticated than North America, and that Italians were more discerning about the food they ate. I didn't want to believe that they are so rapidly descending into the food mess that I thought I left behind in Canada. Weren't Europeans supposed to be more selective when it came to food? Weren't they supposed to resist all this?

The Problem in Europe

I love fall in Italy. I think it is really my favorite season. For us, over the years, the season has come to mean weekend trips to Umbria or Tuscany. Fall smells like wood smoke and it tastes like black truffles. As I stood on the steps of a four-hundred-year-old former convent near the lake town of Bolsena near Umbria one October day, the air smelled like both. I came to *Lago di Bolsena* for a conference on food in Europe. Though it was meant to be a conference about the problems of food in Europe and was provoked more by anxiety than gastronomy, I had a feeling that I would be eating very well.

It was quite chilly inside the unheated stone walls of the convent on the first evening, and we gathered in what had been the original kitchen around an enormous fire roaring in the giant fireplace. Enzo, the man who would be preparing most of our meals, laid out two varieties of a local sheep's cheese for the participants in the conference, who were from Estonia, Latvia, Moldova, Poland, Italy, the Czech Republic, England, the Netherlands, Finland, and Germany. One sheep's cheese was aged, but the other was so young it almost squeaked against the teeth. He put out a basket with some focaccia and sliced some bread that we toasted over the fire and then rubbed with garlic, drizzled with oil, and sprinkled with salt. We washed it down with a glass of the local fizzy white wine.

Afterward we moved on to dinner. Enzo had prepared lentil soup topped with Parmesan and olive oil. For a second course, we had frittata with zucchini and thyme and a salad of greens, radicchio, and tomato. To end the meal, Enzo brought out fruit bowls filled with pears, apples, and late-season plums and peaches. There were pitchers of red wine on the table and pitchers of water. The meal embodied the delightful simplicity that is the best part of Italian cuisine. Enzo lives in the small town of Bolsena, down the hill from the convent, and likes to cook using only ingredients from around the lake. In fact, he said he would be going down to the lake at five thirty the next morning to meet the fishermen and get first pick of the local *coregone* to use in the pasta for lunch the next day. Sabrina Aguiari, the conference organizer, nudged him playfully in the ribs and said, "Here we're lucky enough to eat the one-mile diet."

Aguiari urged everyone to enjoy the food. She reminded us that we were there to talk about food and to understand what's happening in Europe, but that enjoying food and camaraderie were part of that process of understanding. The lack of enjoyment of food was part of the problem.

Every day, people gave presentations and discussed the traditional foods in their countries. These were foods that held personal meaning for them and that also, they felt, represented their country. A woman from Poland brought a special ridged roller and explained how she uses it to cut pastry dough for making the biscuits that her family eats between Christmas and Lent. Mila, a woman in her mid-thirties from western Bohemia in the Czech Republic, brought photographs of women making a special cake called *Chodsky kolac* for the Chodsko Folk Festival, which is held every August. She felt conflicted about the cake. She said it is really good and she has very fond memories of making the cakes every year with her mother and other women in her community. She knows how to make the cakes and the special homemade plum jam that goes with them, but she doesn't make them anymore. I looked again at the photograph of the women bent over the table kneading the dough to give the cake its special airy quality. "I don't make these cakes anymore," she said, "and neither does anyone I know." Only the older women were keeping the tradition barely alive. The cake takes a lot of work and Mila saw the effort as somehow oppressive. She said few people have time to make food like this anymore, though she also seemed saddened by that fact. The cake was at risk of becoming a folkloric representation of a dead food culture if it wasn't somehow integrated into a larger culture of home cooking.

Melena, a woman from Finland who was in her early thirties, also spoke about experiences she had had with her mother and siblings, but her memories were of picking berries and currants. "In the summer we would pick mushrooms. My family had such a knowledge of mushrooms and the local berries." They would make juice from the berries in a special jug. She said the children always asked if they could put sugar in the juice and her mother always said no. Now what was interesting to her was how she longed for the sourness, the slight tang of those berries and their sweet and sour juice.

Angela, a Moldovan woman in her late twenties, said she had wanted to bring something special from her country for the rest of us to try, but she couldn't really find anything that you can't buy everywhere else in Europe. She talked about her happy memories of making bread with her parents and baking it in a wood oven. "Waiting for that bread to come out of the oven are some of the best memories of my childhood with my family," she said. But now, she complained, no one really makes bread anymore because everyone is eating the same kind of bread.

Many of the participants spoke longingly of the bread from their childhoods. Few people actually make bread anymore, because everyone eats sliced bread from the supermarket. Not even bread from bakeries tastes as good as the homemade bread people remember. Their complaints were all based on their own subjective recollections, but the fact that everyone mentioned bread seemed to point to a change in the quality of bread in various parts of Europe. In Rome, most of the bread is not very good; it's made with white flour and has no substance. Even whole-wheat bread has a dry, overly crumbly quality to it. The bread that Enzo was buying for us from a bakery near the lake reminded me of the bread I don't like much in Rome. It's possible to buy really good, well-made bread, and I know where to buy it, but it's not easily available.

Toward the end of the week, we had a visit from an Italian nutritionist. She mentioned that many Italians are also complaining about the quality of bread. So she brought us some bread from a bakery in nearby Viterbo to try. It was made with a variety of hard wheat called "Senatore Cappelli," which hadn't been grown in Italy in about thirty or forty years. The wheat was allowed to disappear almost entirely after the Second World War in favor of the limited range of higher-yield varieties now grown in abundance (though not abundant enough for this nation of pasta eaters: much of the pasta in Italy is now made with flour from wheat grown in Canada and France). She was interested in the wheat because it produces less gluten than the other varieties, and Italy has been facing a rise in gluten intolerance. We tasted the bread: it was made with rough, stone-ground Cappelli flour (not quite whole wheat, but not refined white), water, salt, and olive oil. It had a firm texture that made it perfect for eating on its own (as we did), dipped in olive oil (as we did) and with cheese (as we also did).

Later we took an excursion to the bakery, Il Sambuco, where the bread was made. We had to drive down a bumpy dirt road, around twists and turns, and under thick vines hanging from trees until finally we came to a little valley and a ramshackle building with smoke coming out of the chimney. It looked more like a potential still for making whiskey than a bakery, but it was the place. The bakery sourced all its ingredients from the Viterbo area and got its different varieties of wheat from as close to home as possible. Baking bread in a wood oven gives it a certain flavor and a fragrant crust. But this bread had a very dense texture with a slight hint of sourness from the natural yeast. I asked about the yeast, and the baker explained that he began by making his own bread starter twenty years ago by allowing wheat and water to ferment with a bit of honey, but he said the *pasta madre* improves in flavor as it ages. So around ten years ago, a friend gave him some starter that was thought to be between fifty to seventy years old, and he found that the sourness became more subtle and the wheat flavor intensified.

In many countries where leavened bread is a staple, it has been a tradition to pass the *pasta madre* down through the generations. A friend actually took the train to Florence once because someone had located a bakery that was willing to give him some *pasta madre* that was about a hundred years old. I've been told there are some families in Sardinia that are still passing down a *pasta madre* that is at least three hundred years old. But for the most part, now that people buy all their bread, this living symbol of a live food culture (quite literally) has died. You can't restart a three-hundred-year-old yeast; you have to start over. Now if you want to make a loaf of bread once in a while, you have to buy an instant yeast that doesn't give the bread the same flavor at all and that causes some people to suffer intestinal problems.

Everyone at the conference talked about the fact that we are all eating packaged foods: bread, breakfast cereals in a box, crackers, and so on. Many of the participants made a point of shopping in smaller markets and buying from farmers when they could, but they all acknowledged that going to the supermarket is the normal way to shop in pretty much every country across Europe. Ruta, a journalist from Latvia, pointed out that during the Communist years, there would be food shortages from time to time, but people would pool together what they had to get through them. They knew that a food shortage would eventually end. Now there is an abundance of food in packages on the shelves of the big supermarkets and they never run out of it, but the problem is that no one has the money to buy it as the global marketplace tends to shift jobs around even more readily than it ships food.

The problems in various European countries are more the same than they are different: there's a growing homogenization of food cultures. After the fall of Communism in Eastern Europe, fast-food companies and supermarket chains rushed in. People often spoke of the "Americanization" of food, though many of the food companies were not based in America: some were based in Europe, some even in Italy. But it didn't matter where the company originated, food production had become mechanized and industrial. The ordinary tradition of cooking food at home is slipping away as people eat out more often and buy prepared foods. The children are eating even more processed foods than the adults, and the foods that one generation took for granted—like good quality bread or homemade pasta—are now specialty items.

Pasta, though a relative newcomer to the Italian kitchen, typifies Italian food to most people outside Italy. Though we had been eating well at the convent in Bolsena, we hadn't been eating fresh pasta. Sabrina Aguiari asked if we wanted to learn how to make it; everyone did. So she started asking around to see who could teach us. The convent administrator's boyfriend's eighty-five-year-old grandmother was, it turned out, available and could show us how it's done. Senora Teresa arrived after lunch. She was a small woman wearing a black skirt with a green sweater. Her silvery white hair was short and pushed back from her face. She put on her apron and came to the marble-topped island in the center of the big kitchen. She started to shake: she had been making pasta her entire life but had never stood before such an eager-looking group of foreigners all staring at her expectantly, as though she would reveal the answer . . . to what? All our problems, perhaps, in more ways than one.

She started by taking a mound of flour and creating a well in the middle. She cracked six eggs into the well and started to quickly work the flour into the eggs with her hands to form the dough. She explained in Italian that this was a rich pasta because of the eggs. She had a puzzled look on her face and began to examine the unmixed flour. She found it very nice to work with, much nicer, she said, than the flour she had been buying in the supermarket. It turned out it was the Cappelli flour we had brought back from the bakery in Viterbo. She told me later that her hands instantly knew the feeling of that flour from years ago, that it was more like the flour she had used when her husband was alive, before she started shopping in the supermarket. Her husband loved pasta and needed to eat a dish of it every day. Senora Teresa loved her husband, so she made it for him every day. Since he had died, she had been making it two or three times a week for her grown children and grandchildren.

When we finished making the rich pasta, we moved onto what she called the poor pasta, which had only one egg and water. Everyone around the kitchen island worked his or her dough as Senora Teresa came around to inspect the texture and to knead it a little herself to get it into shape. When it was finally ready, she had us roll out the dough, and she cut some of it by hand. The rest she put through a machine that cut the sheets of dough into ribbons. Then she tossed it with a few spoonfuls of flour so it wouldn't stick together and left it to rest in bowls under tea towels.

Making pasta was much harder work than I had expected. When Senora Teresa did it, she made it look easy. But everything, from getting the texture right at the mixing stage to kneading it and rolling it out without it sticking, took skill. The only person who was able to do it reasonably well was Sarah, a young woman from northern Italy. She was very quiet throughout the pasta-making lesson, working her dough with a sense of ease and satisfaction. At the end, she thanked our instructor and then walked out into the garden. I followed her to see what she thought.

Sarah was extremely moved by the devotion of this woman to her family and her husband. She saw all of this expressed in her pasta making. She makes it look easy, said Sarah, but it takes strength and skill to make it as well as she does. You don't achieve that by taking a few lessons. It's a craft that you have to practice all the time. Sarah had made pasta with her own grandmother and for special occasions such as Christmas with her family, but she never made it for herself or her friends. "My generation doesn't do this. It's too much trouble," she said. "We want to eat it, but we don't want to make it." She complained that the ease of buying dried pasta, though it is very good, meant that few people bothered to make it fresh, even though fresh, homemade pasta could be considered something entirely different from what we buy in boxes. Sarah vowed that even though she is a busy woman, working on her PhD and with an active social life, she is going to make fresh pasta once a week.

Food Revival

Maybe Alice Waters is right that this generation of young people in Europe just needs a reminder. They might not be cooking with their parents at home, but many of them have enjoyed the incomparable feasts of their devoted grandparents. For Sarah, watching Senora Teresa make pasta, recognizing her skill but also her fragility, made her realize that if she wanted to see traditions carry on into the future, she would have to carry them herself.

While I've been watching Italian supermarkets grow bigger with ever more junky kids' foods, and formerly beautiful fresh food markets transform into outdoor supermarkets with mostly industrially produced foods, interest has been growing among younger Italians in their own food traditions and in finding good quality, local foods. It's hard to say if the trend mirrors what's been happening in North America, but it is interesting that they call the new markets by an English name: "farmers markets" rather than calling them *mercati contadini*.

My favorite Roman farmers' market is in one end of the former slaughterhouse of Testaccio. The big, stone barnlike structure, which once housed cattle on their way out of the world, is filled with farmers selling their own fresh produce. I can buy certified organic vegetables and fruits, and I can also buy uncertified produce, which the farmers tell me isn't exposed to pesticide spray or chemical fertilizers. I've bought garlic that has been barely a few hours out of the ground, pale-green zucchini with the flowers still attached, and mixtures of wild greens that I have to cut with spinach because they are still a little bitter for my taste, though I love them cooked with garlic and chilies and piled on toasted bread with a bit of olive oil and Pecorino Romano shaved on top.

As these markets grow in popularity, they expand their hours and attract more vendors. Now I can buy freshly baked bread made with whole-grain farro flour, fresh farro, or spinach pasta. There is also a buffalo farmer selling his own mozzarella and a dairy farmer who sells milk, butter, and cheese. It's become a ritual to go there every Sunday morning with James and Nico. Nico enjoys sampling the olives, the homemade jam, and the fruit, working his way down the center of the building until he arrives at the bread baker at the far end who always gives him a piece of *pizza bianca*.

The farmers' markets are not just popular; they are growing at the expense of the *cibo industriale*. The Italian National Institute of Statistics reported that food sales in 2010 had gone down all over Italy, but that sales at farmers markets grew by 28 percent. Coldiretti, which is the association of farmers and artisanal cheese makers who sell directly to the public, reported a dramatic increase in their sales. They were the only segment of the Italian food industry that did grow. Sales of out-of-season produce imported from Argentina, Brazil, South Africa, and Spain have dropped, in some cases, by nearly 75 percent. The prices in the farmers' markets are comparable to and, in some cases, lower than the prices at supermarkets. Most importantly, all of this has happened through word of mouth. People go and find fresh foods they haven't seen before or haven't seen in a long time, they find that everything tastes great, and they tell their friends. Farmers' markets haven't become popular because of advertising, imagery, and illusions. Going to one is almost like going to a social event. And people are attracted to the fact that the food is local; *la filiera corta* (the short chain) is what it's called. Local food isn't simply a quirky trend here; its roots are in tradition, and here in Italy those roots are deep.

The way I shop has changed since we first came to Rome, but it has changed for the better. I still go to the traditional outdoor markets and buy from my few trusted growers. The farmers' market is only open on weekends, and we make the trip every Saturday or Sunday. Right next door is Spazio Bio, an organic/local food supermarket that is open Tuesday through Sunday. The fresh produce at Spazio Bio is grown on a farm on the edge of Rome. I can buy grains and dried beans at the store that have all been sourced from local producers. It sells an amazingly diverse range of honey, though I'm rather stuck on the thyme variety from the Abruzzo just now. I can buy fantastic olive oil from Sabina and wine from the Lazio area. The store sells mainly ingredients rather than products, but the few products it does sell, such as dried pasta, cheese, and yogurt, all come from small, local, organic producers. If all these vendors aren't enough, I can order a five-kilogram box of fresh, organic produce plus some wine, bread, cheese, prosciutto, nuts, and more online from what's known as a "GAS" in Italy—a collective buying group—and have it delivered to James's office.

There's an air of tradition around these new markets but also an air of the new. I still see old ladies dragging their shopping carts around the farmers' markets, but now there are young families, too, on weekends buying bags of fresh fruit such as apricots and cherries to be doled out to the children for snacks, while the adults drink their coffee in the bar around the corner in a part of the slaughterhouse complex now known as *La Città dell'Altra Economia* (the City with an Alternative Economy). I've even seen people I know there, like parents from Nico's school. I still see lots of junk food and packaged foods in the children's *merenda* boxes, but people are talking about these markets. Once you start shopping this way and eating this great food, it's hard to go back to the supermarket.

FOURTEEN

The Pleasure of Food

Cooking

THERE'S NO GETTING around it: if we want to eat well, we have to cook. If we want our children to grow up with the skills to look after their health, we have to show them that cooking is normal. We don't have to become chefs, just competent home cooks. And then we have to get organized.

It helps to make a plan, to decide on what to make for dinner for the next few days and then shop for those ingredients. I wish I could say that I do this every week, because the fifteen minutes spent on planning saves hours in last-minute shopping and fretting over what to cook. Half the time, I'm making it up as I go along, but I now have enough experience to be able to do this with a minimum amount of banging around and cursing in the kitchen.

Favorite cookbooks are handy for planning, but the Internet is even better. There is no shortage of recipes in the public domain nor of ideas about what to eat. Most of us just need a little practice, and we need to make cooking a habit. The Internet excels at helping us find meals that we can prepare at home in less than an hour, even less than half an hour.

I've also found it convenient to have pots of herbs growing in my kitchen window. A rosemary branch tucked into a pan of braising chicken will fill the house with its aroma and infuse the chicken with it, too. Some chopped parsley stirred into a pot of rice or sprinkled on top of soup makes ordinary, plainly cooked food taste a little more special.

Fresh basil or mint in a salad is a flavor enhancer. These are the little things that can make cooking and eating more of a pleasure. The only big thing is making the decision to cook more often.

Soup

We have been lucky enough to make some really good friends in the time we've been living here in Rome. And we've also been lucky to share some wonderful meals with many of them. My friend Valeria is an amazingly good cook. In fact, her husband dreams of getting her to abandon her career with horses so they can open a restaurant together. We often eat out with them, trying new restaurants or old ones, and we always take our children. They come to our house for dinner and we go to theirs. But I have come to realize that our shared love of food has also led to a kind of formality when it comes to eating together. Valeria and Andrea always set the table in their dining room with a beautiful linen cloth, and Valeria cooks the full load of courses when friends are coming over. She invited us to eat fish with them one night, and when we arrived, Andrea gave us a glass of Franciacorta, and Valeria handed around a plate of bruschetta topped with salt cod, garlic, and herbs. Then we ate pasta with fresh tomatoes and white fish, followed by baked fish—a big, flat, round *rombo*—with bright green *broccoletti* served with olive oil and lemon. The meal was fantastic and we were groaning with pleasure by the end of it.

My friend Raffaella has invited us for memorable dinners, one of which started with ravioli, moved through pork chops with Gorgonzola and speck, several vegetables, salads, fruit, and dessert. Sarah has invited us for fresh pasta with freshly made pesto, and chicken cooked with white wine and squishy black figs. The food is always served on beautiful tables and eaten by candlelight, even with the children.

I realized one day that in all my efforts to understand the way people eat from day to day, and with all the questions I had asked them, I had never really had an ordinary, rushed weeknight meal with my friends and their families. So after James, Nico, and I had spent a beautiful food-filled Sunday in southern Tuscany with Andrea, Valeria, and Luca, I asked Valeria if she could show me how to make soup. I asked her as we sat on a stone wall during a food festival in Manciano with Luca and Nico sitting across from us, hungrily eating bowl after bowl of bean and farro soup. We had bought it from an elderly woman attending a stove and pot that she had dragged halfway outside on the sidewalk, and we had to keep going back for more.

Valeria looked puzzled and said, "Everyone knows how to make this soup." Andrea jumped in and said even he knew how to make this soup. No one had ever taught them how to make it; they had picked it up as they went through life in Italy eating these great soups. Valeria invited us to come for dinner the following week so we could make the soup together. She called Sarah and invited her to come too, with her son and her husband, Luis.

So, there we were at the end of a workday for all of us—Valeria's with the horses, Sarah's on a film set where she works as a set designer, and mine at my desk writing—in Valeria's kitchen with our three excited children, who had spent the day together in school and were revved up about spending the evening together too. Soon after we had arrived at about six thirty, Andrea called to say he was stuck in traffic on his way home from work, as was James. Luis had to work a little later and told us not to wait for him.

Valeria said she was going to cook an average meal that she would make on any fall or winter night. Though her family usually ate in the kitchen, we would be eating in the dining room since there were so many of us. Nico, Luca, and Dylan were setting up train tracks in the living room and playing raucous games that involved flying the trains through the apartment, around the kitchen, and back to the living room.

Valeria put a few glugs of olive oil in a fairly deep pot; then she took some carrot, celery, onion, and garlic and put them through a little chopper. "It's not very romantic," she said, "but it's faster." She let the chopped vegetables cook slowly in the warm pot with the lid on for about ten minutes. Then she added the beans, which she had left to soak before leaving for work that morning, and the farro grains, and stirred them around. She chopped tomatoes and added them to the pot along with some water (she never actually measured anything) and put the lid back on to let the mixture come to a boil. Valeria said that you could add some herbs if you wanted. She also said to wait until the beans were completely cooked before adding the salt. At this point, Valeria poured us each a glass of Prosecco to sip on while the soup cooked. I asked her if she usually has an *aperitivo* on a weeknight, and she laughed, saying it depends on the day. She put some Pecorino Romano and some carrots on a plate along with some bread. The boys zoomed in for carrots and cheese and zoomed out again. Then Valeria pulled out a mixing bowl and put some ground meat in it. "What's that?" I asked her, thinking it was the mystery ingredient in the soup. "Ground turkey," she said. For meatballs. Yes, usually she would just make the soup and vegetables, but she felt she couldn't just serve soup to her friends; she needed something more. Again she chopped some onions and garlic in the little chopper, and she added them to the ground turkey along with breadcrumbs soaked in milk, two eggs, some grated Parmesan, some lemon rind, and a little salt. Then she quickly and expertly rolled enough little meatballs to fill a big, shallow baking dish, drizzled olive oil over them, covered them loosely with foil, and popped them into the oven. Next she washed and chopped some broccoli to cook in salted water.

Andrea and James arrived at the same time and joined us in a glass of Prosecco. The boys shouted from the living room that they were hungry and wanted more carrots and cheese. Valeria checked the soup, which after an hour of cooking wasn't quite ready yet. She cut up more cheese, carrots, and bread, and then we set the table. I had to stop her from pulling out the nice linens and made her use the everyday tablecloth. The meatballs were done in less than half an hour, and by then the soup was ready too. Valeria took it off the heat and stirred in some salt. She ladled it into bowls and we called the children to the table. Luis arrived just in time. Andrea opened a bottle of red wine that he had bought the weekend before when we were in Tuscany, a Morellino di Scansano that goes with this Tuscan-style soup. Everyone added olive oil and Parmesan to their bowls, and it was delicious. The meatballs were also delicious, as was the broccoli with olive oil and lemon. We toasted the long line of Italian women who had passed the savory soup down through the years. We ate heartily, as did the children who wanted seconds of everything. We toasted Valeria and her unflappably gracious skills as cook and host. Then Sarah, who can't help herself, brought out a French apple cake that she baked the night before, after Dylan had gone to bed, because even though it was supposed to be an ordinary night's dinner, it's always a special occasion when we sit around a table together.

I'll have to take their word for it that they don't usually go to all this trouble on an ordinary weeknight. Valeria said she might actually make the soup on a Sunday and then reheat it later in the week for an easy dinner.

Cooking as a Chore

Cooking is drudgery to a lot of people. I too find cooking to be drudgery sometimes. Laundry is always drudgery, making my bed is drudgery, brushing my teeth is drudgery. Half my day, it seems, is taken up with repetitive, life-maintenance chores. But I accept them because I don't want my teeth to fall out; to sleep in a bed with rumpled, twisted sheets; or to walk around in dirty clothes. Though cooking can be drudgery, eating is a pleasure. The need to eat necessitates some work on my part, but often with fairly minimal effort, I can reap great rewards.

Besides, I have a child. James can fend for himself. He was a pretty good cook when we first met, and he still is when I move over in the kitchen and give him half a chance. But my son can't cook for himself, and it's our responsibility to feed him. If I didn't actually like to cook and said, "Enough with this drudgery, I'm a liberated woman and I'm not acting in this role of servitude any longer," I'm sure James would step in and do what he could. I try (though not always successfully) to relinquish control of the kitchen once in a while and let him cook our dinner. But if James said, "Sorry, I'm too busy with work to cook," where would that leave Nico? He's a young child. He can shell his own peas, he's dying to use a knife, but he can't yet light the gas stove.

The one thing I feel I cannot do is abandon my little boy to the food industry. Individuals can do what they want. They can microwave frozen dinners or order in Thai food. But parents have to protect and nurture their children, and feeding them is part of that job. Many parents try to do it within the confines set by the food industry, but I don't think an industry can give us the foods our children really need to eat.

I never used to see myself as a matriarch, with my crisp apron (actually mine is quite uncrisp), my wooden spoon, my stockpots, and my herb garden. Yet somehow I've ended up being the chief cook in my family (but not the bottle washer—James does that part). It is a lot of work, though if I plan ahead, it is much easier. My strategy is to stick to simple meals, save new recipes for the weekend, and try to get invited to Valeria's or Sarah's houses for dinner as often as possible.

Food activists and food lovers sometimes blame feminism for our collective loss of cooking skills and for the rise of processed and fast foods. I don't know about that. I read through Betty Friedan's *The Feminine Mystique* and found her portrayal of women post–World War II and through the 1950s to be truly horrifying. She revealed a narrow world for women who were shut out of the workplace and not allowed to express their identities. If they chose to be career women, they couldn't get married. If a woman wanted marriage, her only option was to be a housewife and mother. Friedan didn't actually say that cooking was oppressing women, but that having no other option but to be the family's servant and cook, make beds, and clean floors was oppressive. She said that a woman does not have to give up her family in order to be happy: "She does not have to choose between marriage and career; that was the mistaken choice of the feminine mystique." She urged women to see housework as a task like any other and to get it over with and out of the way so they could get on to other things. She urged women to embrace household conveniences and to use "the vacuum cleaner and the dishwasher and all the automatic appliances, and even the instant mashed potatoes for what they are truly worth—to save time that can be used in more creative ways." Maybe this is where our conflicted feelings come from.

Friedan lumped the cooking in with the other drudgery because it's part of the housework and of the housewife's oppressive "career." In the fifty years since Friedan published *The Feminine Mystique*, there hasn't been much reason to reevaluate her position on the vacuum cleaner or the dishwasher, but it is certainly time to take a second look at those instant mashed potatoes. In 1963, the world's children were not facing an epidemic of obesity and malnutrition, so it was easy to see convenience foods as simply convenient, or to see eating out in a family-friendly restaurant as a break from the kitchen. How could Friedan have predicted in 1963 that the food industry would use feminism to peddle all of its less-than-ideal food products to emancipated mothers?

Most of us are trying to find a balance among work, cooking, and cleaning. Women still end up shouldering most of the burden of housework, though it doesn't have to be that way. We still have to eat and our children have to eat, and we can make that experience horrible, tolerable, or a pleasure. I have friends who defiantly refuse to cook for themselves and their families: they buy frozen pizza, canned soup, salad in a bag, and factory-made cookies. I don't think that's the way to go. It seems like refusing to brush your teeth or wash your clothes. Cooking is a life skill for men and women. It's one we should practice and definitely share with our children, not least because they might grow up and cook for us one day.

Giuliano Hazan, Marcella Hazan's son, once wrote that his fondest childhood memories are of spending time in the kitchen with his mother, carefully stirring the risotto. Marcella, who is now in her late eighties, recently posted a note on her Facebook page about how she couldn't wait for Giuliano to come home from teaching his cooking course in Italy and cook dinner for her. I can only hope for the same thing when my son grows up.

Cooking for a family is a chore and a pleasure like any other, but it has become freighted with meaning. One Sunday we decided to make our own pizza. Nico and I mixed the dough in the morning. We mixed together whole-wheat flour, a pinch of salt, water, the yeast, and a spoonful of honey, and then we kneaded the dough for ten minutes and left it covered in a bowl to rise. James, Nico, and I went out to the park and ran into some friends with children. After the children had played for a while, we all decided to go out for lunch. When we returned home after being out for about five hours, the dough was big and puffy. I let Nico punch the air out of it, and then we left it to rise some more while I read a book and James and Nico tended to the flowers on the balcony, painted some pictures, built a giant structure from blocks, washed the car, and I can't remember what else. When it was time to make dinner, we got out our dough, divided it into three pieces, and took turns rolling it out as thinly as possible to put on our pizza trays. We brushed the pizzas with olive oil and put some sliced tomatoes and buffalo mozzarella on top (Nico skipped the tomatoes). I added leftover asparagus to mine, Nico put green olives on his, and James added red peppers to his. Then we baked them until the crusts were crisp and starting to blister. While we were preparing them, a friend from Toronto called via Skype on the computer and we told her what we were doing. Nico showed her his pizza before it went into the oven. She said to me, quite sarcastically, "It must be nice to have the time."

I felt as though I might as well have been wearing a bonnet and plaid apron. What time? It was Sunday, and the dough actually took very little preparation time. We had left it alone to rise while we enjoyed a full and active day. What was so important that we were supposed to be doing? Should I have been working? Should James have gone into the office? Making pizza was just another activity, like painting pictures, planting flowers, building block towers, or washing the car, except we could eat the pizza for dinner with a salad.

I suppose I'm lucky because I do like cooking. Sometimes when I'm making chicken schnitzel yet again, of course I find it dull. But I'm fortunate to have access to some good markets and wonderful farmers with bountiful produce. Trying to cook within Italian culture and Roman traditions is also a challenge I've enjoyed. In fact, for the work I have put into it, it has added so much more to my life. Cooking the Italian way has been a pleasure and an education—a journey through a world that was only visible to me by living here and participating in the daily ritual of marketing, thinking, chopping, cooking, and eating. When I was in New York, I talked casually with people about cooking, particularly about making dinner on weeknights—the daily grind. I was surprised by how hostile many people were about the idea that we should make real food for our families, and that we can't just buy packages off the shelf and expect everything to be okay. People seem to like going to restaurants and they like dinner parties, but they don't like cooking for their families or they don't think they should have to cook for their families. While I don't think women should be the only ones doing the cooking, I think that one of the grown-ups in the house has to take it on. It's still kind of retro and unfeminist for a woman to cook for other people unless, of course, she is cooking something wildly complicated and serving it with expensive wine and a lot of fanfare. If I cooked the way I do now but only for myself, I would probably be seen as interesting, but since I do it for my family, I'm seen as servile in some eyes, even though I have a career. Some people are posturing, I think, when they say there isn't time to make real food for dinner every night, to have solidarity with low-income families who have to work really long hours to make ends meet. Of course, I have sympathy for people who have to work so hard, but I don't think we should condemn them and their children to a life of ill health from bad food.

More Than Cooking

I've spent a lot of time talking about the need to cook and to make dinner. But we need much more than just dinner; we need lunch, breakfast, and snacks, too. To hand all that responsibility to the food industry is infantilizing; it makes us dependent, because so many people have lost the habit and the skill of cooking. It's something we need to do for ourselves. That's not to say we need to do it alone. People are forming cooking collectives in which everyone makes one main-course meal a week in a quantity large enough to divide among a few families. Then everyone gets together to swap the food, and it all goes into their freezers. For one day of cooking, you can have seven days of home-cooked meals. Starting a collective takes cooperation and coordination, and it also helps if you live within a food culture in which people share similar tastes. I first read about the idea in New York, but there the problem was that people had different food preferences. My friend Luis, who is Spanish, sent me an article about cooking collectives in Madrid. There the food was all based on Spanish recipes from their shared food culture, and the issue of different tastes didn't come up.

One time when Sarah and Luis were busy working on a film with a short deadline and knew they wouldn't have much time to cook for themselves and Dylan, they hired a woman to cook a variety of meals for their freezer. Either Sarah or Luis tried to pick up fresh vegetables a couple of times a week, but otherwise a home-cooked dinner was already prepared.

I have bought meatballs made by my butcher's wife the morning of the day we plan to eat them. She uses the same ingredients we would use to make them. Though we still like to make meatballs ourselves, especially if we want to experiment with the ingredients, it's nice to know that I can count on her if I need a quick dinner.

Now that more people are searching for better foods with more natural ingredients, there is a market for them. We don't all have to make our own bread if we can find a good baker willing to do it for us who will adhere to the standards we would follow if making it for ourselves. Or we can avail ourselves of some home appliances, as Betty Friedan suggested, and buy a bread maker. You can put ingredients in a bread maker one day, press a button, and wake up the next morning to fresh bread. Or you can start a yeast culture, make some bread (which is as easy as pizza dough), and pass the yeast on to your children when they move out and start families of their own.

While we've never stopped eating, many of us have stopped cooking. But it's a basic skill that we all need to acquire. Some people are able to transform cooking into an art, but it's not necessary to cook like a five-star chef to enjoy the numerous benefits of preparing your own food. I've watched people make lunch for their families with a few good-quality ingredients: slices of melon with prosciutto draped like a veil over top, slices of tomato layered with buffalo mozzarella and basil leaves, and toasted bread rubbed with garlic and olive oil and topped with roasted zucchini, anchovies, and lemon. I once interrupted two mechanics down the street from where I live who were on their lunch break. I happened to walk in as they were piling yellow and red cherry tomatoes on two plates covered in arugula. One of them added sliced boiled eggs and a chunk of bread to each plate, while the other brought down a bottle of olive oil that he kept on the shelf with the tools and carefully poured a thin stream over everything. They had pulled a metal work table out from the wall and covered it with a clean, blue cloth. I was struck by the contrast of the environment: the cement floor with grease stains, the car on the hoist behind them, the tools hanging on the walls, the coveralls worn by both men, and the table set with two plates of carefully arranged salad and two water glasses. It was a civilized scene and a very Italian one, even though one of the men was from Senegal.

We need to know our way around food to be able to prepare a meal so easily. If we lived in a functioning food culture, we would have grown up with an appreciation for good-quality food and we would have learned how to prepare it with little effort. For children in North America, cooking classes in school would be a good way to pass on a few essential skills. We had home economics class when I was growing up, though I think it was actually called "Family Studies" then. Educators could rename it "cooking class" and invite the boys in this time, too. If children learn to do a little cooking, they might soon discover that they prefer what they can make to fast food, especially when they are teens.

Nico is looking forward to the summer when he is eight so that he can go to the day camp cooking classes at the Stop Community Food Centre in Toronto. The classes, which are also offered as an after-school program, teach children about growing, cooking, and shopping for healthy food and have a dose of food politics thrown in. We found a video of children at the Stop expertly chopping garlic and preparing meals together. Nico wanted to watch it again and again because he loved seeing children only slightly older than he is moving confidently around a kitchen, wielding knives, stirring giant pots, and making food to share with each other. I wanted to watch it again and again because I enjoyed seeing children from different ethnic backgrounds cooking food together; it was a glimpse of a complex community of children working together to make a shared meal from local ingredients. Children feel powerful when they learn to cook for themselves. They feel a sense of belonging when they stop thinking only about their own individual preferences and make a meal for everyone to share. They also learn something about the creative possibilities of food and begin to understand the wonderful, pleasurable, health-giving role it could play in their lives in the future.

Teaching children about the politics of food and the workings of the food industry is bound to be controversial, but it's necessary if these children are to grow up to be informed and aware food consumers, happy cooks, and contented eaters. As they grow up, they will need to be vigilant and protective of their right to good, fresh, nourishing food, and they will have to ensure that their right to it takes priority over the food industry's interests. We can't go to the supermarket, buy products off the shelf, and pop them in our mouths. We have to know everything, or as close to everything as possible, about the food we eat. If we can buy it from the people who grow it, that's even better. If we can visit the farms where our food is grown and raised, that's better again. And of course, if we grow some of our own food and cook it too, we take some of the mystery out of the process and we awaken to our own creative potential, making way for a food culture to emerge. That's really where the fun starts. It's in a food culture that our children will learn to enjoy food without fear of it harming their health or making them fat, they will learn to develop shared tastes with their peers and the rest of their community, and we won't need to turn them into judgmental foodies in order to protect their health.

The Dream Continues

When I first came to Italy, I would go to sleep at night with a warm feeling in my stomach that was only partly caused by the food. I thought I had never seen a sky so blue or felt sun so warm. I had never imagined that old, decaying buildings could inspire such awe and reverence. I was impressed by the cooking, by the approach to food, and by the general knowledge that everyone seemed to share about things that eluded me (for example, boil a potato in the water with the spaghetti if you are serving it with pesto, save Parmesan rinds in the freezer and use them later for making soup stock, do not under any circumstances ever try to cook without salt, don't pair fish with cheese, and drink your cappuccino in the morning while standing at the bar and chatting with your neighbors).

Before we came to Italy, I liked to cook well enough. I liked having dinner parties. I used to throw some great ones with friends who also liked to cook. But those were special events; they were fun and a little bit showy. I've always loved the way conversations unravel over a table as people eat together. I love lingering at the table long into the night with friends as we drain the last of the bottle of wine to wash down those last few morsels of cheese. It always makes me sad when someone suggests we move to the living room or somewhere more comfortable.

Living in Italy has made me see how dinner parties are possible with children, too. I see the importance of having them at the table with the adults and of teaching them to eat slowly and to enjoy the food and the company. One iconic image of Italy is a long table set out under a tree,

211

laden with food and surrounded by dinner guests ranging from the very old to the middle-aged to the young and the children. I've been very lucky to sit at such tables on occasion.

I hope that Nico will grow up to see that he was lucky, too. He takes the blue sky, the warm sun, and the beautiful architecture for granted. He sees good food as his birthright. He is lucky to experience the great food of Italy, and he is also lucky to know Canada as it has started to discover the great food it grows and produces. He has experienced an old food culture and will also get to see the birth of a new one. I hope he won't take either of them for granted, that he will work to protect them, and that, in return, they will protect his health and give him great pleasure for a long time to come.

Acknowledgments

Firstly, I have to say that it was my husband, James Heer, who urged me to stop complaining about children's food and to start writing about it. Without his insight, I would have spent my energy ranting over the dinner table instead of redirecting it onto the page. I have been fortunate to be able to work with wonderful editors who have helped me to tell this story about food and children. Alexis Rizzuto at Beacon Press inspired me both on the page and in the kitchen. May her garden forever overflow with tomatoes. At Random House Canada, Angelika Glover and Pamela Murray helped keep my momentum going with their genuine interest in food and children. Kristin Campbell made numerous trips to the library in Toronto while I was in Rome. Stacey Cameron and Jane Gebhart gave the book a polish with their careful copy editing. Jackie Kaiser and Chris Casuccio are not only the world's two best agents; they are also great cooks. I treasure their advice, and I am grateful for their enthusiasm.

I've been lucky to cook with so many friends over the years. I owe a huge debt to Grainne O'Donnell for showing me what is possible in the kitchen. Brenda Ferguson showed me how to eat my way around Paris more than once and then made me think I was still there when I was really in her kitchen in Toronto. Brenda Copeland taught me how to roast a leg of lamb at a crucial time in my life. I want to thank Lorraine Johnson for her friendship and her infectious interest in everything that grows. I want to thank Andrew Leyerle for taking us to dinner, at his father's request, at Taberna de' Gracchi. It was a happy time.

I have to thank my family, too, for all those memories around the dinner table: Mary Marshall, my mom, who really did know how to cook; my sister Marion Marshall, who made the strangest things taste really good; my brothers, for their belief in me: David, Danny, George, and even you, Ken, wherever you are. I also want to thank my adorable niece Kim, who knows her way around Rome; my nephew Brandon, for his sharp insight and lively e-mail correspondence; and my nephew Aaron for declaring at the end of a meal at a farmhouse in Umbria that it was one of the best experiences of his life.

In Rome, Sarah Webster and Luis Prieto, Andrea Maroni Ponti and Valeria Del Gatto, Marjorie Shaw, Maho Sato, and Raffaella Menichini have fed me, talked with me and taught me so much. Mona Talbott at the American Academy of Rome talked with me about food and introduced me to Alice Waters. I would like to thank growers like Loredanna, Domenico, Carlo, and the countless others whose names I don't even know but whose food I eat and enjoy every day.

I'd like to thank Dianne de Fenoyl for teaching me so much about writing. And for being wonderful.

Mostly, I'd like to thank my son, Nico, for opening my eyes, and for eating his broccoli.

References

The following are the sources that supplied me with facts and information but also influenced my thinking.

Chapter One: Discovering a Food Culture

Hazan, Marcella. *Essentials of Classic Italian Cooking*. New York: Alfred A. Knopf, 1994.

Chapter Two: The Packaged-Food Revolution

Avens, Jenni. "The Legacy of Craig Claiborne." *Saveur Magazine*, June 17, 2009. http://www.saveur.com.

Benoit, Jehane. *The Canadiana Cookbook*. Ottawa: New American Library of Canada, 1975.

Berton, Pierre, and Janet Berton. *The Centennial Food Guide: A Century of Good Eating*. Toronto: McClelland and Stewart, 1966.

Block, Melissa. "Something from the Oven: The Rise of Packaged-Food Cuisine in 1950s America." National Public Radio. April 19, 2004. http://www.npr .org.

Duncan, Dorothy. *Canadians at Table: A Culinary History of Canada*. Toronto: Dundurn Press, 2006.

Friedan, Betty. *The Feminine Mystique*. New York: W. W. Norton & Co., 1997.

Flammang, Janet A. *The Taste for Civilization: Food, Politics and Civil Society*. Chicago: University of Illinois Press, 2010.

Gotlieb, Sondra. *The Gourmet's Canada*. Toronto: New Press, 1972.

Hazan, Marcella. *Essentials of Classic Italian Cooking*. New York: Alfred A. Knopf, 1994.

Henderson, Mary F. *Practical Cooking and Dinner Giving*. New York: Harper & Brothers, 1877.

Kenneally, Rhona Richman. "There Is a Canadian Cuisine, and It Is Unique in All the World. Crafting National Food Culture during the Long 1960s." In *What's to Eat? Entrées in Canadian Food History*, edited by Nathalie Cooke, 167–91. Montreal: McGill-Queen's University Press, 2009.

Rebora, Giovanni. *Culture of the Fork: A Brief History of Food in Europe*. New York: Columbia University Press, 2001.

Root, Waverly, and Richard De Rochemont. *Eating in America: A History*. New York: Ecco Press, 1981.

Rozin, Paul, Rebecca Bauer, and Dana Catanese. "Food and Life, Pleasure and Worry, among American College Students: Gender Differences and Regional Similarities." *Journal of Personality and Social Psychology* 85, no 1 (July 2003): 132–41.

Shapiro, Laura. *Something from the Oven: Reinventing Dinner in 1950s America.* New York: Viking, 2004.

Smith, Andrew F. *Eating History: 30 Turning Points in the Making of American Cuisine.* New York: Columbia University Press, 2009.

Chapter Three: Scientific Mothers

Apple, Rima D. *Mothers and Medicine: A Social History of Infant Feeding 1890–1950.* London: University of Wisconsin Press, 1987.

Berry, Nina J., and Karleen D. Gribble. "Breast Is No Longer Best: Promoting Normal Infant Feeding." *Maternal and Child Nutrition* 4 (2008): 74–79.

Bosely, Sarah. "Bottle-Feeding Babies Can Lead to Adult Obesity, Says Study." *Guardian* (UK), September 30, 2010. http://www.guardian.co.uk.

"Breastfeeding Moms Fight Back with Protest at H&M's Vancouver Store." *Province* (Canada), August 7, 2008. http://www.canada.com.

Centers for Disease Control and Prevention National Immunization Survey. "Breastfeeding Report Card, United States: Outcome Indicators, 2010." http://www.cdc.gov.

Dewar, Gwen. "Flavors in Breast Milk and Baby Formula: How Early Feeding Experiences Shape Your Baby's Preferences for Solid Foods." *Parenting Science.* 2009. http://www.parentingscience.com.

Dykes, Fiona, and Victoria Hall Moran. *Infant and Young Child Feeding: Challenges to Implementing a Global Strategy.* West Sussex, UK: Blackwell Publishing, 2009.

Flexnews. "Nestlé: Nutrition Division to be Significant Growth Driver; Infant Nutrition Segment to Play Major Role." Global Data Systems. June 20, 2008.

Fortin, Joseph, director. *Formula for Disaster.* DVD. Philippines: UNICEF Philippines in association with JRF Productions, 2007.

Golden Rice Project. "Almost Everything You Wanted to Know about Golden Rice." Accessed October 28, 2011. http://www.goldenrice.org.

Institut National de la statistique et UNICEF. *Enquête par grappes à indicateurs multiples 2006. Rappoert principal.* Cameroon: Institut National. http://www.who.int.

Kram, Kathryn M., and George M. Owen. "Nutritional Studies on United States Preschool Children: Dietary Intakes and Food Procurement, Preparation and Consumption." Quoted in Apple, *Mothers and Medicine.*

Moorhead, Joanna. "Milking It." *Guardian* (UK), May 15, 2007. http://www.guardian.co.uk.

Muller, Mike. *The Baby Killer.* Report. London: War on Want, 1974. http://www.babymilkaction.org.

Nestlé. "Full Year 2011: 7.5% Organic Growth, +60 Basis Points Margin Improvement." Press release. February 16, 2011. http://www.nestle.com.

————. "Nestlé to Acquire Pfizer Nutrition in Strategic Move to Enhance Its Position in Global Infant Nutrition." Press release. April 23, 2012. http://www.nestle.com.

Nestle, Marion. *What to Eat: An Aisle by Aisle Guide to Savvy Food Choices and Good Eating.* New York: North Point Press, 2006.

Pollan, Michael. *In Defense of Food: The Myth of Nutrition and the Pleasures of Eating.* London: Allen Lane, 2008.

Public Health Agency of Canada. *What Mothers Say: The Canadian Maternity Experiences Survey.* Ottawa: Public Health Agency of Canada, 2009. Accessed 2010. http://www.who.int.

Spiegel Online International. "The Politics of Breast-Feeding: Italian Mothers Hold Mass Public Nursing." June 25, 2008. http://www.spiegel.de.

World Health Organization. *International Code of Marketing of Breast-milk Substitutes.* Geneva: World Health Organization, 1981. http://www.who.int.

Chapter Four: When Children Learn to Taste

Brillat-Savarin, Jean Anthelme. *The Physiology of Taste: Or Meditations on Transcendental Gastronomy.* Translated by M. F. K. Fisher. New York: Alfred A. Knopf, 2009.

Eisenberg, Arlene, Heidi E. Murkoff, and Sandee E. Hathaway. *What to Expect: The Toddler Years.* New York: Workman Publishing, 1996.

Frankenburg, Frances Rachel. *Vitamin Discoveries and Disasters: History, Science, and Controversies.* Santa Barbara, CA: Praeger, 2009.

Greco, Luigi, and Gabriella Morini. "Lo sviluppo del gusto nel bambino." *Medico e Bambino* (blog), November 4, 2010. http://medicoebambino.blogspot.com.

Kuhnlein, Harriet V. "Here Is the Good News." *World Nutrition, Journal of the World Public Health Nutrition Association* 1, no. 2 (June 2010). http://www.wphna.org.

Lean, Michael E. J., ed. *Fox and Cameron's Food Science, Nutrition & Health.* 7th ed. London: Hodder Arnold, 2006.

Morini, Gabriella. Phone interview with author. Bra, Italy. 2011.

Morini, Gabriella. "L'educazione del gusto nella prima infanzia." *Alimentazione,* January 2009: 43–48.

Pollan, Michael. *In Defense of Food: The Myth of Nutrition and the Pleasures of Eating.* London: Allen Lane, 2008.

Power, Michael L., and Jay Schulkin. *The Evolution of Obesity.* Baltimore: Johns Hopkins University Press, 2009.

Chapter Five: The Art, Science, and Tradition of Eating

Apple, Rima D. *Mothers and Medicine: A Social History of Infant Feeding 1890–1950.* London: University of Wisconsin Press, 1987. *Including references to Justus von Liebig.*

Carpenter, Kenneth J. *The History of Scurvy and Vitamin C.* Cambridge, UK: Cambridge University Press, 1986.

Frankenburg, Frances Rachel. *Vitamin Discoveries and Disasters: History, Science, and Controversies.* Santa Barbara, CA: Praeger, 2009. *Including references to Stephen Babcock.*

Gadsby, Patricia. "The Inuit Paradox: How Can People Who Gorge on Fat and Rarely See a Vegetable Be Healthier Than We Are?" *Discover* 25, no. 10 (October 2004).

Health Canada. "Vitamin D and Calcium: Updated Dietary Reference Intakes." Accessed October 31, 2011. http://www.hc-sc.gc.ca.

House, A. A., et al. "Effect of B-Vitamin Therapy on Progression of Diabetic Nephropathy." *Journal of the American Medical Association* 303, no. 16 (April 27, 2010): 1603–609.

Institute of Medicine. *Dietary Reference Intakes for Calcium and Vitamin D.* Washington, DC: Institute of Medicine. November 30, 2010. http://iom.edu.

Kolata, Gina. "Extra Vitamin D and Calcium Aren't Needed, Report Says." *New York Times,* November 29, 2010.

Latham, Michael. "The Great Vitamin A Fiasco," *World Nutrition, Journal of the World Public Health Nutrition Association* 1, no. 1 (May 1, 2010). http://www.wphna.org.

Lean, Michael E. J., ed. *Fox and Cameron's Food Science, Nutrition & Health.* 7th ed. London: Hodder Arnold, 2006.

Monteiro, Carlos. "The Big Issue Is Ultra-processing: The Hydrogenation Bomb." *World Nutrition, Journal of the World Public Health Nutrition Association* 2, no. 4 (April 2011). http://www.wphna.org.

Mowbray, Scott. *The Food Fight: Truth, Myth and the Food-Health Connection.* Toronto: Random House of Canada, 1992.

Nestle, Marion. "IOM: Vitamin D, Calcium Supplements Not Needed!" *Food Politics.* November 30, 2010. http://www.foodpolitics.com.

Patel, Raj. *Stuffed and Starved: The Hidden Battle for the World's Food System.* Toronto: HarperCollins Publishers, 2007.

Pollan, Michael. *In Defense of Food: The Myth of Nutrition and the Pleasures of Eating.* London: Allen Lane, 2008.

Reynolds, John E., III, et al. "Human Health Implications of Omega-3 and Omega-6 Fatty Acids in Blubber of the Bowhead Whale (*Balaenamysticetus*)." *Arctic* 59, no. 2 (June 2008). http://pubs.aina.ucalgary.ca.

Stolzt, Veronica D., ed. *New Topics in Vitamin D Research.* New York: Nova Science Publishers, 2006.

Weeks, Carly. "B Vitamins Linked to Heart, Kidney Damage in Diabetics." *Globe and Mail* (Toronto). April 27, 2010. http://www.theglobeandmail.com.

Chapter Six: Selling Food to Children

Bakan, Joel. *The Corporation: The Pathological Pursuit of Profit and Power.* London: Constable, 2004.

"Ban on Fast Food TV Advertising Would Reverse Childhood Obesity Trends, Study Shows." *Science Daily,* November 29, 2008. http://www.sciencedaily.com. *National Bureau of Economic Research Study.*

Council of Better Business Bureaus. Children's Food and Beverage Advertising Initiative. Accessed October 31, 2011. http://www.bbb.org.

Dittmann, Melissa. "Protecting Children from Advertising." *American Psychological Association* 35, no. 6 (June 2004). http://www.apa.org.

Fast Food FACTS. Yale Rudd Center for Food Policy & Obesity. Accessed October 31, 2011. http://www.fastfoodmarketing.org.

Feigenbaum, Harvey. "America's Cultural Challenge Abroad." *Political Science Quarterly* 126, no. 1 (Spring 2011): 107–29.

Girls Intelligence Agency. Accessed October 31, 2011. http://www.girlsintelligenceagency.com.

Kessler, David A. *The End of Overeating: Taking Control of the Insatiable North American Appetite.* Toronto: McClelland and Stewart, 2009.

Layton, Lyndsey. "David Kessler: Fat, Salt and Sugar Alter Brain Chemistry, Make Us Eat Junk Food." *Washington Post,* April 27, 2009.

"Let There Be Toys! Judge Throws Out Lawsuit Brought against McDonald's Happy Meals by Concerned Mom." *Daily Mail* (UK), April 5, 2012. http://www.dailymail.co.uk.

"Marketing Food Products to Children: Are the UN Agencies Helpless?" *World Nutrition: Journal of the World Public Health Nutrition Association.* May 2010. http://www.wphna.org.

Mayo, Ed, and Agnes Nairn. *Consumer Kids: How Big Business Is Grooming Our Children for Profit.* London: Constable & Robinson, 2009.

McNeal, James. *The Kids Market: Myths and Realities.* Ithaca, NY: Paramount Market Publishing, 1999.

Nestlé Italia. "Il Gelato: Una merenda sano e gustosa per il tuo bambino." May 26, 2009. Accessed July 13, 2009. http://www.nestle.it.

Nestle, Marion. "McDonald's Happy Meal Changes." *Food Politics,* July 27, 2011. http://www.foodpolitics.com.

Packard, Vance. *The Hidden Persuaders.* London: Penguin Books, 1961.

Pepsi baby bottles and vintage new Pepsi baby bottle. Photographs. Accessed October 31, 2011. Etsy.com and eBay.com.

Reuters. "Unilever Wants French to Love Ice-Cream Like Italians." May 6, 2009. Accessed September 11, 2009. http://www.flex-news-food.com.

Schor, Juliet B. *Born to Buy: The Commercialized Child and the New Consumer Culture.* New York: Scribner, 2004.

"Soda Pop Industry Branded Baby Bottles with Soft Drink Logos." *Natural News.* November 28, 2010. http://www.naturalnews.com.

"TV Food Advertisements Increase Obese Children's Appetite by 134 Percent." *Science Daily,* April 25, 2007. http://www.sciencedaily.com. *University of Liverpool study.*

World Health Organization. "Set of Recommendations on the Marketing of Foods and Nonalcoholic Beverages to Children." 2010. www.who.org.

Chapter Seven: The Tragic Results

Abraham, Carolyn. "Childhood Obesity." *Globe and Mail* (Toronto), September 12, 2008. http://www.theglobeandmail.com.

Beil, Laura. "Surgery for Obese Children?" *New York Times*, February 15, 2010.

Belluck, Pam. "Child Obesity Seen as Warning of Heart Disease." *New York Times*, November 12, 2008.

Bittman, Mark. "Don't End Agricultural Subsidies, Fix Them." *Opinionator* blog, NYTimes.com. March 1, 2011.

Brody, Jane. "To Preserve Their Health and Heritage, Arizona Indians Reclaim Ancient Foods." *New York Times*, May 21, 1991.

———. "Weight Problems May Begin in the Womb." *New York Times*, September 6, 2010.

Brown, Harriet. "For Obese People, Prejudice in Plain Sight." *New York Times*, March 15, 2010.

"By 2020, 80% of Men Will Be Overweight, Study Shows." *Guardian* (UK), February 16, 2010. http://www.guardian.co.uk.

Center for Health Promotion and Wellness at MIT Medical. "Set Point Theory." Accessed October 31, 2011. http://www.medweb.mit.edu.

Chang, Guo-Qing, et al. "Maternal High-Fat Diet and Fetal Programming: Increased Proliferation of Hypothalamic Peptide-Producing Neurons that Increase Risk for Overeating and Obesity." *Journal of Neuroscience*. November 12, 2008. http://www.neuro.cjb.net.

Cheng, Maria. "Obesity Could Become Top Cancer Cause." *Globe and Mail*. September 24, 2009. http://www.theglobeandmail.com.

Delpeuch, Francis, et al. *Globesity: A Planet Out of Control?* London: Earthscan, 2009.

Dor, A., et al. "A Heavy Burden: The Individual Costs of Being Overweight and Obese in the United States." Department of Health Policy. George Washington University School of Public Health and Health Services. September 21, 2010. http://www.gwumc.edu.

Finkelstein, Eric A., et al. "Annual Medical Spending Attributable to Obesity: Payer-and Service-Specific Estimates." *Health Affairs* 28, no. 5 (September/October 2009): w822–w831.

Franks, Paul W., et al. "Childhood Obesity, Other Cardiovascular Risk Factors, and Premature Death." *New England Journal of Medicine* 362, no. 6 (2010): 485–93.

James, Janet, et al. "Preventing Childhood Obesity: Two Year Follow-up Results from the Christchurch Obesity Prevention Programme in Schools (CHOPPS)." *British Medical Journal*. October 8, 2007. http://www.bmj.com.

Kessler, David. *The End of Overeating: Taking Control of the Insatiable North American Appetite*. Toronto: McClelland and Stewart, 2009.

Laskawy, Tom. "Scientists Claim Junk Food Is as Addictive as Heroin." *Grist*, October 27, 2009. http://www.grist.org.

Lee, Douglas S., et al. "Trends in Risk Factors for Cardiovascular Disease in Canada: Temporal, Socio-demographic and Geographic Factors." *Canadian Medical Association Journal*. July 20, 2009. http://www.cmaj.ca.

Lumeng, Julie C., et al. "Weight Status as a Predictor of Being Bullied in Third through Sixth Grades." *Pediatrics* 125, no. 6 (June 1, 2010): e1301–e1307. Accessed May 3, 2010. doi:10.1542/peds.2009_0774.

O'Connor, Anahad. "The Claim: Chia Seeds Can Help You Lose Weight." *New York Times,* January 24, 2011.

Parker-Pope, Tara. "Extra Weight Adds to Economic Woes." *Well* blog, NYTimes .com, July 22, 2010.

Picard, Andre. "The Face of Heart Disease Gets Younger." *Globe and Mail*, January 25, 2010. http://www.theglobeandmail.com.

Piepenburg, Erik. "An Endless Cycle of Failed Diets." *Well* blog, NYTimes.com, October 5, 2010.

Rabin, Roni Caryn. "Baby Fat May Not Be So Cute After All." *New York Times*, March 22, 2010.

———. "Risks: Asleep, and Helping to Keep the Weight Off." *New York Times*, September 6, 2010.

———. "Central Heating May Be Making Us Fat." *New York Times*, January 26, 2011.

———. "Prognosis: Study Finds Troubles with Gastric Band Surgery." *New York Times*, March 24, 2011.

Sassi, Franco. *Obesity and the Economics of Prevention: Fit not Fat.* Paris: Organisation for Economic Co-operation and Development, 2010.

Sherry, B., et al. "Vital Signs: State-Specific Obesity Prevalence among Adults— United States, 2009." Centers for Disease Control and Prevention. August 3, 2010. http://www.cdc.gov.

Tarkan, Laurie. "A Rise in Kidney Stones Is Seen in U.S. Children." *New York Times*, October 28, 2008.

Trust for America's Health and the Robert Wood Johnson Foundation. "F as in Fat 2009: How Obesity Policies Are Failing in America." July 2009. http://www .healthyamericans.org.

US Department of Health and Human Services, National Institutes of Health. "Obesity Threatens to Cut U.S. Life Expectancy, New Analysis Suggests." News release. March 16, 2005.

Wang, Youfa, and Tom Lobstein. "Worldwide Trends in Childhood Overweight and Obesity." *International Journal of Pediatric Obesity* 1, no. 1 (2006): 11–25.

Weeks, Carly. "On the Children's Menu: Dangerous Levels of Salt." *Globe and Mail*, September 21, 2009. http://www.theglobeandmail.com.

World Health Organization. *Global Strategy on Diet, Physical Activity and Health.* Geneva: World Health Organization, 2004.

———. "Obesity and Overweight." Fact sheet no. 311. Updated March 2011. http://www.who.int.

Chapter Eight: Normal Food

Aley, Ian. Interview with author. Toronto. 2010.

Bain, Jennifer. "Cafeteria Serves Cuisine: Pilot Project Proves Kids Will Eat Healthy Food When It Tastes Good." *Toronto Star*, October 20, 2009. http://www.foodshare.net/media_archive100.htm.

Beck, Leslie. "How to Eat Less Salt." *Globe and Mail* (Toronto), February 3, 2010. http://www.theglobeandmail.com.

———. "Why You Should Read Nutrition Labels between the Lines." *Globe and Mail*, May 3, 2011.

British Heart Foundation. "Mums Hoodwinked by Manipulative Food Manufacturers." News release. December 20, 2009. http://www.bhf.org.uk.

Field, Debbie. Interview with author. Toronto. 2010.

Flammang, Janet A. *The Taste for Civilization: Food, Politics and Civil Society*. Chicago: University of Illinois Press, 2010.

Henry, Sarah. "Berkeley's New School Food Study: A Victory for Alice Waters." *Atlantic Monthly*, September 23, 2010. http://www.theatlantic.com.

Knickerbocker, Peggy. "Educating Fanny." *Food & Wine*, September 2003. http://www.foodandwine.com.

The Mario Batali Foundation. Accessed October 31, 2011. http://www.mariobatalifoundation.org.

National School Lunch Program. USDA Food and Nutrition Service. Accessed October 1, 2011. http://www.fns.usda.gov/cnd/lunch.

"Parents'Misled' by Food Nutrition Labels." BBC News. December 19, 2009. http://www.bbc.co.uk.

Parker-Pope, Tara. "Six Meaningless Claims on Food Labels." *Well* blog, NYTimes.com, January 28, 2010.

Pollan, Michael. *In Defense of Food: The Myth of Nutrition and the Pleasures of Eating*. London: Allen Lane, 2008.

Rosenberger, Bill. "Schools Still Serve 'From-Scratch.'" *Herald-Dispatch* (Huntington, WV), May 22, 2011. http://www.heralddispatch.com.

Silverglade, Bruce, and Ilene Ringel Heller. *Food Labeling Chaos: The Case for Reform*. Washington, DC: Center for Science in the Public Interest, 2010. http://www.cspinet.org.

"Some Baby Foods Worse Than Junk Foods: Survey." Reuters.com. May 4, 2009. http://www.reuters.com.

Waters, Alice. *Edible Schoolyard: A Universal Idea*. San Francisco: Chronicle Books, 2008.

Waters, Alice. Interview with author. Rome. 2010.

Weeks, Carly. "Granola Bars: A Healthy Snack or Dressed-up Junk Food?" *Globe and Mail* (Toronto), December 12, 2010. http://www.theglobeandmail.com.

Chapter Nine: An Industrial View

Bakan, Joel. *The Corporation: The Pathological Pursuit of Profit and Power*. London: Constable, 2004.

Berry, Susan. "USDA Pushes Food Stamps at Farmers Markets." *Breitbart*, September 1, 2012. http://www.breitbart.com.

Estes, Ralph. *Tyranny of the Bottom Line: Why Corporations Make Good People Do Bad Things*. San Francisco: Berrett-Koehler, 1996.

Friedman, Milton. *Capitalism and Freedom*. Chicago: University of Chicago Press, 1962.

———. "The Social Responsibility of Business Is to Increase Its Profits." *New York Times Magazine*, September 13, 1970.

Gonsalves, Colin. "Right to Food Forum, Food and Agriculture Organization of the United Nations." Speech. Rome, October 2008.

Helstosky, Carol. *Garlic & Oil: Food and Politics in Italy*. New York: Berg, 2004.

Henshaw, Caroline. "Incoming FAO Chief Says Brazil Program Offers Model for Fighting Global Hunger." *Wall Street Journal*, July 21, 2011. http://www.wsj.com.

Kaufman, Leslie. "Greening the Herds: A New Diet to Cap Gas." *New York Times*, June 4, 2009.

Mapsone, Naomi. "Old Roots Tap New Consumers." *Financial Times*, September 28, 2010. http://www.ft.com.

Marinetti, Filippo Tommaso. *La Cucina Futurista*. Milan: Casa Editrice Sonzogno s.d., 1932.

Monteiro, Carlos. "'Nutrient Profiling,' and 'Fortified' Soft Drinks for Africans." *World Nutrition, Journal of the World Public Health Nutrition Association* 2, no. 1 (January 2011). http://www.wphna.org.

———. "There Is No Such Thing as a Healthy Ultra-Processed Product." *World Nutrition, Journal of the World Public Health Nutrition Association* 2, no. 7 (August 2011).

Moss, Michael. "Peanut Case Shows Holes in Safety Net." *New York Times*, February 8, 2009.

Otsuki, Kei, and Alberto Arce. "Brazil: A Desk Review of the National School Feeding Programme." United Nations World Food Programme. July 2007. http://www.wfp.org.

Patel, Raj. *Stuffed and Starved: The Hidden Battle for the World's Food System*. Toronto: Harper Collins, 2007.

Patel, Raj, Eric et al. "Ending Africa's Hunger." *Nation*, September 21, 2009. http://www.thenation.com.

Pepsi Refresh Project. Accessed July 10, 2011. http://www.refresheverything.com.

Schlosser, Eric. *Fast Food Nation*. New York: Penguin, 2002.

Seabrook, John. "Snacks for a Fat Planet: PepsiCo Takes Stock of the Obesity Epidemic." *New Yorker*, May 16, 2011. http://www.newyorker.com.

US Department of Agriculture Agricultural Marketing Service. "Farmers' Markets and Local Food Marketing." http://www.ams.usda.gov.

US Department of Agriculture Economic Research Service. "Organic Agriculture." Updated November 30, 2009. http://www.ers.usda.gov.

US Department of Health and Human Services, US Food and Drug Administration. *FDA 101: Animal Feed*. June 2009. http://www.fda.gov.

Yach, Derek. Interview with author. White Plains, NY. 2010.

Chapter Ten: Natural Food Cultures

Englberger, Lois. "Revisiting the Vitamin A Fiasco: Going Local in Micronesia." International Scientific Symposium (slides). *Biodiversity and Sustainable Diets: United against Hunger.* Food and Agriculture Organization of the United Nations, Rome, November 3–5, 2010.

Fee, Margery. "Stories of Traditional Aboriginal Food, Territory, and Health." In *What's to Eat? Entrées in Canadian Food History*, ed. Nathalie Cooke. Montreal: McGill-Queen's University Press, 2009.

Food and Agriculture Organization of the United Nations. "How to Feed the World in 2050." 2009. http://www.fao.org.

Kuhnlein, Harriet V., et al., eds. *Indigenous Peoples' Food Systems: The Many Dimensions of Culture, Diversity and Environment for Nutrition and Health.* Rome: FAO, 2009. Specific studies: Chotiboriboon, Sinee, et al., "Thailand: Food System and Nutritional Status of Indigenous Children in a Karen Community," 159–83; Englberger, Lois, et al. "Documentation of the Traditional Food System of Pohnpei," 109–38; Kuhnlein, Harriet V., et al. "'Gwich'in Traditional Food for Health: Phase 1," 45–58; Turner, Nancy J., et al. "The Nuxalk Food and Nutrition Program, Coastal British Columbia, Canada: 1981–2006," 23–44.

Patel, Raj. *Stuffed and Starved: The Hidden Battle for the World's Food System.* Toronto: Harper Collins, 2007.

———. *The Value of Nothing: Why Everything Costs So Much More Than We Think.* Toronto: Harper Collins, 2009.

"Sponsors: Commitment to Micronesia." 2010 Guam Micronesia Island Fair. *Pacific Daily News.* Accessed June 2, 2011. http://www.guampdn.com.

Streib, Lauren. "World's Fattest Countries." Forbes.com. August 2, 2007.

United Nations Conference on Sustainable Development. "Rome-based Organizations Submit to Rio+20 Outcome Document." Accessed October 4, 2012. http://www.uncsd2012.org.

Young, T. Kue, et al. "Geographical Distribution of Diabetes among the Native Population of Canada: A National Survey." *Social Science & Medicine* 31, no. 2 (1990): 129–39.

Chapter Eleven: How the World Eats

"Apple Varieties." Orange Pippin. Accessed July 28, 2011. http://www.orange pippin.com.

Bioversity International. *Agriculture, Agricultural Biodiversity and Sustainability.* Rome: Bioversity International, May 2010.

Bittman, Mark. "E. Coli: Don't Blame the Sprouts!" *Opinionator* blog, NYTimes .com. June 7, 2011.

DeSchutter, Olivier. "Report Submitted by the Special Rapporteur on the Right to Food." United Nations Human Rights Council. December 20, 2010. http:// www.srfood.org.

Gale, Jason. "India's Diabetes Epidemic Cuts Down Millions Who Escape Poverty." *Bloomberg Markets Magazine*, November 7, 2010. http://www.bloomberg.com.

Jackson, Tim. *Prosperity without Growth: Economics for a Finite Planet*. London: Earthscan, 2009.

Malkin, Elisabeth. "Mexico Puts Its Children on a Diet." *New York Times*, March 13, 2011.

McKibben, Bill. *Deep Economy: Economics as If the World Mattered*. Oxford, UK: Oneworld Publications, 2007.

Moore, Mike. *A World without Walls: Freedom, Development, Free Trade and Global Governance*. Cambridge, UK: Cambridge University Press, 2003.

Neogi, Saikat. "India, World Diabetes Capital." *Hindustan Times*, September 3, 2007. http://www.hindustantimes.com.

Nestlé Global. *Nestlé Creating Shared Value and Rural Development Report 2010*. http://www.nestle.com.

Pingali, Prabhu, and Yasmeen Khwaja. "Globalisation of Indian Diets and the Transformation of Food Supply Systems." Inaugural Keynote Address, 17th Annual Conference. Indian Society of Agricultural Marketing, Hyderabad. February 5–7, 2004. http://www.fao.org.

Reardon, Thomas, Peter Timmer, and Julio Berdegue. "The Rapid Rise of Supermarkets in Developing Countries." *Journal of Agricultural and Development Economics* 1, no. 2 (2004): 168–83.

Rodrik, Dani. *The Globalization Paradox: Why Global Markets, States, and Democracy Can't Coexist*. Oxford, UK: Oxford University Press, 2011.

Romero, Simon, and Sara Shahriari. "Quinoa's Global Success Creates Quandary at Home." *New York Times*, March 19, 2011.

Rosenwald, Michael S. "Why America Has to Be Fat." *Washington Post*, January 22, 2006.

Sen, Amartya. *Poverty and Famines: An Essay on Entitlement and Deprivation*. New York: Oxford University Press, 1981.

Siebert, Charles. "Food Ark." *National Geographic*, July 2011.

Stiglitz, Joseph E., Amartya Sen, and Jean-Paul Fitoussi. "Report by the Commission on the Measurement of Economic Performance and Social Progress." 2009. www.stiglitz-sen-fitoussi.fr.

Traill, W. Bruce. "The Rapid Rise of Supermarkets?" *Development Policy Review* 2, no. 24 (2006): 163–74.

Unilever. "MDGs Index." Unilever Global. Accessed October 31, 2011. http://www.unilever.com.

United Nations. "We Can End Poverty: 2015 Millennium Development Goals." Accessed October 31, 2011. http://www.un.org.

United Nations Food and Agriculture Organization. Nutrition and Consumer Protection Division. *Biodiversity and Nutrition: A Common Path*. Information package. http://www.fao.org.

United Nations Secretary General. "Impact of Globalization on the Achievement of the Internationally Agreed Development Goals, Including the Millennium

Development Goals." 63rd Session, United Nations General Assembly, August 26, 2008. Report no. A/63/333. http://www.un.org.

Vepa, Swarna Sadasivam. "Impact of Globalization on the Food Consumption of Urban India." In *Globalization of Food Systems in Developing Countries: Impact on Food Security and Nutrition*. FAO Food and Nutrition Paper 83. Rome: Food and Agriculture Organization of the United Nations, 2004. http://www.fao.org.

World Health Organization. "10 Facts about Diabetes." Accessed August 2, 2011. http://www.who.int.

———. "Diabetes Programme." Accessed August 2, 2011. http://www.who.int.

World Hunger Education Service. "2011 World Hunger and Poverty Facts and Statistics." http://www.worldhunger.org.

WTO official. Phone interview with author. Geneva. 2011.

Chapter Twelve: The Global Market

Associated Press. "Coke Profit Fails to Meet Expectations." *New York Times*, April 20, 2010.

Balducci, Maria Letizia. Interview with author. Rome. 2011.

"Bhutan Aims to Be First 100% Organic Nation," *West Australian*, October 4, 2012. http://www.au.news.yahoo.com.

Brillat-Savarin, Jean Anthelme. *The Physiology of Taste: Or Meditations on Transcendental Gastronomy*. Translated by M. F. K. Fisher. New York: Alfred A. Knopf, 2009.

Brody, Jane E. "Still Counting Calories? Your Weight-Loss Plan May Be Outdated." *New York Times*, July 18, 2011.

Faber, M., and S. Laurie. "A Home Gardening Approach Developed in South Africa to Address Vitamin A Deficiency." In *Combating Micronutrient Deficiencies: Food-based Approaches*, edited by Brian Thompson and Leslie Amoroso, 163–82. Rome: FAO and CABI, 2011.

Fleige, Lisa. "PepsiCo and the Millennium Development Goals." *Food Frontiers*, PepsiCo blog. September 29, 2010. http://foodfrontiers.pepsicoblogs.com.

Kariuki, John. Phone interview with author. Kenya. 2011.

Lay's Mobile Farm. "Lay's Brand Brings the Simple Happiness of Farm Life to Big Cities Across America with Mobile Greenhouse Exhibit." News release. July 26, 2010. http://www.pepsico.com.

"Lo spot dei 'Flauti' Mulino Bianco Barilla è scorretto e va ritardo. Non si possono definire sane quelle merendine, lo dice l'EU." Il Fatto Alimentare, September 25, 2012. http://www.ilfattoalimentare.it.

Ludwig, David S., and Marion Nestle. "Can the Food Industry Play a Constructive Role in the Obesity Epidemic?" *Journal of the American Medical Association* 300, no. 15 (October 15, 2008): 1808–11. http://jama.ama-assn.org.

MacDonald, A. C., et al. "Small-Animal Revolving Funds: An Innovative Programming Model to Increase Access to and Consumption of Animal-source Foods by Rural Households in Malawi." In *Combating Micronutrient Deficiencies:*

Food-Based Approaches, edited by Brian Thompson and Leslie Amoroso. Rome: FAO and CABI, 2011.

Marinetti, Filippo Tommaso. *La Cucina Futurista*. Milan: Casa Editrice Sonzogno s.d., 1932.

Monteiro, Carlos A., Fabio S. Gomes, and Geoffrey Cannon. "The Snack Attack." *American Journal of Public Health*. April 15, 2010. http://ajph.alphapublications.org.

Mozaffarian, Dariush, et al. "Changes in Diet and Lifestyle and Long-term Weight Gain in Women and Men." *New England Journal of Medicine* 364 (June 23, 2011): 2392–404.

Nestlé. *Nestlé Annual Report 2010*. Nestlé Global. http://www.nestle.com.

Nestle, Marion. "More on Oxfam's Anti-poverty Partnership with Coca-Cola." *Food Politics* (blog). April 21, 2011. http://www.foodpolitics.com.

Nierenberg, Danielle, Brian Halweil, and Linda Starke. *State of the World 2011: Innovations that Nourish the Planet: A Worldwatch Institute Report on Progress toward a Sustainable Society*. New York: W. W. Norton, 2011.

PepsiCo. *PepsiCo 2010 Annual Report*. http://www.pepsico.com.

Thompson, Brian. Interview with author. Rome. 2011.

Unilever. *Annual Report and Accounts 2010*. Unilever Global. http://www.unilever.com.

"We Will Feed the Nation, Create Jobs—Akinwumi Adesina, Agric Minister," *TELL, Nigeria's Independent Weekly*, July 23, 2012. http://www.tellng.com.

Yach, Derek, et al. "Can the Food Industry Help Tackle the Growing Global Burden of Undernutrition?" *American Journal of Public Health*. April 15, 2010. http://ajph.aphapublications.org.

Zmuda, Natalie. "At 125 Years Old, Coke's Story Is Still Being Written: After Winning Cola Wars, Company Aims to Double Revenue in 10 Years and Continue History of Breaking Marketing Ground." *Advertising Age*. May 2, 2011. http://www.adage.com.

Chapter Thirteen: Changing Eating Habits in Europe

Barilla. http://www.academiabarilla.com.

"Foreign News: Futurist Food." *Time U.S.*, January 12, 1931. http://www.time.com.

"Frutta e verdure tra le merendine: Progetto pilota di Ministero e Regione." *La Repubblica Firenze*, February 7, 2011. http://www.repubblica.it.

Grass Root Solutions. "Heritage Wheat Varieties." http://www.grassroot-solutions.com.

Helstosky, Carol. *Garlic & Oil: Food and Politics in Italy*. New York: Berg, 2004.

Kerr, William A., and Jill E. Hobbs. *The North American–European Union Dispute over Beef Produced Using Growth Hormones: A Major Test for the New International Trade Regime*. Oxford, UK: Blackwell Publishers, 2002.

Kostioukovitch, Elena. *Why Italians Love to Talk about Food: A Journey through Italy's Great Regional Cuisines, from the Alps to Sicily*. New York: Farrar, Straus and Giroux, 2006.

Marinetti, Filippo Tommaso. *La Cucina Futurista*. Milan: Casa Editrice Sonzogno s.d., 1932.

"McDonald's McItaly Burger Fails to Impress Italian Critics." *Telegraph* (UK), February 5, 2010. http://www.telegraph.co.uk.

McNeil, Donald G., Jr. "Research in Italy Turns Up a New Form of Mad Cow Disease." *New York Times*, February 17, 2004.

Menichini, Raffaella. Interview with author. Rome. 2011.

Mulino Bianco. *Buona Merenda: Una sana abitudine*. Mulino Bianco. April 2010. http://www.mulinobianco.it.

Petrini, Carlo. "Lettera al panino McItaly." *La Repubblica*. February 3, 2010.

Rubino, Monica. "Farmer's market in controtendenza cresce la spesa a chilometri zero." *La Repubblica*. May 25, 2011.

Schmidhuber, Josef. "The EU Diet: Evolution, Evaluation and Impacts of the CAP." Paper presented at WHO Forum "Trade and Healthy Food and Diets," Montreal, November 7–13, 2007. Published by the Global Perspectives Studies Unit, FAO. Rome. 2008. http://www.fao.org.

Seed, Diane. Interview with author. Rome. 2011.

Società Coop. Il Sambuco. http://www.biofornoilsambuco.it.

Università di Urbino. "'Senatore Cappelli': Il grano che ha una storia." http://www.uniurb.it.

Chapter Fourteen: The Pleasure of Food

Friedan, Betty. *The Feminine Mystique*. New York: W. W. Norton, 1997.

Hazan, Giuliano. "You Are How You Eat." *New York Times*, July 6, 2004.

Stop Community Food Centre. "After School Program & Summer Camp." http://www.thestop.org.

Woolever, Laurie. "Saving Time and Stress with Cooking Co-ops." *New York Times*, June 22, 2010.